# Innovations in Health Care

# Innovations in Health Care
## A Reality Check

Edited by

### Ann L. Casebeer
*Associate Director, Centre for Health and Policy Studies*
*Associate Professor, Department of Community Health Sciences*
*Faculty of Medicine, University of Calgary, Alberta*
*Faculty Director, SEARCH Canada, Alberta*

### Alexandra Harrison
*Director, Patient Experience, Calgary Health Region*
*Adjunct Associate Professor, Department of Community Health Sciences*
*Faculty of Medicine, University of Calgary, Alberta*

### Annabelle L. Mark
*Professor of Healthcare Organization, Middlesex University Business School,*
*United Kingdom*

palgrave
macmillan

First published 2006 by
PALGRAVE MACMILLAN
Houndmills, Basingstoke, Hampshire RG21 6XS and
175 Fifth Avenue, New York, N.Y. 10010
Companies and representatives throughout the world

PALGRAVE MACMILLAN is the global academic imprint of the Palgrave
Macmillan division of St. Martin's Press, LLC and of Palgrave Macmillan Ltd.
Macmillan® is a registered trademark in the United States, United Kingdom
and other countries. Palgrave is a registered trademark in the European
Union and other countries.

ISBN-13: 978–1–4039–4748–2
ISBN-10: 1–4039–4748–1

This book is printed on paper suitable for recycling and made from fully
managed and sustained forest sources.

A catalogue record for this book is available from the British Library.

Library of Congress Cataloging-in-Publication Data
Innovations in health care : a reality check / edited by Ann L. Casebeer, Alexandra
Harrison, Annabelle L. Mark.
    p.   cm.
Includes bibliographical references and index.
ISBN 1–4039–4748–1 (cloth)
1. Medical care.  2. Medical innovations.  I. Casebeer, Ann L., 1952–
II. Harrison, Alexandra, 1950–  III. Mark, Annabelle L.
RA395.A3I52 2006
362.1—dc22                                                                    2005045618

10  9  8  7  6  5  4  3  2  1
15  14  13  12  11  10  09  08  07  06

Printed and bound in Great Britain by
Antony Rowe Ltd, Chippenham and Eastbourne

*For our children –*
*Emma, Zach, Stewart, Ted and Louise –*
*innovators of the future...*

# Contents

## Part I    When Does Research Make a Difference?

## Part II    When Does Practice Lead the Way?

# List of Figures, Tables and Boxes

## Figures

## Tables

**Box**

# Foreword: We Know Better, Why Don't We Do Better? Assessing the Contributions of Organizational Behaviour to Health Policy and Practice

*Stephen M. Shortell*

There is an urgent need for a reality check on innovations in health care. The health care sector is particularly rich soil for the development of organizational theory and the advancement of organizational practice in relation to change and innovation. It is complex, very visible politically, with a large number of professionals from different disciplines all contributing to extremely fragmented organizational structures. It is filled with paradoxes; for example, it is highly institutionalized but with great technical demands and pressures. It is also 'hyper-turbulent' (Powell, 2003) with significant technological innovations that, at the same time, co-exist with organizational structures for physicians that have not changed for a hundred years and are often hampered by the extremely slow spread of new knowledge and technologies. In summary, 'it's real messy out there!'

The literature on organizational behaviour is also diverse and challenging to navigate for targeted messages relevant to understanding health care situations. Add to this the growing literature on the nature of innovation and the 'messyness' increases. When assessing the contributions of organizational behaviour to health policy and practice, I often ask: 'If we know better, why don't we do better?' Part of my answer is that the transfer and exchange of knowledge is a highly complex social, political and technical process that requires considerable skill.

To understand innovation in complex situations nested in complex organizational forms, our theories and practices relating to change must become equally complex. There are a variety of approaches to bringing about change. Gustafson et al. (2003), found the following factors associated with the likelihood of successful health care improvement: a deep understanding of the problem and needs; the credibility and commitment of the change agents; the relative advantage of the change compared with the status quo; the fit with the current philosophy and culture; the flexibility of design; the complexity of the implementation plan; and, if the supporters will gain more than opponents will lose if the project succeeds. Many of these factors are consistent with those identified by Rogers (1995). In our own experience some reasons why change does not occur include: people do not really understand the change or what it means for their job; people do not really agree with the change; people fear they cannot adapt to the change; and, people are not clear about 'what's in it for me'.

Kaiser Permanente, an integrated delivery system in the US, used a 'linkage' model as the conceptual framework for improving the patient care experience. The Care Experience Council applied an evidence based approach to find out what matters to its members and employees and what leadership actions are important. Multiple internal studies and external research identified four leadership behaviours that have the highest correlation with patient and employee satisfaction. These include: creating a focus on customers, service and quality; building commitment through employee involvement and effective two-way communication; and, achieving results through accountability and performance management. Effective leaders see their role as enabling physicians and employees to deliver high quality service. Their behaviours and interventions reflect this focus. The Care Experience Council identified the following learnings: an evidence based approach provides a strong foundation for improving member satisfaction; the patient – patient care provider relationship is at the heart of the care experience; high performing teams are essential to creating a superior care experience; and, leadership is the key to creating a superior care experience. Employees and patients need the same thing – to be cared about, listened to and involved in decisions that affect them.

The 'comfort zone' theory of change (Shortell, Morrison and Friedman, 1990) provides some insights about why some changes last and others do not. The less that the current state is disrupted, the more likely the change will stick. The greater the demonstrated instrumental value to key stakeholders, the more likely the change is to stick. The greater the extent to which changes are introduced within social networks supportive of innovation, the more likely the changes are to stick. The greater the extent to which the changes become an expected 'way of doing business', the more likely the changes are to stick.

Some of our own field research and that of others has lead toward development of a 'multi-level theory of change' at four levels: Individual, Group or Team, the Organization, and the larger System or Environment. One also needs to consider the content (large versus small changes and the amount of complexity); the context (the time frame and relevant stakeholders); as well as the process (top down versus bottom up, planned versus unplanned, and the degree of participation). Change within levels is a function of that level's capacity and motivation relative to the perceived rewards, and the costs of moving to the new state. Each level has its own 'comfort zone'. Change within levels is about reaching that level's tipping point or threshold for action. Change across levels involves knowledge of the collective 'comfort zones' of multiple levels and designing strategies through the use of information flows, social networks and incentives that increase interdependence. Each level needs to see that its interests are better met (relative to alternatives) by expanding its comfort zone to include co-operative behaviour with other levels, thereby facilitating the innovation to occur. Key concepts of the levels approach to change include interdependence, alignment and the role of social networks.

An example of the multi-level approach is provided by efforts to improve the quality and outcomes of care. These include individual level instruction and use of treatment guidelines; group/team level efforts in using quality improvement processes; organizational level adoption of electronic information technology; and system level initiatives to reward performance on the part of players. For example, forty teams participated in a study that evaluated a collaborative to improve care for patients with chronic illness. The study used the chronic care management model and Institute for Health Improvement PDSA (plan, do, study, act) cycle change approach. The chronic diseases studied included patients with asthma, congestive heart failure, depression and diabetes. Findings revealed that a patient centred focus is key to team effectiveness; identifying and supporting team champions is important; meaningful involvement of a small number of physicians on each team is important; maintaining a balanced culture of group participation, innovation, achievement orientation and some rules promotes team effectiveness; and teams of intermediate size (for example, seven to ten) were associated with greater effectiveness. Self-assessed team effectiveness, in turn, was associated with making more changes and in-depth changes to improve chronic illness care.

In summary, to understand innovation and change in health care organizations we must draw on multiple theoretical constructs and learn from multiple examples in practice. Successful change depends on both external incentives and internal capabilities. It affects and is informed by theory, by policy and by practice. Any reality check on the state of innovation in health care needs to explore complex possibilities with a wide range of objectives and within multiple contexts. The fourth International Conference of Organizational Behaviour in Health Care (2004) made an excellent start in tackling these issues. This book takes the next step by sharing more widely some lessons from both research and practice concerning innovation in health care settings around the world. It provides a foundation for further discovery and understanding of the ongoing process of innovation.

# References

Gustafson, D., Sainfort, F., Eichler, M. et al. (2003) 'The development and testing of a decision-theoretic model to predict the success of health care improvement change efforts', *Health Services Research*, 38(2), pp. 751–76.

Powell, M. (2003) 'The influence of healthcare management research on organization theorizing', Paper presented at the Annual Meeting of the Academy of Management, Seattle, WA.

Rogers, E.M. (1995) *Diffusion of Innovations*, 4th edn (New York: Free Press).

Shortell, S.M., Marsteller, J.A., Lin, M. et al. (2004) 'The Role of Perceived Team Effectiveness in Improving Chronic Illness Care', *Medical Care*, 42(11), pp. 1040–8.

Shortell, S.M., Morrison, E.M. and Friedman, B. (1990) *Strategic Choices for America's Hospitals* (San Francisco, CA: Jossey Bass).

# Notes on the Contributors

**Orvill Adams** is Director of Orvill Adams & Associates, a consultancy that specializes in working with policy makers and senior managers to formulate policies and implement innovative and sustainable solutions to the complex health systems and health workforce challenges they face. Orvill has 25 years of experience in senior positions in the public and private health sector. He was Director of Medical Economics with the Canadian Medical Association; Principal in the consulting firm Curry Adams & Associates, which focused on health, education and social services issues; and Director of the Department of Health Services Provision, then the Department of Human Resources for Health at the World Health Organization. He is an adjunct lecturer at the Department of General Practice in Primary Health Care, Quality and Management of Human Resources, University of Helsinki. Orvill Adams is widely published in the area of health workforce development, management, policy and planning. He holds postgraduate degrees in economics and international affairs.

**Pauline Barnett** is Senior Lecturer at the Department of Public Health and General Practice, Christchurch School of Medicine and Health Sciences, University of Otago, New Zealand. Her research interests include health restructuring, particularly governance issues and health policy, with an emphasis on primary health care.

**Allan Best** is Senior Scientist at the Centre for Clinical Epidemiology and Evaluation, Vancouver Coastal Health Research Institute; and Clinical Professor, Health Care and Epidemiology, at the University of British Columbia, Canada. For the past several years, Dr Best has focused his research and training program on community partnerships for health research. Current initiatives focus on prevention and management strategies for chronic disease, evidence based decision making by local health authorities, and systems approaches to promoting knowledge integration in the research to policy and practice cycle.

**Judy Birdsell** is Principal Consultant and President of On Management Ltd. She has acted as a consultant on organizing and policy in health, health research and voluntary sectors since 2001, and is Adjunct Associate Professor, Haskayne School of Business, University of Calgary, Alberta, Canada. Her consulting practice includes assisting clients with knowledge utilization, organization strategy and analysis, process facilitation and applied research. Prior to 2001, Judy was employed in health research for 15 years with the Alberta Cancer Board, and in knowledge translation for three years with the Alberta Heritage Foundation for Medical Research. She has 20 years of experience in the voluntary sector, including membership on Boards of Directors for the Canadian Cancer Society, the National Cancer Institute of Canada and the Canadian Breast Cancer Research Initiative. Presently she is Chair of the Board of the Stem Cell Research Network, a Network of Centres of Excellence; Vice-Chair of the Board of MCF Housing for Seniors; and Vice-President of the Alumni Council of the University of Alberta. Judy was awarded a Commemorative Medal for the 125th Anniversary of the Confederation of Canada in 1992 and the Queen's Golden Jubilee Medal in 2003. She has a PhD in organizational analysis.

**Richard Bolden** is a research fellow at the Centre for Leadership Studies, University of Exeter. Richard is an experienced researcher and educator in the fields of leadership and organizational psychology. His current projects include evaluating the effectiveness of leadership development in higher education, investigating the use and application of leadership competencies and standards, and exploring leadership for beneficial social change in Africa.

**Ann L. Casebeer** is Associate Professor in the Department of Community Health Sciences, and Associate Director of the Centre for Health and Policy Studies, both at the University of Calgary, Alberta, Canada. Ann has worked in the United States, the United Kingdom, Australia and Canada in a variety of university and health system settings. Her previous experience as Policy Director within the UK National Health Service grounds her applied health research interests in organizational and community level change for health gain. Research efforts continue to test capacity to demonstrate and transfer innovation for health improvement across sectors and systems. She has considerable experience in creating bridges across disciplines and between diverse groups and is particularly interested in supporting learning for innovation and in sharing that learning across boundaries and borders. Her role as Faculty Director for SEARCH Canada (a public service organization dedicated to improving knowledge development and use in practice) involves enhancing knowledge creation and exchange within research collaboratives and by health providers, managers and their organizations.

**Costanza Ceda** is a lecturer and researcher in public administration and health care in CERGAS, the University of Bocconi's Research Centre on Healthcare Management. She has a degree in Modern Literature from the Università degli Studi, Parma, and is in the Masters Program in Economics and Management in Non-Profit Organizations at the School of Management, University of Bocconi, in Milan, Italy. Her main subject is non-profit and social services management, and her lectures concentrate on human resources and the relationship between the public and private sector.

**David Chambers** is Head of the Dissemination and Implementation Research Program at the National Institute of Mental Health (NIMH), National Institutes of Health, part of the US Department of Health and Human Services in Bethesda, Maryland. His work has focused on how change occurs in clinical practice, how diffusion of innovations occurs, and how barriers and facilitators to improving evidence based practice affect dissemination and implementation efforts. Prior to his work with NIMH, Dr Chambers was a member of a research team based at the University of Oxford in the UK that evaluated several NHS funded initiatives attempting to translate research findings into medical practice.

**Sara Christian** completed an undergraduate degree in nursing at King's College London and is now a research associate there in the Nursing Research Unit. Over the past decade she has been involved in two large evaluation studies and has become particularly interested in the process of change across clinical settings. She is currently writing up her PhD study which investigates the findings from the South Thames Evidence Based Practice (STEP) evaluation using the 'innovation journey' model developed by the Van de Ven group. She hopes that the research findings will further the understanding of the process of change and its subsequent long-term sustainability in clinical practice.

**Pamela I. Clark** is Senior Research Scientist at the Battelle Center for Public Health Research & Evaluation, Columbus, Ohio, USA. Dr Clark is a leading tobacco researcher, whose most recent work on the roles of parents, schools and communities in youth tobacco use has helped to refocus prevention efforts to a balance of individual personal attributes and the broader community context of substance use and other risk behaviours.

**Jacqueline Cumming** has academic backgrounds in economics and public policy, and 12 years' experience in health services research. She has worked as a policy analyst/economist in the Treasury, the Department of Labour, the Department/Ministry of Health and the Public Health Commission in Wellington, New Zealand. She has a PhD in public policy and is Director of the Health Services Research Centre/Te Hikuwai Rangahau Hauora, a thriving health services research centre based in the School of Government at Victoria University in Wellington. Current interests include priority setting and resource allocation, economic evaluation of health services, health reforms and health system performance, and access to care. Jackie is involved in a range of health services research projects and is currently leading an evaluation of the 2001 New Zealand health reforms and an evaluation of the implementation and intermediate outcomes of the Primary Health Care Strategy. She co-ordinates a course on health policy in the School of Government at Victoria University and teaches health economics to graduate students in economics and public policy.

**Huw Davies** is Professor of Health Care Policy and Management at the University of St Andrews, and was Harkness Fellow in Health Care Policy when he was based at the Institute for Health Policy Studies at the University of California, San Francisco, USA. He is Co-Director of both the Centre for Public Policy & Management (CPPM) and the Economic and Social Research Council-funded Research Unit for Research Utilisation (RURU) at the University of St Andrews, as well as being Associate Director of the Social Dimensions of Health Institute (SDHI) at the Universities of Dundee and St Andrews. In addition to these roles, Huw is Deputy Director of the Service Delivery and Organisation (SDO) Research Funding Programme on secondment to the Department of Health, London. Huw's research interests are in public service delivery (especially health care), encompassing evidence based policy and practice, performance measurement and management, accountability, governance and trust. He also has a particular interest in the role of organizational culture in the delivery of high quality services.

**Jean-Louis Denis** is Full Professor at the Department of Health Administration and a researcher in the Groupe de recherche interdisciplinaire en santé (GRIS) in the Faculty of Medicine at the Université de Montréal, Canada. He holds a chair on the transformation and governance of health organizations from the Canadian Health Services Research Foundation and the Canadian Institutes for Health Research. He has taught the transformation of organizations and health systems to health administrators and researchers for more than 15 years. His current research is in the area of leadership and change in health care organizations and integrated health networks, and the role of evidence in the adoption of clinical and organizational innovations in the health care sector. He is a member of the Royal Society of Canada and the academic co-ordinator of the EXTRA program, an initiative to train executives in the use of research based evidence in health care organizations.

**Francesco Ripa di Meana** – no biographical details are available for this contributor.

**Bernard Dowling** is a research fellow at the National Primary Care Research and Development Centre at the University of Manchester. He specializes in social policy, with a particular interest in health policy. Bernard's research interests include the organizational and governance arrangements of healthcare institutions, their accountabilities, the quality and equity of access to care, and the use of quasi-markets in the planning and provision of services.

**David Evans** has worked in the National Health Service (NHS) in the UK since 1995 in the field of research and development, evidence based practice and related learning. He is Founder and Director of Effective Health Care CHAIN (Contacts, Help, Advice and Information Network) which is located within the NHS, and works in partnership with a sister network, CHAIN Canada, which is based at the University of Ottawa. CHAIN provides a network for people interested in research, evidence based practice and workplace based learning in health care. David's research interests include research related networks in health and social care. A key interest is the implementation of changes to improve health and health care based on research evidence, and the creation of infrastructures and resources which enable and encourage busy professionals and managers to engage with research.

**Gülin Gedik** works at the Department of Human Resources for Health at the World Health Organization headquarters in Geneva, Switzerland. She is a physician with postgraduate training in public health and health economics. She started her career as a general practitioner, then worked for the Turkish Ministry of Health in the National Health Policies Co-ordination Committee, and then as Deputy Co-ordinator of the health reform project at the Ministry of Health. She continued at the WHO Regional Office for Europe and co-ordinated the MANAS health reform project in Kyrgyzstan for two years, after which she undertook responsibility for health reforms in Central Asian countries at the WHO Regional Office in Copenhagen, Denmark. After that she was the General Co-ordinator of a consulting company in the area of health policy, systems and management.

**Liane Soberman Ginsburg** is Assistant Professor in the School of Health Policy and Management at York University in Toronto, Canada. Professor Ginsburg received her PhD in healthcare organization and management from the University of Toronto. Her research interests focus on patient safety culture, and group and organization level learning from adverse events.

**Jonathan Gosling** is Director of the Centre for Leadership Studies at the University of Exeter. Jonathan has designed and directed development programs for many companies, with a particular focus on international and rapidly changing businesses. His current research looks at how leadership can foster continuity through tough transitions. Jonathan was co-founder of the International Masters in Practicing Management (IMPM), a collaboration of business schools around the world.

**Gail Greig** is presently a doctoral candidate in the Centre for Public Policy and Management (CPPM) at the University of St Andrews. Gail's research interests include primary health care organizations and their professionals, and organizational learning. Previously, Gail worked within the NHS and primary care in the UK in various managerial posts.

**Jeremy Grimshaw** is Director of the clinical epidemiology program of the Ottawa Health Research Institute and Director of the Centre for Best Practice, Institute of Population Health, University of Ottawa, Canada. He holds a tier 1 Canadian research chair in health knowledge transfer and uptake and is Full Professor in the Department of Medicine, University of Ottawa. Dr Grimshaw received a MBChB (MD equivalent) from the University of Edinburgh, UK. He trained as a family physician prior to undertaking a PhD in health services research at the University of Aberdeen. His research focuses on the evaluation of interventions to disseminate and implement evidence based practice. He is Director of the Canadian Cochrane Network and Centre and Co-ordinating Editor of the Cochrane Effective Practice and Organisation of Care (EPOC) group. He has been involved in over 20 cluster randomized trials of different dissemination and implementation strategies conducted in a wide range of settings, and has evaluated interventions relating to a wide range of behaviours. He has also undertaken research into statistical issues in the design, conduct and analysis of cluster randomized trials. More recently his research has focused on assessing the applicability of behavioural theories to health care professional and organizational behaviour.

**Alexandra Harrison** is Director of Patient Experience in the Calgary Health Region, and Adjunct Associate Professor in the Faculty of Medicine at the University of Calgary, Alberta, Canada. Her research interests and professional responsibilities relate to the organization, improvement and evaluation of health care organizations; leadership skills for health care professionals; medical education; and patient involvement in health care processes.

**Sarah Hayward** is Chief Executive Officer for SEARCH Canada and is located in Edmonton, Alberta. She has combined roles in research, education and practice over the last 15 years to build bridges between health research and service delivery. Currently, Ms Hayward leads SEARCH Canada, a not-for-profit corporation dedicated to developing capacity for producing and using research throughout the health system, through training, organizational development and multi-sectoral networks. SEARCH Canada is jointly funded and governed by the Alberta Heritage Foundation for Medical Research (AHFMR), Alberta's health regions, universities and government. As previous Director of Applied Health Research Programs for AHFMR, Ms Hayward established various province-wide initiatives to create networks of expertise for applied research, research ethics and research transfer. Previously a public health nurse researcher, her research focused on evaluation and outcomes of public health nursing, especially in parent-child health, and she later established a technology transfer company providing knowledge systems for healthcare. Currently, Sarah is interested in the connections between a research culture and leadership development, and the challenge of connecting individual and organizational capacity.

**Bob Hinings** is Professor Emeritus in the Department of Strategic Management and Organization, Faculty of Business, University of Alberta, Edmonton, Canada. He is also a member of the Health Organization Studies Group and Senior Research Fellow in the Centre for Entrepreneurship and Family Enterprise. His interests are in organizational design and organizational change and he is currently carrying out research on strategic organizational change in health systems, professional service firms and the Canadian wine industry.

**Bev Holmes** is a PhD candidate at the School of Communication, Simon Fraser University, Burnaby, British Columbia, Canada. Ms Holmes is a former freelance health writer and communications consultant. Her Masters' research topic was 'on-line illness narratives' and the production, dissemination and use of health information. She is currently working on a project examining the role of the Internet in lay-user consumption of cancer-related information.

**Timothy R. Huerta** is a research scientist with the Child and Family Research Institute at the Provincial Health Services Authority in British Columbia, Canada. Dr Huerta has appointments with the University of British Columbia's Faculty of Medicine and the Vancouver Coastal Health Research Institute to study knowledge and inter-organizational networks among health agencies. With formal training in organizational theory and behaviour, system and network theory, complexity, statistics, public policy, game theory and computer simulation, he focuses on generating holistic and interdisciplinary approaches to collaboration.

**Paula Hyde** is Senior Lecturer in leadership and experiential learning at Manchester Business School, University of Manchester, England. Her teaching interests are in management of change, experiential learning and personal leadership development. In broad terms, her research interests are organizational dynamics and change, human resource management and performance, and organizational leadership. She is particularly concerned with psychoanalytic approaches to understanding organizational life; specifically, organizational defences, and approaches to humanizing organizations. She is currently researching human resource management and performance, changing skill-mix, and failure and turnaround in the NHS. Research sponsors include the Department of Health Policy Research Unit, the Chartered Institute for Personnel Development and the Health Professional Managers Association.

**Diane Kelly** is Assistant Director Postgraduate Medical Education (Continuing Professional Development) at NHS Education for Scotland, West Region General Practice Section. The core purpose of the GP Section is to provide leadership, through a supportive educational infrastructure, for GPs and their teams to enable them to manage change and make improvements in the service they provide. Imbedded within this is a commitment to a culture of rigour and research, the results of which will inform the process of change. Her research interests include translating learning organizations theory into practice and building learning capacity in primary care.

**Lise Lamothe** is Associate Professor at the Health Administration Department, Faculty of Medicine, University of Montreal, Canada. She is Chair of GETOS (Governance and Transformation of Healthcare Organizations), and a researcher in GREAS (a research group on equity of access and organization of primary health care services), CEFRIO (a liaison and transfer centre focused on social and organization innovation), and CAPP (Canadian Association of Petroleum Producers). Her general area of research is the governance and transformation of health care organizations. Her specific focus is on professional dynamics associated with the transformation of health care organizations; dynamics associated with mergers of institutions and the formation of networks of integrated services; structuring effects of NCIT in the transformation of clinical work processes; and dynamics associated with public and private partnerships for the management of change projects.

**Jennifer Landau** is Senior Lecturer at the School of Management and a researcher at CERGAS, the Healthcare Management Research Centre, at the University of Bocconi, Milan, Italy. She has a BA in social anthropology from Harvard University and an MA in organizational psychology from Columbia University. Jennifer is currently completing her doctoral thesis in economics of public administration at the University of Parma, Italy. Her research interests include quality of life and change management in health care.

**Ann Langley** is Professor of strategic management and research methods at HEC Montreal (Hautes Études Commerciales de Montréal), Canada, and Director of the PhD and MSc programs. She obtained her undergraduate and masters degrees in the UK and her PhD in administration at HEC in 1987 after working for several years as an analyst/health systems consultant both in the private and public sectors. Her research deals with strategic decision making, innovation, leadership and strategic change in pluralistic organizations and notably in the health care sector. Recent publications have appeared in Academy of Management Journal, Health Care Management Review, Human Relations, Policy and Politics, and Public Administration.

**Francis Y. Lau** is Associate Professor and Director of the School of Health Information Science, University of Victoria, British Columbia, Canada. Dr Lau specializes in the design, implementation and evaluation of health information systems. His research interests include action research, virtual teams, e-learning, knowledge management and use of IT in organizations.

**Scott Leischow** is Senior Advisor for Tobacco Policy, Department of Health and Human Services (HHS), Washington, DC. Dr Leischow played a senior role in creating several statewide tobacco treatment and evaluation programs in Arizona. He joined US NCI (National Cancer Institute) in 2000 as Chief – Tobacco Control Research Branch, and in 2004 became Senior Advisor for Tobacco Policy in the Office of the Secretary, where he has led efforts to implement a national quitline network and a tobacco-free workplace policy at HHS.

**Murray Lough** is Assistant Director in the west region of NHS Education for Scotland (NES) based in Glasgow. NES is a special health board within NHS Scotland responsible for ensuring lifelong learning for all employees in the NHS in Scotland. His research interest includes risk analysis in general practice; in particular, exploring drug error between pharmacists and general practitioners. His main work is to introduce a module on critical thinking into the GP training curriculum.

**Annabelle L. Mark** is Professor of Healthcare Organization at the Middlesex University Business School, The Burroughs, Hendon, England, and is Director of the Pilot NHS Human Resource Management Training Scheme from which the NHS develops leaders of tomorrow. She is also Fellow of the Institute of Healthcare Management, and Fellow of the Royal Society of Medicine. She is the founding academic of the Organizational Behaviour in Health Care Conference and elected Chair of the newly formed Learned Society for Studies in Organising for Healthcare (SHOC). Following a ten-year career as a manager in the NHS, she now undertakes consultancy and research, and writes almost exclusively on health management issues. Her current interests are changing roles for the professions in health care, leadership and teamworking, the management of emotion, and the management of demand for health care.

**Laura McAuley** has an MSc in epidemiology from the University of Ottawa, Ontario, Canada. She studied and now works in the area of methodological aspects of synthesizing research findings, with a specific focus on systematic review. She was Co-ordinator of the Cochrane Effective Practice and Organisation of Care Group at the time CHAIN Canada was launched and this paper was prepared. Laura is currently working at the Canadian Health Services Research Foundation in the area of evaluation, with a focus on demonstrating and measuring research use and evidence based decision making culture.

**Jessie McGowan** is Research Librarian at the Institute of Population Health/ Ottawa Health Research Institute, Ontario, Canada. She is also Adjunct Professor in the Department of Medicine at the University of Ottawa and Associate Editor with the Journal of Clinical Epidemiology. She works with the Cochrane Collaboration's Effective Practice and Organisation of Care Group and is the facilitator for CHAIN Canada. She has worked on Cochrane reviews as an author and providing librarian support. She also works in the area of knowledge translation and how best to meet the information needs of researchers, clinicians and decision makers.

**Susan McLaren** is Professor of Nursing and Director of the Center for Leadership and Practice Innovation at the London South Bank University. Her teaching covers postgraduate work in leadership and management studies, ethics, biosciences, and research philosophies and methodologies. She has completed externally-funded research projects in the areas of organizational change, role development and design, stroke rehabilitation and nutrition support for patients.

**Gregg Moor** is Project Co-ordinator, Centre for Clinical Epidemiology and Evaluation, at the Vancouver Coastal Health Research Institute, British Columbia, Canada. Mr Moor has long been interested in disease prevention and wellness maintenance, particularly the role of mind and spirit in achieving and maintaining health. He brings a background in psychology, gerontology, business, communications and non-profit management to his current work on the application of systems theory to facilitate multidisciplinary and multi-organizational collaborations.

**Peter Norton** is Head of the Department of Family Medicine at the University of Calgary in Alberta, Canada. He holds the rank of Professor at the University. His current research and teaching focuses on quality improvement, patient safety and medical adverse events across Canada. He is active in the Calgary Health Region's quality initiatives and is helping to design a patient safety program there.

**Petra O'Connell** has been a health care consultant for Belfield Resources Inc., Calgary, Alberta, Canada, for the past 12 years. She has assisted health regions, health care organizations and government sectors in Alberta and Ontario on numerous projects related to business case development and program planning, service model development, program evaluation, organizational and operational reviews, and strategic planning. Prior to this, Petra worked in hospitals in Edmonton, Alberta, in the areas of ambulatory care, facilities management, resource management and strategic planning, and for the Alberta Ministry of Health and Wellness in health technology assessment.

**Susan Pickard** has been a research fellow in the National Primary Care Research and Development Centre since 1997. She specializes in lay/informal care and its interfaces with professional care, and lay involvement in health care decision making. Susan is a social anthropologist by background and training. She is currently working on projects looking at the impact of user involvement in research and dissemination, and on policy transfer.

**Michael Powell** is Professor of Management and Dean of Griffith Business School in Brisbane, Australia. He has published in the areas of professional service firms, governance of health care organizations and organizational change. His current research interests lie in examining health care leadership, especially with respect to macro organizational change.

**David Rea** has a PhD from the University of Kent and lectures in health care management at the University of Swansea. He has research interests in accountability and quality in health and social care, with a particular interest in the involvement of and accountability to patients and service users. He has recently completed a large-scale evaluation of service delivery in rural areas for elderly people with mental health problems. His current research is with establishing a network of researchers interested in patient and public involvement, which includes service users and caregivers as researchers. He is also currently researching the processes of constructing knowledge about service user views collaboratively, so that provider organizations can learn and change service delivery and professional practice.

**Sally Redfern** is Emeritus Professor of Nursing, now semi-retired and working part-time in the Nursing Research Unit at King's College London. After qualifying as a registered general nurse and working as a staff nurse and ward sister in different hospitals, she gained a BSc in behavioural science (psychology) followed by a PhD in occupational psychology, both at Aston University. She joined Chelsea College, University of London (later King's College) as a lecturer, then senior lecturer, and spent a year as a visiting professor in the Centre for Care Research at the University of Lund in Sweden. She moved to the Nursing Research Unit in 1989 as its Director.

She has researched and written in the areas of assessing quality of nursing, evaluating developments in nursing and health care, and continuing care of older people. Her current research is concerned with evaluating new roles in nursing and practice developments, with an emphasis on linking context, process and outcomes in health care.

**Fiona Ross** is Professor of Gerontological Nursing in Primary Care and Director of the Nursing Research Unit (NRU) in the Florence Nightingale School of Nursing and Midwifery at King's College London. The NRU is funded by the Department of Health Policy Research Programme and has expertise in the study of the working lives and careers of nurses, pathways of change, role innovation and user involvement in research with a focus on outcomes for older people. Fiona did an undergraduate degree in nursing at Edinburgh University and a PhD at King's College London, and has worked in primary care in a variety of clinical and academic posts. In 1996, she was appointed to the first Chair of Nursing in primary care at St George's Hospital Medical School in its partnership with Kingston University, where she was involved in building research capacity, inter-professional initiatives, and developing a framework for service user involvement in the design and delivery of education. Fiona is a fellow of the European Academy of Nursing Sciences and Editor-in-Chief of the Journal of Interprofessional Care.

**Rosemary Rushmer** is a lecturer in organizational behaviour and organizational development in the Centre for Public Policy and Management (CPPM) at the University of St Andrews. Rosemary's research interests include organizational learning in health care organizations, inter-professional working, and the extent to which health care organizations provide facilitative or hindering work environments. She is a member of the Institute for Healthcare Improvement Safer Patients Initiative in the UK and is working collaboratively with NHS 24 in Scotland on service re-design and the production of an evidence base surrounding an integrated model of telehealth across Scotland.

**Nancy Santesso** is a knowledge translation specialist for the Musculoskeletal Group and the Effective Practice and Organisation of Care Group for the Cochrane Collaboration. Her current work focuses on transferring evidence to consumers of health care for informed decision making. She is a registered dietitian, and practised clinically before completing a Masters of Library and Information Science. Her interests include information access, translation and dissemination.

**Rod Sheaff** is Senior Research Fellow at the (English) National Primary Care Research and Development Centre (NPCRDC) where he co-ordinates the Centre's research on the organization of primary care. His disciplinary background is in politics, nowadays with a focus on the micropolitics and organization of health organizations. He has researched the organizational effects of health system reform in a number of European countries and is now embarking on studies of the social networks within primary care. NPCRDC is a joint undertaking between the Universities of Manchester and York and is based in the medical school at Manchester. It undertakes policy-related research, mainly for the (English) Department of Health.

**Stephen M. Shortell** is the Blue Cross of California Distinguished Professor of Health Policy and Management and Professor of Organization Behavior at the School of Public Health and Haas School of Business at the University of California-Berkeley. He is also the Dean of the School of Public Health at Berkeley and holds appointments in the Department of Sociology at UC-Berkeley and the Institute for Health Policy Research, UC-San Francisco. A leading health care scholar, Dr Shortell has been the recipient of many awards including the Distinguished Baxter-Allegiance Prize for his contributions to health services research; the Distinguished Investigator Award from Academy Health; the Gold Medal Award from the American College of Health Care Executives; and, the Honorary Lifetime Membership Award from the American Hospital Association. Dr Shortell received a commendation from the California State Senate for his contribution to health through leadership of the technical committee on 'Pay for Performance'. He is an elected member of the Institute of Medicine of the National Academy of Sciences and past Editor of Health Services Research. Dr Shortell is currently conducting research on the evaluation of quality improvement initiatives and on the implementation of evidence based medicine practices in physician organizations.

**David Snowden** has been one of the leading figures in the movement towards integration of humanistic approaches to knowledge management with appropriate technology and process design. Known as a 'formidable realist', he seeks to link academic and practitioner perspectives into a single, comprehensible purview. He left IBM in July 2005 to allow greater freedom to explore new transdisciplinary and participatory approaches to research and the creation of an open source approach to management consultancy. His work now draws on the cognitive sciences, complexity theory, anthropology and other disciplines to create new perspectives and approaches to management science and practice. Dave Snowden has an MBA from Middlesex University and a BA in philosophy from Lancaster University. He is Adjunct Professor of knowledge management at the University of Canberra, an honorary fellow in knowledge management at the University of Warwick, Adjunct Professor at the Hong Kong Polytechnic University and MiNE Fellow at the Università Cattolica del Sacro Cuore in Italy. He teaches on various university programs throughout the world. In addition, he is on the editorial board of several journals and is one of the three main editors of E:CO (Emergence: Complexity and Organization). He regularly consults at the board level with some of the world's largest companies as well as to government and NGOs, and was recently appointed as an advisor on sense making to the Singaporean Ministry of Defense.

**Ramkrishnan V. Tenkasi** is Professor, Department of Management and Organizational Behavior, College of Business, Technology and Professional Programs, Benedictine University, Lisle, Illlinois, USA. Dr Tenkasi's research focuses on the impact of cognitive, affective and communicative processes in organizational change, knowledge and learning and their mediation by organizational design choices. He is currently exploring these issues in arenas such as knowledge development in research and development efforts, and in fundamental organizational transitions.

**Richard Thornley** is Manager, Evaluation, Analysis and Information Services for the Alberta Heritage Foundation for Medical Research, Edmonton, Alberta. He has a BSc degree in biology-chemistry, an MLIS degree and a MPH in health policy research. His interests are in program evaluation, knowledge management, social informatics and health research policy.

**Deborah Tregunno** is Assistant Professor in the School of Nursing at York University in Toronto, Canada. Deborah is a registered nurse. She received her PhD in healthcare organization and management from the University of Toronto. Her research interests focus on patient safety culture and leadership for quality and safety improvement.

**William K. Trochim** is Professor, Department of Policy Analysis & Management, Cornell University, Ithaca, New York, USA. Dr Trochim's research is broadly in the area of applied social research methodology, with an emphasis on program planning and evaluation methods. He is recognized for the development of a multivariate form of concept mapping, a method for mapping the ideas of a group of people on any topic of interest that integrates traditional group processes with state-of-the-art statistical methods.

**Joyce Wilkinson** is currently a lecturer in clinical governance and evidence based practice at the School of Nursing and Midwifery, University of Dundee, and also a doctoral candidate in the Centre for Public Policy and Management (CPPM), University of St Andrews. Joyce's research interests include research utilization and evidence implementation in health care, primary health care, and the concept of learning in organizations in health care settings.

**Martin Wood** is Director of Research and Senior Lecturer in social theory and organization, Department of Management Studies, University of York. Previously he was a member of faculty at Exeter and Warwick Universities. He was awarded his PhD for work on new modes of knowledge production in health care. Martin is interested in the development of an analytically rigorous and imaginative social theory of organization and management, one that importantly recognizes organizing and managing as social processes, distinct from the traditional view which focuses on organizations and managers as discrete and bounded economic entities. His current research explores management and leadership in relation to issues of identity and difference, digital technologies, and the perceived acceleration of events in contemporary life.

**Wilfred Zerbe** is Professor of human resources and organizational dynamics in the Haskayne School of Business at the University of Calgary, Canada, and Visiting Professor, Theseus International Management Institute, Nice, France. His research interests focus on emotions in organizations, organizational research methods, service sector management, and leadership. His publications have appeared in books and journals, including the Academy of Management Review, the Industrial and Labour Relations Review, the Canadian Journal of Administrative Sciences, the Journal of Business Research, the Journal of Psychology, the Journal of Services Marketing, and the Journal of Research in Higher Education. He is also an active consultant and executive educator.

# Introduction

*Ann L. Casebeer, Alexandra Harrison and Annabelle L. Mark*

*Innovations in Health Care: A Reality Check* is the fourth in an ongoing series begun in 1998 from the biennial conference Organizational Behaviour in Health Care. This book describes how innovations actually occur within health care settings, analyzing how and where research and theory make a difference; identifying when practice experience leads the way; defining evidence based management; and exploring managing across boundaries. It compiles descriptions of innovations within complex health care settings that are working, providing some valuable examples of what can be and has been accomplished through organizational change. It also explores a range of examples where innovations were hindered, blocked, or not sustained across time, and examines where current theories and practices are falling short and why there are problems that remain unsolved.

This book draws its content from the best of the papers delivered in Banff, Alberta, the site of the fourth International Conference on Organization Behaviour in Health Care. The overarching theme of the conference was about taking a reality check on innovations in health care settings. The book's title and its objective are drawn from this theme and, mindful of the earlier volumes in the series, the authors describe new directions that help fill previously identified theory gaps and build knowledge bridges between research and practice. The book targets a subject that is key to every academic and organizational effort to improve health care – understanding how to identify, sustain and diffuse innovations that are working – providing some credible and valuable examples of what can be and has been accomplished through organizational change. Perhaps most usefully, some selections within the book critically examine where our current theories and practices are falling short and why there are problems that remain unsolved.

This fourth book represents some additional breakthroughs. The fourth conference was the first of the series to be held outside the United Kingdom. Bringing the conference to a North American venue has put a truly international stamp on the work, widening the draw of US and Canadian academics and practitioners who contributed, while retaining the strong UK and European core, including contributors from across the globe.

Papers addressed one of four themes relating to the broader interest in innovations in health care:

- When does research make a difference?
- When does practice lead the way?
- What is evidence based management?
- How do organizations manage across boundaries?

The four parts of the book are organized around these themes and are briefly described in the following sections.

## When does research make a difference?

Part I of the book focuses on contributions that link research findings to actual change in practice. The gap between research theory and practice action is one of the longest standing in the field of organizational change.

Denis, Lamothe and Langley share the experience of 15 years of in-depth, linked research into mechanisms of change in complex health care system environments in Canada. Their work has yielded valuable observations concerning the possibilities for change in practice. The hard work of the authors has paid off. They identify three levers for change – structures, interactions and incentives – and a pivotal organizational capability – leadership – that are necessary for effective and lasting change to occur. They emphasize that leadership is much more than 'simply the business of people in formal organizational roles. Participation of formal and informal leaders at the clinical level is essential' and that 'the different levers of change are part of a tool box that needs to be skilfully mastered' by all leaders for change.

As with Denis and colleagues, Bolden, Wood and Gosling focus on the pivotal roles of leadership and the need to draw on a broader theory base when trying to encourage effective leadership within the complex national health system of the United Kingdom. These authors take the reader across a bridge of literature capturing long-standing philosophical argument to inform where we should be focusing our practice efforts on the ground. They argue that the targeted focus on recruiting and training 'leaders' is insufficient to 'make a difference' and, in fact, misses the critical characteristics and dynamics required for the emergence and exercise of leadership.

Like Bolton and his colleagues, Mark and Snowden utilize some specific innovations in health care to show how new concepts can help in understanding not only what something is but, perhaps more importantly, what it is not. They argue that the usual science base we draw on when either attempting or assessing innovation in health systems is blinkered and insufficient if we are really to understand what is appropriate and where in this complex environment. They offer the concept of Cynefin as a way of understanding, interpreting and enacting appropriate responses to innovation which are dependent on both its purpose and context. In his chapter, David Chambers provides insight into the critical role of transfer exchange if actual use of research in practice is to occur. As Chief of the Dissemination and Implementation Research Program at the National Institute of Mental Health (NIMH) in the US, he is well placed to take what is already known about 'what makes a difference' to bridging the gap between our research and our practice and then extending our learning and capacity to do a better job in the future. Through several initiatives and workshops, NIMH has identified sets of priorities and key questions that are used to guide and evaluate their own research dissemination and implementation efforts. Their experience is shared along with some critical evidence from the literature in order to encourage additional use and extension of research efforts focused on truly 'making a difference' to practice.

## When does practice lead the way?

Part II reverses the orientation. Here, the reader will find innovations in practice that in turn become the basis for advances in knowledge and the pilots for further research. These types of practice breakthroughs fuel re-examination of current theories of organizational behaviour as well as expanding our knowledge bases.

The first chapter in this section is the flipside of the first chapter in Part I. Barnett, Powell and Cumming provide us with the lessons from a historical review of practice that tells us about the nature of health reforms in New Zealand. They sketch out an empirical journey of politically led health reforms – looking hard to see lessons and progress for health care delivery across time. They raise the pivotal question of whether four sets of health reforms over two decades have indeed improved system reforms. While their answer at a systemic level is 'probably not', they do identify pockets of actual reform. These relate to performance improvement in primary care and increased organizational learning and awareness concerning the roles of governance, management and delivery systems and the potential to encourage greater efficiencies in service arrangements.

In the next chapter, Landau and colleagues use Normann's model of 'internal marketing' stressing 'working relationships' as the key to organizational success. The authors take us through a practice initiative incorporating action research that truly makes a difference to practice and puts the 'humpty dumpty' problems of primary care back together again in a local health authority setting in Northern Italy.

Liane Ginsberg and colleagues focus attention on the important area of patient safety practice. Their interest is in discovering whether educational interventions can advance patient safety in hospital settings. Given the stakes, this is an issue where practice must take the lead and where research needs to be undertaken to ensure that practice moves forward and patient safety in all settings is assured. This chapter sheds light on a key question concerning the nature of patient safety culture, sharing data that suggests the existence of subcultures may confound the potential for a dominant and/or shared system-wide culture to emerge. The practical implications of this for advancing safety in health care organizations are substantial and at odds with current thinking in the literature.

Rushmer and colleagues address a critical potential for future practice improvement – learning. They remind us that 'clever health systems are needed' if we are to meet critical health and health care goals. Their work within primary care practices has led to the creation of a learning practice inventory – a tool that may be able to help increase our ability to identify what learning is taking place and what consequences for practice it has. Their thesis that learning in practice will truly lead the way is a space where research and practice fuse to the benefit of health services delivery and improving health.

## What is evidence based management?

Chapters in Part III look at the pivotal role of evidence in decision making, but also consider the underlying importance of other factors such as values, both personal and professional, as well as organizational context and culture.

The chapter by David Rea explores the concept of clinical governance, which he defines as a systematic framework used to combine organizational and clinical aspects of health care delivery. Although he concludes that the use of evidence in managing health care is increasing, he stresses the need to 'examine the processes by which evidence is classified, examined, verified and validated'. He cautions that disproportionately weighting evidence such as the randomized control trials may lead to less opportunity for patients' wishes to be incorporated into decision making processes.

In their chapter, Judy Birdsell and colleagues describe the development of a conceptual framework that was designed to understand and enhance the capacity of health regions to use research evidence in delivering services. This framework is used to evaluate a province-wide learning and development program that works with health care practitioners helping them to access, use and participate in research (SEARCH). Both the conceptual framework and the evaluation of the SEARCH (Swift Efficient Application of Research in Community Health) program provide important contributions to understanding evidence based management in a health care environment.

The chapter by Sally Redfern et al. reports on a study commissioned by the UK NHS to implement and evaluate an evidence based practice development program that encompassed nine partnership projects. Although nine different clinical areas were involved, all used the same research design. The intervention was the introduction of evidence based guidelines. The project leaders were the change agents, and implementation included training staff to use the guidelines. Project leaders were interviewed to identify factors perceived as helping or hindering the use of the guidelines, with follow-up, confirmatory interviews with university and trust leaders. Factors perceived as facilitating or hindering the use of guidelines are identified and discussed in relation to Van de Ven's 'road map' of the typical innovation journey. This contribution helps to understand the process of change in the midst of a dynamic health care system.

The chapter by Rod Sheaff et al. asks if the goal of evidence based decisions about organizational innovation may at times be a delusion. It identifies reasons for introducing evidence based management, including identifying which policies are likely to 'work', and using evidence based policy and management as a rationale for encouraging evidenced based medicine in the clinical sphere. It also outlines challenges for evidence based management, including using a false 'programme theory' to support policy; the methodology for evidence based management presents more research design difficulties than clinical research; and, lastly, organizational innovations and health policies rely on ideology or belief systems with a substantive normative component, not just technical knowledge. The research studied nine English Primary Care Trusts, and examined if evidence existed for organizational innovations that were introduced. The research found that most innovations examined (62 per cent) were at least minimally evidence based. The authors note that evidence basing of organizational innovations is a matter of degree both in volume of evidence and its formality. They also note that defining the intended outcomes of organizational innovations is a precondition to deciding what evidence is.

## How do organizations manage across boundaries?

The ability to manage across the many organizational and professional boundaries found within health care is one of the most difficult challenges for organizational behaviour theory and implementation. Chapters in Part IV present a very timely 'reality check' about organizational measures and forms (such as networks and collaborations) that facilitate cross boundary action.

Allan Best and colleagues provide an in-depth description and analysis of a two-year, nation-wide initiative in the United States that applies system thinking to a strategy for tobacco control. Three approaches are described – system dynamic modelling, network analysis and knowledge management. The chapter provides an insightful synthesis of relevant literature and offers valuable conceptual maps, frameworks and diagrams to guide researchers and professionals, as well as policy makers, on how to accomplish system-wide change by linking across boundaries.

Paula Hyde explores a number of definitions and concepts of boundaries with particular reference to professional boundaries in health services. The chapter presents a series of case studies applying a psychodynamic approach to examine boundaries in four areas of a mental health service in one organization – the psychiatric ward, the occupational therapy department, the hostel and the community team. The author suggests that this psychodynamic analysis can help to explain resistance to organizational change that occurs with health care restructuring.

David Evans et al. describe a free-of-charge membership, web based network available to people from a range of backgrounds who wish to use research evidence to improve health. The network spans professional as well as geographic boundaries with centres in both the United Kingdom and Canada. The chapter outlines the history of the network as well as how the members use it, and provides contact information for those who wish to participate.

The final chapter, from Orvill Adams and Gülin Gedik, looks at four commonly used organizational interventions that have been introduced as part of health system reform strategies in countries around the world, including decentralization, ownership, integration, and information for consumer empowerment. It uses the WHO 2000 framework for assessing health systems performance that includes both health system functions and objectives.

This collection of chapters as a whole provides both practice and theory based examples to demonstrate the application of innovation theories to actual innovations in progress. However, and perhaps more importantly, authors also frequently question the epistemological basis of what is currently used to justify practice in the real world. Identifying not just the outcomes, but also where the outcomes are flawed through false assumptions and methods, is a critical role for academics to contribute to the practice community.

# Acknowledgements

We want to acknowledge all the participants of the 4th International Conference on Organizational Behaviour in Health Care, held in Banff, Alberta, Canada in the spring of 2004. The editors are indebted to those who joined us on the Conference Planning Committee and we thank Sue Dopson, Louise Fitzgerald, Ewan Ferlie and Judy Birdsell for all their hard work. Thanks also to Diane Lorenzetti for her help with referencing the text. A special tribute is reserved for Wendy Spragins for her contribution to a successful conference as well as her copy-editing and co-ordination skills which allowed us to put the book together working with editors from three different sites across two countries and authors from around the world.

Two final mentions are critical. First, we wish to recognize all of the authors who have contributed their work to this book. Without their insights into the state of innovation within health care settings, there would be no text and no useful ideas to share with readers. And finally, we wish to thank and encourage everyone out there trying to support further innovation within our health and health care organizations and communities. Whether you are academics pushing the envelope on theory or providers enhancing the practice, or working 'in the gap' to bridge these two spaces for innovation, your energy and your lessons will shape the future.

# Part I

# When Does Research Make a Difference?

# 1
# Reforming Health Care: Levers and Catalysts for Change

*Jean-Louis Denis, Lise Lamothe and Ann Langley*

## Introduction

In Canada, as in a majority of OECD (Organisation for Economic Co-operation and Development) countries (Saltman and Figueras, 1998; Saltman, 2002), health care systems are under increased pressure to implement changes in their structures and modes of functioning for service delivery. But at the same time, they seem to face a high level of inertia (Denis, 2002; Sinclair, 2002; Tuohy, 2002). Over the past 15 years, numerous public commissions at the federal (National Forum on Health, 1997; Commission on the Future of Health Care in Canada, 2002; Kirby, 2002) and provincial levels of government (Rochon, 1988; Clair, 2000; Fyke, 2001; Mazankowski, 2001 among others) have suggested various directions for change: expansion and restructuring of primary care services, implementation of integrated health networks, and reinforcement of accountability structures for health providers and organizations. These directions for change are generally considered appropriate as means to achieve the objectives of better access, continuity and reduction of costs of services. The convergence in recommendations has stimulated waves of attempts by politicians and technocrats to implement large-scale reforms. So far, lack of success in achieving the objectives has created fatigue among clinicians and managers responsible for implementing changes. However, although continuing demand for change is pressuring the system and its organizations, some progress has been made.

In this chapter, we analyze the potential and limits of various levers for change in health care systems and their organizations. Our analysis is based on a long-term research program focusing on change processes in the health care industry. Over the past 15 years, our studies have allowed us to be close witnesses of reform in the Quebec system. Our experience strongly suggests that, in order for research to 'make a difference' to complex organizational practice in health care settings, long-term, in-depth efforts are required.

We first briefly describe health care organizations as pluralistic organizations and discuss some of the particular challenges they face in managing change.

Second, we analyze the potential of three levers to intentionally stimulate change in this type of organization – the structural lever, the interactive lever and the incentive lever. Our analysis leads us to a consideration of appropriate leadership practices in health care organizations when there are strong pressures to implement changes successfully. We argue that the three levers are the essential ingredients that need to be combined to produce change, but that skilful leadership is also needed to act as a catalyst to make these ingredients effective.

## Managing change in health care organizations

As many authors argue (Mintzberg, 1979; Quinn, 1992), managers in health care or professional organizations do not have undisputed sway over people or unlimited autonomy to control strategic orientations or their implementation. Indeed, these organizations can often be described as inherently 'pluralistic' in nature (Denis, Lamothe and Langley, 2001a) as they are characterized by the existence of multiple objectives and diffuse power structures, often extending beyond organizational boundaries (Rainey, 1991; Nutt and Backoff, 1992). As Cohen and March (1986, p. 195) indicated in their discussion of the dilemmas underlying the university president's role: 'When purpose is ambiguous, ordinary theories of decision making and intelligence become problematic. When power is ambiguous, ordinary theories of social order and control become problematic.' Therefore, pluralism in health care systems and their organizations raises specific challenges as it can lead to organizational inertia in at least three ways:

*Individual autonomy may generate collective paralysis.* While pluralistic organizations provide broad scope for 'individual' action, encouraging local development and flexibility, this same autonomy becomes a barrier to integrated 'organizational' action as people are free to dissociate themselves from centrally established orientations (Hardy et al., 1984; Cohen and March, 1986). Therefore, managing change in a co-ordinated and integrated way appears difficult to achieve.

*Participative processes to reconcile divergent positions and visions may generate disparate and unrealistic change projects or orientations.* While participative management appears unavoidable to ensure that all actors are involved and committed to emerging organizational changes, experience shows that, in practice, consensus is often achieved at the expense of realism in change initiatives; broad participation tends to have an inflationary effect on the definition of change projects as attempts are made to reconcile a diversity of interests and ideas about change (Denis, Langley and Contandriopoulos, 1995).

*Diffuse power and divergent objectives may lead to dilution of change initiatives during the implementation process.* As a result of the existence of diffuse power structures in pluralistic organizations, strategic change must often be negotiated with the same people and through the same processes that are considered responsible for the need for change. Thus, changes are often diluted as they are implemented, producing a 'sedimented' layering of partially digested structures and strategic orientations or changes (Cooper, Hinings, Greenwood and Brown, 1996; Denis, Lamothe and Langley, 2001a). Health care organizations with their complex web of professional relationships and strategic initiatives face these three sources of inertia. This suggests that managing strategic change may require the use of a set of more or less intrusive or indirect means to orient change deliberately while maintaining coherence with the fundamental dynamics of these organizations. In the next sections, we analyze the potential of three levers to stimulate changes in health care organizations – the structural lever, the interactive lever and the incentive lever.

## The potential of various levers for managing change in health care organizations

### The structural lever: producing change by moving formal boundaries

By the structural lever, we mean a deliberate modification of the formal boundaries of organizations as in the case of mergers among organizations, and the creation of health networks and regional health authorities (Denis, Lamothe, Langley and Valette, 1999). Our discussion here of the potential and limitations of the structural lever is based on a stream of research on the process of merging teaching hospitals (Denis, Lamothe and Langley, 1999, 2001a). We consider such change as being radical because it threatens current patterns of functioning and interests that have been constituted through time (Denis, Lamothe and Langley, 1999; Denis, Lamothe, Langley and Valette, 1999). It imposes two critical tasks on these organizations – recomposing a viable organizational culture and reconstructing communities of practice in the clinical core of these hospitals.

Mergers destabilize organizational routines and dynamics at the strategic and operational/clinical levels. The process of moving from a state of destabilization to a new regime of functionality is a major challenge. Mergers imply the integration of diverse organizational cultures that favour different conceptions of roles and patterns of relationships between professionals and between professionals and management. Despite the fragmented state of pluralistic organizations, our study of mergers revealed that organizational members are attached to the negotiated orders (Strauss et al., 1964) that form the basis of an acceptable and relatively predictable way of doing things in a given organizational setting. Managing change in such contexts implies the working out of a new organizational order in coherence with the functional needs of the emerging new organizational entities.

Our studies of mergers show that modifying formal organizational boundaries may also produce changes that are at odds or distant from the organizing principles of the clinical core of these hospitals. Health care organizations may be conceived as a cluster of communities of practice (Wenger and Snyder, 2000). Mergers necessarily imply the relocation or restructuring of clinical services or units. This fundamentally upsets the organization of clinical practices. In hospitals, distinctive forms of co-ordination among professionals (negotiated orders) emerge organically around different categories of patients (Lamothe, 1996). We have observed that few professionals see any interest in transforming practice habits that seem effective from their clinical point of view. The success of the merger seems then to depend on the informal dynamics of restructuring the clinical operating core, and management seems to actually have relatively limited control over these dynamics (Mintzberg, 1982; Denis, Lamothe and Langley, 1999). Mergers must thus deal with these emergent social units and forms of collaboration. They must also deal with the intrinsic power relationships (Lamothe, 1996) and incentives that structure emergent collaboration and produce these local and varied negotiated orders (Denis, Lamothe, Langley and Valette, 1999).

Overall, the shifting of formal organizational boundaries reveals the complexity of managing change in health care organizations. The functioning of these organizations rests upon various and emerging rules and patterns of collaboration in a context of fragmented power and relative dilution of managerial control (Denis, Lamothe, Langley and Valette, 1999; Denis, Lamothe and Langley, 2001b). While environmental constraints or opportunities and political pressures are able to push organizations toward a major structural change in a relatively short period of time, the re-stabilization of the internal dynamics of the new organizational entities operates at a very different pace. While change in organizational boundaries provides new space for action, it is a rather indirect and blunt way to steer change at a distance. It does not in itself capture the social processes that are at the basis of the day-to-day operations of health care organizations. It is limited in its capability to change what people value about their work. To reconstruct a legitimate equilibrium within the new organizational entity other means than the structural lever need to be used (Denis, Gagnon, Lamothe and Langley, 2003). We now look in more detail at the potential of the interactive lever when it is used inside current organizational boundaries.

### The interactive lever: producing change through deliberations and conversations

By the interactive lever we mean the use of face-to-face interactions and extensive exchanges or communications between actors in order to stimulate and implement changes. Our discussion of the potentials and limits of the interactive lever is based on a series of empirical studies on strategic planning and quality improvement experiences in health care organizations (Lozeau, Langley and Denis, 2002; Denis, Langley and Lozeau, 1995). These studies look at the implementation of managerial techniques that aim to act upon organizational members' aspirations and behaviours in a very non-intrusive manner.[1]

## The experience of strategic planning in hospitals

The basic hypothesis behind strategic planning is that changes will be defined and achieved by relying on internal processes of deliberations coupled with formal analysis to define plausible options for change. We analyzed 26 experiences of strategic planning in hospitals. Overall, the use of the interactive lever has not generated a strong commitment to bring about significant changes. Only two appeared to involve forceful attempts at 'transformation' – one of these being quite successful, the other much less so. The cases of the remaining hospitals illustrate situations where plans were used as negotiation tools with the institutional environment represented mainly by government or as an occasion to promote professional aspirations and development outside the organization. In varying degrees, strategic planning was in most cases a rhetoric used to position the organization against some forces in the environment or an assemblage of numerous ambitious projects that required significant increases in the resource base of the organization.

Looking at the internal dynamics of planning operations in hospitals and considering the wide physician participation and continuing power, political negotiations tended to dominate the content and the use of strategic planning. It was difficult in a majority of cases to use planning to exercise choice among competing interests and visions. In most cases, planning effort became diluted by the pressures exerted by different powerful groups that wished to find in a plan the confirmation of their aspirations instead of a tool to arbitrate multiple demands with respect to available resources. Interactions were not sufficient, despite the support provided by legitimate formal authority. This suggests that interactions need to be coupled with other levers in order to align current patterns of representations and interests with change initiatives.

## The experience of Total Quality Management (TQM) in hospitals

Quality management is another process that relies extensively on interactions (in multidisciplinary teams, for example) to achieve change. Overwhelmingly, the quality management programs we observed during our 1995 to 1996 studies were introduced in response to institutional pressures, mainly from the Canadian Council for Hospital Accreditation (CCHA).

For most hospitals then, the quality management effort was driven more by the need to satisfy the CCHA than by pressure to satisfy customers, whose power in the public hospital system is rather weak. Even where leaders might buy into the quality philosophy, the diffuse power structure meant that this philosophy could not easily be made to infuse the entire organization, especially in the absence of strong pressures from customers (Lozeau, Langley and Denis, 2002). Implementation according to strict TQM principles would have involved transferring power from top and middle managers to lower level employees, and from dominant professionals (physicians) to teams. Politically, no one was in a position to impose such a transfer other than at the margins. Success in the implementation of TQM tended to be localized in some clinical units where professionals were individually committed to such process and/or where incentives or leadership pushed toward substantive changes.

Overall, our observations on strategic planning and TQM converge. Both techniques tend to be captured by the organizational dynamics into which they are inserted rather than transforming those dynamics in any fundamental way. Interactions among organizational members are shaped by the diffuse power structure of hospitals and by legitimate but potentially conflicting aspirations of various autonomous professional groups in the operating core of these organizations. Some outlier cases driven by a crisis situation or strong leadership seem to have induced some changes through these soft interactive levers. Mutual understanding or appeal to voluntarism fit well with the social fabric of these organizations but is frequently not sufficient to generate significant or substantive changes. Of course, individuals adapt to organizational situations by interacting to resolve problems and by getting involved in processes like the ones induced by strategic planning and TQM. However, one must take into account, as in the case of the structural lever, that it is difficult to penetrate clinical production in order to bring deliberate changes in practice or in the ways that professionals relate to organizational imperatives. Interactions probably need to be coupled with others levers. We now consider the potential of incentives as an alternative to stimulate changes in health care organizations.

### The incentives lever: producing changes through information, money and prestige[2]

Incentives are generally seen as a very effective lever to implement changes in health care systems and organizations. Very often when policy makers discuss dysfunctions or failures in the health system, they tend to see in incentives a potential solution (Giacomini, Hurley, Lomas et al., 1996). Reformers of public management (so-called New Public Management) also cite the need to reshape incentive systems in order to induce desired changes (Ferlie, Ashburner, Fitzgerald and Pettigrew, 1996). Incentives are seen as having the potential to align professional preferences and organizational strategies with objectives pursued in health care reforms without creating the major shocks associated with structural changes. However, incentives have been difficult to change in the Canadian health care system. The issue of changing the mode of payment for physicians is a clear example of this.

The difficulty of changing incentives is indeed so strong that our own research on organizational change has come across few cases where changes in incentives were part of the initiative. Moreover, when plans to change incentives were present initially, they tended to disappear from view prior to implementation. For example, in our studies of teaching hospital mergers, there was initially much talk of introducing practice plans for physicians, but no such plans were ever introduced.

Nevertheless, in this section we will examine a major policy experiment in the Canadian health care system, namely the experience of the Health Transition Fund that in some sense at least partially introduced incentives for change. Between 1997 and 2001, the HTF funded approximately 140 pilot projects and/or evaluation studies across Canada. Because this program offers the opportunity for professionals and organizations to propose innovative projects and obtain new financial resources on a competitive basis, it can be conceived as an attempt to generate and implement changes by using incentive (in this case a financial incentive). The HTF did not provide an a priori blueprint for the modification of current formal structures, roles and missions of health care organizations. Our analysis focuses on the lessons learned from a cross-case analysis of HTF projects (n = 40) carried out in Quebec.[3]

The HTF experience reveals that, despite the attribution of a high level of inertia in health care organizations, professionals and organizations were capable of generating innovative projects and were highly motivated by the idea of implementing changes developed at the clinical core of these organizations. The HTF was an opportunity to stimulate and formalize emergent changes that responded to the main preoccupations of professionals and managers in their working context. Many of these projects aimed to increase the integration of care for specific patient or disease groups or to reinforce the role of primary care in the health care system.

In a period where many health care organizations and professionals had faced severe resources constraints, they were highly sensitive to the supply of new resources provided by the HTF. However, the sensitivity of actors in the health care system for the opportunities and incentives provided by the HTF was not enough to ensure full implementation of the various innovative projects. Like the other two levers of change we just discussed, incentives do not operate in a vacuum. The injection of new financial resources to support pilot projects does not mean that the implementation context has all the ingredients to ensure the achievement of objectives and substantive changes at a desired scale. Incentives had to interact with other facilitating factors in the organizational and health care system environment. For example, innovative projects require professionals and managers to learn to work differently. Organizations may have to develop new forms of co-operation as is often the case in projects aiming at increasing the integration of care. In order to learn or co-operate, people have to have the opportunity to interact in flexible structures well adapted to the challenges of change. Organizational contexts do not all offer opportunities for such informal and decentralized exchanges. Moreover, while there may be incentives for sponsors to apply for money to test innovations, individuals involved in the experiments themselves may not necessarily perceive the rewards associated with making the innovations work. Also, the potential of incentives can be limited by current formal organizational boundaries. For example, in some projects, constructive exchanges between professionals across organizational boundaries were not coupled with the same openness from the boards of the concerned organizations. Moreover, the health care environment is often described as being characterized by a high degree of interdependency. Concretely, this means that the generation of changes is not under the responsibility and the control of a single authority structure or local organization. In many cases, despite high commitment and efforts by local actors to implement a pilot project, it appears that there are limits to what may be achieved locally. The 'marge de manoeuvre' of health care organizations and professionals in local settings is partly dependent on rules and decisions that are taken at other governance levels. Rules contained in labour contracts or modes of regulation of the status and payment of physicians are important constraining factors that were identified in many projects. In a striking example, two Quebec projects intended initially to test capitation payment methods never succeeded in implementing these new incentive schemes because of dominant contextual forces.

Overall, the HTF experience suggests that there is a significant potential for change inside current health care organizations, a potential that may have been underestimated by many large-scale reforms. However, incentives have their own limits. Stimulating interests by injecting new money is different from sustaining the alignment of actors' and organizations' behaviours with a project's objectives. The possibility of investing in long term change process may represent an important source of motivation. HTF projects were limited in time but after two years it seems that many projects were functional.

Our analysis of the potential of the various levers for change shows that they do not work in a vacuum. They operate in a complex pluralistic context where many levers for change need to be used simultaneously and coherently. The progression of a change process depends not only on the combination of the various levers but also on their strategic use through time. The selection of the various levers and their real potential will depend on how they are used – this is the realm of leadership.

## Leadership as catalyst in mobilizing and managing the levers for change

The specificities of pluralistic organizations discussed at the outset of this chapter suggest that the implementation of significant changes will only happen when key actors are sufficiently dedicated and competent to overcome the forces for fragmentation. Change in this context needs agency. In previous work (Denis, Lamothe and Langley, 2001a), using a 'processual' perspective, we define leadership as a collective and supraorganizational phenomenon in which actors join together in groups to respond to different challenges using multiple sources of expertise and legitimacy associated with the management of change.

As we saw, the levers of change do not move by themselves. They need to be created, manipulated and managed by people in leadership roles at all levels of organizations. Throughout our research, we have been fascinated by the way in which, despite the limitations noted above, certain individuals or groups of individuals working in concert have succeeded in moving organizations in certain directions by articulating the various levers for change.

For example, clinical leaders in several of the HTF experiments saw the opportunities in this program and the more astute and determined of them were able to not only benefit from the resources made available but to leverage those resources through interactions and the creation of structures that promoted continuity of their ideas. In some cases, top managers in hospitals involved in major restructuring were able to contribute significantly to reorienting the mission of their organizations and to ensure adaptation to new contingencies and opportunities.

Finally, despite the sad stories we told of abortive strategic planning and quality management initiatives, there were some exceptions in which the natural inertial logic of interactive mechanisms was overcome. For example, one hospital we studied had over a period of 20 years fundamentally changed its behaviour, adopting a 'planning culture' that involved the wide acceptance of formal analysis as an input to decisions and the use of plans in all areas as both determinants of action and control devices to measure progress. It appeared that shared values of procedural justice partly based on rational choice, but also based on peer review routines, had taken hold. This pluralistic but analytic model of decision making can be related to the ideal of collegiality sometimes invoked in classic visions of professional organizations (Satow, 1975). This was not achieved instantly, but through persistent incremental efforts by the CEO over many years.

We should also reiterate that, in professional contexts, leadership is not simply the business of people in formal organizational roles. Participation of formal and informal leaders at the clinical level is essential. Too often, we have seen managers ignore this to the detriment of change processes. If the clinicians themselves are not on the leading edge co-creating the change, the 'changes' may unfortunately remain hollow – stuck at the structural level without touching modes of practice. Our example of mergers shows that it was difficult to stimulate new modes of practice partly because of a lack of appropriate incentives, but also partly because many clinical leaders were not convinced that the change was necessary.

In summary, we suggest that leadership seems to be the catalyst that enables the levers of change to function and achieve successful articulation. The different levers of change are part of a toolbox that needs to be skilfully mastered by organizational leaders. Leaders must know the potential and the limits of each lever and work on an appropriate and dynamic combination of these levers through time. In addition, because leadership in health care organizations can be conceived as a collective enterprise (Denis, Lamothe and Langley, 2001), managers must accept to share the use of levers with formal and informal leaders within their organizations. The progression of a change project may require changes over time in the leadership constellation in order to favour the use of some lever. For example, while the capacity to decree changes in structures may lie mainly with people in positions of formal authority, interactions are probably more effective when a physician leader promotes a change project within the medical community. Because managers do not have the monopoly of the use of the various levers, the articulation of a coherent strategy to manage the change process is a challenge in itself.

This has implications for the role of managers in sustaining change in health care organizations. This role may sometimes mean manipulating the definition of change projects so that they fit with the interests and values of a dominant coalition of players (creating indirect micro-incentives), rather than attempting to manipulate those interests directly – an approach consistent with actor-network theory (Latour, 1987). A collectivity can be moved in certain directions by the creation of viable options for change that link them together, at least temporarily in actor-networks (Denis, Langley and Rouleau, *in press*). In this vision of leadership the leader must see him or herself as embedded in an ongoing process shared with others (an active node in a multifaceted constantly shifting network), not as an external authority able to impose his or her will. He or she has access to certain levers. The trick is to work with these in collaboration with others.

Overall, structures provide frameworks within which people are assigned authority and potential scope for action, but these are useless without the self-directed behaviour of people who occupy the positions of influence at all levels and use them skilfully. Interactions provide opportunities for learning; but, to be productive, they have to be sustained by a clear vision of what the organization needs or is trying to achieve. Finally, while the macro incentives underlying the health care system are extremely difficult to change, successful leaders can sometimes generate micro-level incentives (designing a project that attracts support) that can help in moving their organizations.

## Conclusions

In this chapter, we build on several previous research initiatives in the health care sector to draw some conclusions about the levers and catalysts for change. Like others, we have noted the immense barriers to change in a pluralistic organizational system. Our analysis shows that gauging the appropriate dosage of various levers in a change process is a challenging task for organizational leaders. Of course, each of our examples (mergers, utilization of managerial tools and of incentives) are not solely based on one lever but place an emphasis initially on one lever. In all cases, it became difficult through time to articulate which of the various levers of change were able to generate in-depth or large-scale transformation. Attempts to change through restructuring have unfortunately often resulted in destruction rather than construction. Attempts to change by focusing on grassroots processes such as interactions and mutual adjustment have unfortunately often resulted in agreements to disagree, log-rolling or inflationary consensus. Attempts to change through incentives have too often become diluted or bought off as those affected by the change make it so costly as to be unworkable.

Our analysis adds some insights into the complementarities of the various levers for change. Structures are needed to create a focus for action and attention; interactions are needed so that individuals can learn to integrate change at the operational level within structures; and incentives are needed to ensure that they have some interest in investing in learning. The three levers are not disembodied however. Our thinking at this point is that when change initiatives work, it is through the agency of leaders who individually and collectively manage to mix and match them effectively in a specific organizational context. Leaders are not only people in formal positions but also in informal networks within and outside formal organizational boundaries. More research is needed to reveal the dynamic of articulating strategically the various levers in a constellation of formal and informal leaders to promote change in health care organizations.

## Notes

1. For a description of the research and data sets, see Lozeau, Langley and Denis (2002), 'The corruption of managerial techniques by organizations', *Human Relations*, 55(5), p. 537.
2. This section is based essentially on a book chapter by Denis (2004), 'Governance and management of change in Canada's health system', in P.-G. Forest, G. P. Marchildon and T. McIntosh (eds), *Changing Health Care in Canada* (Toronto: University of Toronto Press).
3. Desbiens, Dagenais, Joubert et al., 2001; Denis, Lamothe and Langley, 2000, 2001b; Touati, Contandriopoulos, Denis et al., 2001, in press; Béland, Bergman, Lebel et al., 2001; Lamarche, Lamothe, Bégin et al., 2002.

## References

Alberta. Premier's Advisory Council on Health (2001) *A Framework for Reform: Report of the Premier's Advisory Council on Health*. Mazankowski report (Edmonton: Report of the Premier's Advisory Council on Health), accessed 2005-07-22, http://www.premiersadvisory.com/reform.html.

Alter, C. and Hage, J. (1993) *Organizations Working Together* (Newbury Park CA: Sage Publications).

Béland, F., Bergman, H., Lebel, P., Lespérance, K., Denis, J-L., Tousignant, P., Contandriopoulos, A-P., Boivin, J-F. and Morales, C. (2001) 'Évaluation d'un système de services intégrés pour personnes âgées en perte d'autonomie (SIPA)', in J-C. Henrard, O. Firbank, S. Clément, M. Frossard, J-P. Lavoie and A. Vézina (eds), *Personnes âgées dépendantes en France et au Québec. Qualité de vie, pratiques et politiques* (Paris: INSERM).

Bryson, J. M. and Crosby, B. C. (1992) *Leadership for the Common Good: Tackling Problems in a Shared Power World* (San Francisco: Jossey-Bass).

Clair (2000) – *see* Québec. Commission d'étude sur la santé et les services sociaux (2000)

Cohen, M. D. and March, J. G. (1986) *Leadership and Ambiguity* (Boston: Harvard University School Press).

Comité sénatorial permanent des Affaires sociales, des sciences et de la technologie/ The Standing Senate Committee on Social Affairs, Science and Technology (2002) *La santé des Canadiens: Le rôle du gouvernement fédérale: Recommandations en vue d'une réform*, vol. 6, Kirby Report (Ottawa ON: Comité sénatorial permanent des Affaires sociales, des sciences et de la technologie).

Commission on the Future of Health Care in Canada (2002) *Building on Values: The Future of Health Care in Canada* (Saskatoon, SK: The Commission), accessed 2005-07-21, http://www.hc-sc.gc.ca/english/pdf/care/romanow_e.pdf.

Cooper, D. J., Hinings, C. R., Greenwood, R. and Brown, J. L. (1996) 'Sedimentation and transformation in organizational change: The case of Canadian law firms', *Organization Studies*, 17(4), pp. 623–47.

Denis, J-L. (2002) *Governance and Management of Change in Canada's Health System, discussion paper #36* (Ottawa: Commission on the Future of Health Care in Canada), accessed 2005-07-22, http://www.hc-sc.gc.ca/english/pdf/romanow/ pdfs/36_Denis_E.pdf.

Denis, J-L., Gagnon, S., Lamothe, L. and Langley, A. (2003) 'Disappear to survive and prosper: managing paradox in a hospital merger', Paper presented at the Annual Meeting of the Academy of Management, Seattle, WA.

Denis, J-L., Hébert, Y., Langley, A., Lozeau, D. and Trottier, L. H. (2002) 'Explaining diffusion patterns for complex health care innovations', *Health Care Management Review*, Summer, 27(33), pp. 60–73.

Denis, J-L., Lamothe, L. and Langley, A. (2003) 'Templates and pilots in the framing of public sector reform', Paper presented at the 19th EGOS Colloquium, Copenhagen, Denmark.

Denis, J-L., Lamothe, L. and Langley, A. (2003) 'Uncovering the deep structure of health care organizations through organizational change processes', Paper presented at the Administrative Sciences Association of Canada Understanding Organizational Change Symposium, Halifax, NS.

Denis, J-L, Lamothe, L. and Langley, A. (2001b) 'Government-funded experiments as resources for renewal in health care?', Paper presented at the Annual Meeting of the Academy of Management, Washington, DC.

Denis, J-L., Lamothe, L. and Langley, A. (2001a) 'The Dynamic of Collective Leadership and Strategic Change in Pluralistic Organizations', *Academy of Management Journal*, 44(4), pp. 809–37.

Denis, J-L., Lamothe, L. and Langley, A. (2000) 'The emerging shape of professional organization in health care', Paper presented at the Annual Meeting of the Academy of Management, Toronto, ON.

Denis, J-L., Lamothe, L. and Langley, A. (1999) 'The struggle to implement teaching hospital mergers', *Canadian Public Administration*, 42(3), pp. 285–311.

Denis, J-L., Lamothe, L., Langley, A. and Valette, A. (1999) 'The struggle to redefine boundaries in health care systems', in D. Borck, M. Powell and C. R. Hinings (eds), *Restructuring the Professional Organizations* (London: Routledge).

Denis, J-L., Langley, A. and Cazale, L. (1996) 'Leadership and strategic change under ambiguity', *Organization Studies*, 17, pp. 673–99.

Denis, J-L., Langley, A. and Contandriopoulos, A-P. (1995) 'La transformation du rôle des instances régionales dans le système de santé au Québec', *Revue française d'administration publique*, 76(4), pp. 599–608.

Denis, J-L., Langley, A. and Lozeau, D. (1995) 'The role and impact of formal strategic planning in public hospitals', *Health Services Management Research*, 8(2), pp. 86–112.

Denis, J-L., Langley, A. and Pineault, M. (2000) 'Becoming a leader in a complex organization', *Journal of Management Studies*, 37, pp. 1063–103.

Denis, J-L., Langley, A. and Rouleau, L. (in press) 'Rethinking Leadership in Public Organizations', in *Oxford Handbook of Public Administration*.

Desbiens, F., Dagenais, C., Joubert, P. et al. (2001) *De l'innovation au changement: final report submitted to the Health Transition Fund (HTF)* (Québec: Ministère de la santé et des services sociaux).

Ferlie, E., Ashburner, L., Fitzgerald, L. and Pettigrew, A. (1996) *The New Public Management in Action* (Oxford: Oxford University Press).

Fyke (2001) – *see* Saskatchewan Commission on Medicare (2001)

Giacomini, M., Hurley, J., Lomas, J., Bhatia, V. and Goldsmith, L. (1996) *The Many Meanings of Money: A Health Policy Analysis Framework for Understanding Financial Incentives. Final Report* (Toronto, ON: Center for Health Economics and Policy Analysis, McMaster University).

Hardy, C., Langley, A., Mintzberg, H., Rose, J. (1984) 'Strategy formation in the university setting', in J. L. Bess (ed.), *College and University Organization: Insights from the Behavioural Sciences* (New York: New York University Press).

Kirby (2002) – *see* Comité sénatorial permanent des Affaires sociales, des sciences et de la technologie (2002)

Lamarche, P., Lamothe, L., Bégin, C., Léger, M. and Vallières-Joly, M. (2002) 'L'intégration des services: enjeux structurels et organisationnels ou humains et cliniques?', *Ruptures*, 8(2), pp. 71–92.

Lamothe, L. (1996) *La structure professionnelle clinique de facto d'un hôpital de soins ultraspécialisés*, PhD Thesis, McGill University, Faculty of Management, Montreal QC.

Latour, B. (1987) *Science in Action* (Cambridge, MA: Harvard University Press).

Lozeau, D., Langley, A. and Denis, J-L. (2002) 'The corruption of managerial techniques by organizations', *Human Relations*, 55(5), pp. 537–64.

Mazankowski (2001) – *see* Alberta. Premier's Advisory Council on Health (2001).

McNulty, T. and Ferlie, E. (2002) *Process Reengineering: The Complexities of Organisational Transformation* (Oxford: Oxford University Press).

Mhatre, S. L., and Deber, R. B. (1992) 'From equal access to health care to equitable access to health: a review of Canadian provincial health commissions and reports', *International Journal of Health Services*, 22(4), pp. 645–68.

Mintzberg, H. (1982) *Structure et dynamique des organisations* (Paris: Éditions d'organisation). (Note: English edition 1979.)

National Forum on Health (Forum national sur la santé) (1997) *La santé au Canada: un héritage à faire fructifier* (Ottawa: Health Canada), accessed 2005-07-22, http://www.hc-sc.gc.ca/francais/soins/forum_sante/publications/finvol2/.

Nutt, P. C. and Backoff, R. W. (1992) *Strategic Management of Public and Third Sector Organizations* (San Francisco: Jossey-Bass).

Quebec. Commission d'enquête sur les services de santé et les services sociaux (1988) *Rapport* Commission Rochon (Quebec: Gouvernement du Québec).

Québec. Commission d'étude sur la santé et les services sociaux (2000). *Les solutions émergentes*. *Rapport final*. Rapport Clair (Quebec: la Commission d'étude sur la santé et les services sociaux), accessed 2005-07-22, http://publications.msss.gouv.qc.ca/acrobat/f/documentation/2000/00-109.pdf.

Quinn. J. B. (1992) *Intelligent Enterprise* (New York: Free Press).

Rainey, H. G. (1991) *Understanding and Managing Public Organizations*. (San Francisco: Jossey-Bass).

Rochon (1988) – *see* Quebec. Commission d'enquête sur les services de santé et les services sociaux (1988).

Rodriguez, C., Langley, A., Béland, F. and Denis, J-L. (2003) 'Managing across boundaries in healthcare: the forces for change and inertia', in N. Paulsen and T. Hernes (eds), *Managing Boundaries in Organizations: Multiple Perspectives* (Basingstoke: Palgrave Macmillan).

Saltman, R. B. (2002) 'Regulating incentives: the past and present role of the state in health care systems', *Social Science & Medicine*, 54(11), pp. 1677–84.

Saltman, R. B. and Figueras, J. (1998) 'Analyzing the Evidence on European Health Care Reforms', *Health Affairs*, 17(2), pp. 85–108.

Saskatchewan. Commission on Medicare (2001) *Caring for Medicare: Sustaining a Quality System*. Fyke Report. (Regina: Commission on Medicare).

Satow, R. L. (1975) 'Value-rational authority and professional organizations: Weber's missing type', *Administrative Science Quarterly*, 20, pp. 526–31.

Shortell, S. M., Gillies, R. R., Anderson, D. A., Erickson, E. M. and Mitchell, J. B. (1996) *Remaking Health Care in America: Building Organized Delivery Systems* (San Francisco: Jossey-Bass).

Sinclair, D. (2002) 'After Kirby and Romanow: where to from here?', *Hospital Quarterly*, 6(2), pp. 42–3.

Strauss, A., Schatzman, L., Butcher, R., Ehrlich, D. and Sabshin, M. (1964) *Psychiatric Ideologies and Institutions* (New York: Free Press).

Touati, N., Contandriopoulos, A-P., Denis, J-L., Rodriguez, R. and Sicotte, C. (in press) 'The integration of health care services as solution to the problem of accessibility in rural areas: what leverage mechanisms do regulatory agencies have in a public system?', *Health Care Management Review*.

Touati, N., Contandriopoulos, A-P., Denis, J-L., Rodriguez, R., Sicotte, C. and Nguyen, H. (2001) 'Une expérience d'intégration des soins dans une zone rurale: les enjeux de la mise en œuvre', *Ruptures*, 8(2), pp. 93–107.

Tuohy, C. H. (2002) 'Political conditions in Canada may now favor some major changes in its health care system', *Health Affairs*, 21(3), pp. 32–46.

Wenger, E. and Snyder, W. (2000) 'Communities of practice: the organizational frontier', *Harvard Business Review*, Jan–Feb, pp. 139–45.

# 2

# Is the NHS Leadership Qualities Framework Missing the Wood for the Trees?

*Richard Bolden, Martin Wood and Jonathan Gosling*

## Introduction

Typically, when thinking of directors, professionals, politicians and other 'leaders', the individual (as post holder) is promoted as the source of 'leadership'. S/he is seen to act as an energizer, catalyst and visionary equipped with a set of abilities (communication, problem-solving, people management, decision making, and so on) that can be applied across a diverse range of situations and contexts. Whilst situational factors (such as the nature of the task, group, culture, and so on) may be considered, they are not generally viewed as barriers to an individual's ability to lead under different circumstances. Thus the term 'leadership' is used to refer to the personal qualities and capabilities of a few key people – whose conduct may be perceived as 'leaderful' by their embodiment of some already present exemplar or archetype. However, leadership can also be considered as a process of social influence between individuals and/or groups within an environmental setting (Yukl, 2002). In this instance a person (or group of people) is deemed 'leaderful' by reason of a fortunate spontaneity with the situation in question.

An increasing emphasis on 'evidence based' policy and practice as the basis for management recruitment, development and education within the UK public sector ensures that the former definition remains dominant, with management (and now leadership) presented as an objective, rational and individual pursuit rather than the consequence of a complex web of contextually-situated inter-relations (Sanderson, 2002). In reply to this treatment we suggest that it is short sighted to think that leadership corresponds to certain distinct personal qualities, capabilities and/or behaviours – this tendency too quickly turns leadership development into a routine hurdle race, quite apart from any question of critical and/or appreciative study. In this chapter we highlight some methodological and theoretical weaknesses of this individualistic approach through reference to the National Health Service (NHS) Leadership Qualities Framework. We also present an alternative base of literature and explore a different 'vocabulary' that together help better capture the nature of leadership and the associated values and relationships that surround and suffuse it.

## Competency frameworks and the individualization of leadership qualities

The main developments in leadership thinking can be traced from the trait approach (Stogdill, 1950), through the behavioural and contingency schools (McGregor, 1960; Blake and Mouton, 1964; Fiedler, 1967), situational leadership (Hersey and Blanchard, 1977) and transformational leadership (Burns, 1978; Bass, 1985; Bass and Avolio, 1994). Throughout this shift, however, leadership continues to be conceived of as a set of values, qualities and/or behaviours exhibited by the leader that encourage the participation, development, and commitment of others (usually termed 'followers'). The leader is expected to display excellent information processing, project management, customer service and delivery skills, along with proven business and political acumen. They build partnerships, 'walk the talk', show incredible drive and enthusiasm, and get things done. Furthermore, the leader should demonstrate innovation, creativity and think 'outside the box' (Rickards, 1999). They are entrepreneurs who identify opportunities – they like to be challenged and they are prepared to take risks. Of interest too is the emphasis on the importance of qualities such as honesty, integrity, empathy, trust and valuing diversity. The leader is expected to show a true concern for people that is drawn from a deep level of self-awareness and personal reflection (Conger and Kanungo, 1998; Goleman et al., 2002).

From this view it is leaders who impress others; inspire people; push through transformations; get the job done; have compelling, even gripping, visions; stir enthusiasm; and have personal magnetism (Maccoby, 2000). This notion of the 'heroic' leader, however, does little to challenge traditional conceptualizations of leadership and, despite it being one of the most researched topics of the past 50 years, the popular view remains relatively unchanged. Whilst personal qualities of the leader are undoubtedly important they are unlikely to be sufficient in themselves for the emergence and exercise of leadership. It is perhaps more likely that these aspiring characteristics, attitudes and behaviours result from the over-simplification of a vast pool of environmental data into a few key people. Mintzberg has made this point several times and repeats it once more when he questions *Fortune* magazine's assertion that 'within four years, Lou Gerstner added more than $40 billion to IBM's shareholder value. *All by himself?*' (Mintzberg, 2004, p. 22 – original emphasis).

Nevertheless, this individualistic concept of leadership has been widely adopted as a basis for management education and development in the UK ever since the Review of Vocational Qualifications report in 1986 (De Ville, 1986) and continues to gain dominance (for example, CEML, 2002; IiP,

2003; MSC, 2004). Following the Council for Excellence in Management and Leadership research, for example, the UK government pledged to address the national management and leadership deficit through a range of initiatives to increase demand and improve supply of management and leadership development (DfES, 2002). As these initiatives are rolled out across the country the emphasis on evidence based policy, measurable performance outcomes and consistency of approach encourages increased reliance on government-endorsed models, frameworks and standards (PIU, 2001; MSC, 2004; Tomlinson, 2004).

One such framework now being used in the UK is the NHS Leadership Qualities Framework (NHS Leadership Centre, 2002), which describes a set of key characteristics, attitudes and behaviours that leaders in the National Health Service should aspire to in delivering the NHS Plan (DoH, 2000). This framework was a central pillar of the NHS Modernisation Agency (recently disbanded) and their strategy to modernize and update the NHS to cope with the demands of the twenty-first century. The framework has a number of applications and forms the foundation for setting leadership standards in the NHS, assessing and developing high performance in leadership, individual and organizational assessment, integrating leadership across the service and related agencies, adapting leadership to suit changing contexts and bench-marking of leadership capacity and capability (NHS Leadership Centre, 2005).

There are 15 characteristics within the framework, clustered around personal qualities (self-belief, self-awareness, self-management, drive for improvement and personal integrity), setting direction (broad scanning, intellectual flexibility, seizing the future, political astuteness and drive for results) and delivering the service (leading change through people, holding to account, empowering others, collaborative working and effective and strategic influencing). It aims to communicate rich data about those characteristics that distinguish what highly effective leaders should actually say, do, think and feel in order to achieve successful outcomes across the service. On the whole, the framework has been well-received, nevertheless, there are some voices of dissent (for example, Richards, 2003) and a series of methodological and theoretical weaknesses that, we believe, greatly undermine the potential of this approach to deliver what it promises.

The literature identifies at least five major weaknesses of the competency approach. Firstly, it is criticized for being reductionist, fragmenting the management role rather than representing it as an integrated whole (Lester, 1994; Ecclestone, 1997; Grugulis, 1997). Secondly, competencies are often generic, assuming a common set of capabilities no matter what the nature of the situation, individuals or task (Swailes and Roodhouse, 2003). Thirdly, it is argued that standards may reinforce rather than challenge traditional ways of thinking about management (Cullen, 1992; Lester, 1994). Fourthly, competencies focus on measurable behaviours and outcomes to the near exclusion of more subtle (and probably more important) qualities, interactions and situational factors, such as the moral and emotional dimensions of leadership (Bell et al., 2002; Holman and Hall, 1997; Bolden, 2005). And a fifth common criticism is the rather limited and mechanistic approach to education that often results whereby managers are 'trained' in order to improve job-related performance rather than 'educated' to develop more general knowledge and cognitive abilities (Grugulis, 1997; Brundrett, 2000).

The implications of such criticisms are quite damning in practice. They imply, in effect, that competency frameworks neither give a realistic picture of the management and/or leadership role (such as described by Mintzberg, 1973; 1975) nor do they offer a credible basis for the selection and/or development of managers and/or leaders. Indeed, it could be argued that rather than clarifying leadership, standards and competencies they actually confuse the issue: 'the problems it promised to resolve are not capable of resolution and its promise consisted largely of a sleight of hand whereby organizational problems were simply restated as management responsibilities' (Salaman, 2004, p. 75).

While the NHS Leadership Qualities Framework may fare better than many competency-based frameworks, most of the criticisms and weaknesses identified still hold true to a certain degree. Thus, for example, although this model is not as generic as some (that is, at least it is organizationally bounded) it is applied across all parts of the NHS despite the initial research on which it is based being derived simply from interviews with Chief Executives and Directors (NHS Leadership Centre, 2003). Furthermore, the information on which it is based is entirely self-report (via interviews and focus groups) rather than through observation of actual leadership in practice and thus tends to post-rationalize and personalize the experience.

In the case of the NHS Leadership Qualities Framework personal qualities and behaviours, such as self-belief, -awareness, -management, -improvement and personal integrity, are central to the model and feed into the processes of setting direction and delivering the service. Whilst this individual focus may usefully articulate some of the things that a person does, is, or aspires to, it may (a) be a somewhat persecutory list of 'oughts', and (b) still do little to achieve effective leadership. One may be visionary, communicative and honest – and still find leadership to be elusive. So these qualities turn out to be descriptive (not necessarily of leadership, but of some qualities associated with people in the top jobs) yet they are often presented as prescriptive. Where leadership is lacking the boss may well need to do these things, but simply doing them does not conjure up 'leadership'. In fact, the possibility of doing them is just as likely to be the outcome of collective desires and beliefs.

## The paradox of leadership standards and competencies

At the heart of the standards/competency approach is a desire to be both descriptive (what leaders actually do) and normative (what leaders should do) but, to a large extent, neither of these are achieved through this approach. Thus, whilst it may be useful to describe what constitutes effective practice in certain situations (for example, examples of 'good practice'), due to the complexity of organizational life, it is unlikely that this will ever correspond closely to the lived experience of other people even if faced with similar challenges. Likewise, prescribing what ought to be done may encourage consistency but is also likely to foster an environment of dependency, so that when faced by uncertainty the 'leader' will be unable to decide which course of action to follow, and will not be inspired to develop his or her own approach.

The NHS Leadership Qualities Framework is founded on research into the qualities and capabilities of individual Chief Executives and Directors from the NHS. Whilst this can be informative as to the general characteristics of these people, it is not definitive and nor does it give much guidance as to how these qualities manifest themselves within a given situation. Such descriptions tend to oversimplify and may prove to be of limited, practical value within the climate of complexity, interdependence and fragmentation that arguably characterizes multi-disciplinary organizations such as the NHS (Blackler et al., 1999).

Furthermore, when assessing leaders against competencies there is a tendency to interpret behaviour according to these predefined categories. Thus, in effect, the framework becomes a self-fulfilling prophecy whereby individuals redefine themselves in terms of the corporate language. Grugulis (1997) reached this conclusion for the National Occupational Standards in Management, identifying them simply as a means for enabling managers to legitimize their role rather than reappraising or improving their practice, and similar conclusions have been reached within the health service (Holman and Hall, 1997).

Rather than considering the behaviours that individual leaders and managers should exhibit, maybe it would be better to consider instead how we have purposefully selected these particular abilities from a welter of environmental data. Looked at from this point of view we can still describe effective leadership and managerial work, but we are now aware that our descriptions are 'a rich totality of many determinations and relations' (Marx, 1973, p. 101); they are a consequence of a process of thinking and no longer the property of a few venerated individuals. As Tolstoy memorably reminds us in *War and Peace*, 'to study the laws of history we must completely change the subject of our observation, we must leave aside kings, ministers, and generals, and study the common, infinitesimally small elements by which the masses are moved'.

One implication of this broadening of focus is that our reductive assessment, selection and measurement of certain leadership and management qualities and capabilities is really a process of fixing and naming production – the working up of our observations into abstract concepts that appeal to us and that we can fasten onto easily. Thus, the usual evaluation has to be reversed. We should no longer judge by selecting and breaking down the complex reality of leadership into a few key people and fragmented 'qualities', as with frameworks and standards, but intuitively grasp it as constantly in the making. Instead of concentrating on the abstract analysis of dissociated leaders' definite qualities and capabilities we should think in terms of their mode of production. Individual leaders are cut from continual process in a way that makes leadership familiar and understandable. But, it is this process, rather than its product, that should be our logical subject. Each time we cut leaders out from the world of experience we detach them from whatever reality it is that they belonged to. This deletes the background, the surroundings, the past, and their connections and links to the rest of the world. In other words, we project our perception onto a few key people ('leaders') so that we see them as substantial things in themselves, as if the qualitative characteristics of their appearance were objective reality and not, more limitedly, as 'a mode of attention' that only frames and fixes a few discrete and familiar individuals.

Thus, for example, in a health care setting perhaps it would be better to reconnect with how a moving, living, multi-disciplinary team such as a maternity department works effectively together over a sustained period to facilitate the effective delivery (so to speak) of a desired outcome. In such a scenario it is undoubtedly the relations of the medical team, patient, organizational systems and a whole host of other factors that makes leadership far more than the personal qualities or intrinsic intentionality of any one of the individuals involved (although a high degree of professional competence and ability is also clearly essential).

An important question to consider is what grounds we have for the belief that in some way leadership really is in those key people as our senses perceive them. For conventional thinkers, no leadership is conceivable without the qualities and capabilities of a few key people. That is to say, leadership qualities are normally referred to as the property of particular individuals. Nonetheless, if our alternative argument is correct, leadership qualities are first and foremost an abstraction, a purposive selection. Once we think we have the key person we call 'leader', our mind recomposes our experience within them.

By fixing upon the actions or qualities of a few key people the result is a 'crude tearing apart' of 'real' relationships (Marx, 1973, p. 87) into discrete processes – for example, 'leader/follower'. But such processes are merely crude and accidental connections; abstract moments. Real relationships, on the other hand, are 'organic relationships of things that belong together and moments that must be grasped in their unity' (Marx, 1973, p. 90). Marx (1973, p. 83) considers that the isolated, detached, definite and limited individual 'belongs among the unimaginative conceits of the Eighteenth Century', which rests on 'a belief in natural individuals not arriving through social production, but posited by nature'. Like Marx, we argue that the leadership focus on a few key people is an illusion (see Wood, 2005 for a further elaboration of these ideas).

Returning to our earlier example, looking for the 'leader' within a 20-hour plus delivery (and the antenatal care preceding and postnatal care following this 'event') is somewhat meaningless. In such a case the responsibility passes between members of the medical and support teams in a more fluid manner as the situation evolves. Instead of a 'magic bullet', leadership is tied to the way we make reference to the 'leader'. Changing our reference could change our identification of/with the leader.

### Beyond individual competencies

We have noted above how conventional leadership studies, and now the competency approach, give us a few key people upon which to anchor the notion of leadership, but this, we have argued, is a misleading notion. Our aim now is to show, methodologically, how a view of leadership as a contextually-situated relational process can enable a more sophisticated purchase on leadership qualities and capabilities than the teleological tendency of standards and competency frameworks.

The first problem is not to seek to understand the preconceived world of passions, intentions and influence of a 'few key people', but rather to explore the significance of some of the other factors in the actual occasions and to look at the values associated with the emerging relationships. Consider, for example, the appropriateness of the sentence 'S/he is the leader'. Adapting Bohm's (1980, p. 29) enquiry into the subject-verb-object structure of language we might ask whom is the 'S/he' that is doing the leading? Following Bohm, would it not be more accurate to say 'Leadership is going on'? Similarly, instead of saying 'Leaders act on followers', we can more appropriately say, leadership is going on within a mutually dependent association that makes any bracketing of the abstractions customarily called 'leaders' and 'followers' difficult to sustain.

With this in mind, the phenomenological appearance of a key person cannot be construed as an isolated thing, present at hand, that gets caught up in life. The person cannot dissociate him or herself from his/her environment, and nor can the environment be dissociated from the people who interact within it. Instead, the appearance (and disappearance) of leaders and followers should be spoken of in terms of ongoing movement or unfolding and not in terms of absolute, distinct entities. Unfolding (or 'becoming') suggests that the essence of leadership does not reside within a few key people, but within the relations of ongoing movement and orientations that is our lived experience.

A process approach to leadership qualities and capabilities might be consistent with Foucault's genealogical strategy (Dreyfus and Rabinow, 1982) and particularly his complex analysis of power (Foucault, 1980), as well as with ideas from critical management research, which emphasize leadership as a social field of activity (Alvesson, 1996; Alvesson and Deetz, 2000). Process methodology starts from two, interrelated axioms. First, like power, leadership is always in the process of being formulated; always 'in the making', and always enmeshed in social practice, rather than in a few key people 'already made'. This focus brings the space of the stage or scene to the centre of analysis and not the unambiguous leader who can be simply located, or the external relations, which obtain between a few key people in specific places. Like power, leadership is an internal relation, constantly 'in-tension' and subject to a myriad of 'meanings, values, ideals and discourse processes' (Alvesson, 1996, p. 472). Second, the key individuals we come to recognize in a specific social context are not the inherent qualities or substantial capabilities of leadership as it really is, but an endlessly complex set of interrelations that we must attend to if we are to reach an understanding of the unfolding events in a particular social field, here and now. The methodological concern, therefore, is not with any reductive, a priori manifestations, but with 'freeing the conditions of emergence' (Foucault, 1972, p. 127) of leadership.

One implication of this reconception is that our experience of leadership always exceeds our categorizing reaches and so the tendency to rely upon hypothetical categories is misplaced. 'Good' and 'effective' leadership cannot be categorically labelled only experienced and lived, here and now. Sandberg (2000), in his analysis of research with car assembly workers, concluded that job competencies arise as a result of the worker's perception of the ultimate purpose of his/her work rather than any independently stated set of capabilities. He thus proposes that what is important is to engage the person in dialogue to reveal and clarify his/her purpose at work rather than presenting him/her with a pre-defined set of competencies to acquire. By ensuring clarity of purpose, it is argued the appropriate competencies will emerge naturally within a given situation. This research would thus imply that 'competence' is a socially constructed set of meanings rather than a definable list of attributes and/or behaviours to acquire. In our example of the maternity department this is arguably what happens – the common sense of purpose and an understanding of roles binding participants together in a relationship that facilitates the emergence of effective and appropriate behaviours (leadership or otherwise) as required.

If we are looking to model a different kind of leadership strategy for the NHS, a second implication is that we might start to look at other forms of social influence such as self-governance and self-determination (that is, autonomy). Exploring leadership as one form of social influence implies a methodological focus on the relations, connections, dependencies and reciprocities that form the appearance of leadership – the set of advantageous circumstances that becomes identical with the 'objective' subject of leadership.

In other words, through such a focus, it is difficult to maintain the simple exteriority of leadership as a clear object of study from the whole domain of institutions, economic processes and social relations, within which a subjective appearance obtains. Instead, we are dealing with a 'density of discursive practices, systems that establish [leadership as] events' (Foucault, 1972, p. 128). Process thought holds that a particular period, encounter, issue, or situation, rather than shared behaviour patterns, attitudes or traits should be our focus.

Practically speaking this means attending to the 'density' of events and background processes through which leadership is socially recognized. In turn, this implies the deployment of a qualitative, interpretive and ethnographic research strategy, with a strong 'situational' focus (Alvesson, 1996). Such an approach seeks to emphasize the degree and form of permeability of a particular appearance, the principle of its articulation and the 'tangle of continuities and discontinuities, modifications' and 'discursive formations' (Foucault, 1972, p. 176), through which it is effectively maintained. It means opening up leadership from multiple angles, searching the 'small details, minor shifts and subtle contours' (Dreyfus and Rabinow, 1982, p. 106) of its surface to see how it was realized. Research questions will emphasize the ambiguous and the precarious quality of leadership as a behaviour/social relation and acknowledge the role of social/institutional norms and their constraints – of variations and contingencies in accounts. The focus is on leadership as a practical accomplishment, constituted in event places, and so avoids the pathological distinction that leaves leaders 'out there' or 'on top'. What is interesting, from a process studies perspective, is how continual patterns and divergent processes form a subjective appearance, or appear to obtain in a substantial set of qualities or capabilities. The NHS Leadership Qualities Framework remains bound up with notions of self-responsibility and comparatively contestable 'standards of identity' in which one's life must be programmed meticulously to measure up to tight and extensive institutional standards of 'normality and entitlement'. Our re-conceptualization encourages a shift not only in how leadership is researched, but also in how it is recognized, rewarded and developed within the NHS. It argues for a more discursive approach to leadership and leadership development that enables people at all levels within the organization to explore the meanings and responsibilities associated with their roles in the search for common understanding rather than consensus. Rather like the (in)famous story of the NASA janitor who, when asked, claimed that his job was about putting a man on the moon, it is quite conceivable that everyone has a role to play in the process of 'leadership' and equally inconceivable that the 'leader' could achieve the outcome without their contribution. Research into leadership in complex health system environments such as the NHS should no longer concentrate on exposing new leadership skills or abilities, but on the myriad incidents and minute facts either overlooked or deliberately ignored.

We thus call for a broadening of the scope of focus for leadership beyond the individual to a fuller consideration of processes of social influence situated in context. This requires a degree of reflection and self-responsibility in all of us; a mode of conduct that stops subordination to a powerful individual and enables professionals to act and engage with others and their priorities collectively. An important task now is to examine the evidence for the claim that leadership, in a much more primary sense than typically endorsed by extant leadership competency frameworks, is to be found within a system of interdependencies and without an individual or collectively organized agent to serve as a centre or pivot.

## Conclusion

It has been argued that whilst management and leadership frameworks, such as that used in the NHS, have been developed to address very practical concerns (providing a benchmark of best practice and a model for assessment and development) they are too conceptually and methodologically flawed to be of much benefit on their own.

In this chapter we have argued for a shift in emphasis from individual leaders to the collective processes of leadership; from leadership in abstraction (as represented by generic competencies) to leadership experienced and lived, here and now and always beyond our categorizing reaches; and from the prescriptive use of competencies (to define what 'leaders should do') to an inductive dialogue (to facilitate an understanding of the challenges of 'leadership as it is').

Within the NHS, the Leadership Qualities Framework marks a significant step towards trying to understand the nature of leadership within this incredibly complex and worthy organization. The longer this model is used, however, the greater the likelihood of it eroding the very thing that the NHS is trying to nurture – that is a culture of responsible shared leadership. In order to progress in a constructive manner there is a pressing need to gain a more thorough understanding of the processes of managerial and clinical leadership across the NHS in the future. The focus on individual behaviours should be extended to permit a broader appreciation of leadership and management. This should include empirically at least (1) studying of a representative range of stakeholders and approaches to managerial and clinical leadership in the NHS to assess their relative success against a range of indicators; (2) establishing whether the effectiveness of leadership style is related to individual qualities or to aspects of the collective network in which the leader is situated; and (3) exploring the implications of the consistent actions, competing accounts and informed interpretations of others for extending our understanding of the leadership function.

There is also a deeper, theoretical issue, however, and its complexity cannot be ignored. The trenchant divisions between professional groups and their experiences of leadership and authority certainly are not going to be solved merely by replacing one set of qualities by another analogous set.

If leadership research and development, as a way of understanding and as a practicable program of development, is not to remain subjugated to the individualistic canon we first must 'relevate'[1] alternative ways of thinking so as to gain new conceptual leverage on leadership's essential relatedness. The difficulty, however, is conceiving a post-individualistic, relational thinking and language adequate for progression beyond the individual without destroying its significance and integral role in the processes of leadership. However, if we accept these propositions, unless the NHS and other organizations using or considering a competency-based approach to leadership engage with the wider theoretical constructs and contexts of leadership they run the risk of missing the very thing they are looking for – in effect, 'missing the wood for the trees'.

## Note

1. A derivation of the verb elevate and the noun relevance it refers to the practice of raising the status and bringing to bear that which appears, in the first instance, to be 'irrelevant' to the world of leadership studies and practice.

## References

Alvesson, M. (1996) 'Leadership studies: from procedure and abstraction to reflexivity and situation', *Leadership Quarterly*, 7(4), pp. 455–85.

Alvesson, M. and Deetz, S. (2000) *Doing Critical Management Research* (London: Sage).

Bass, B. M. (1985) *Leadership and Performance Beyond Expectations* (New York: Free Press).

Bass, B. M. and Avolio, B. J. (1994) *Improving Organizational Effectiveness Through Transformational Leadership* (Thousand Oaks, CA: Sage Publications).

Bell, E., Taylor, S. and Thorpe, R. (2002) 'A Step in the Right Direction? Investors in People and the Learning Organization', *British Journal of Management*, 13, pp. 161–71.

Blackler, F., Kennedy, A. and Reed, M. (1999) 'Organising for incompatible priorities' in A. Mark and S. Dopson (eds), *Organisational Behaviour in Health Care: The Research Agenda* (Basingstoke: Macmillan).

Blake, R. R. and Mouton, J. S. (1964) *The Managerial Grid* (Houston, TX: Gulf).

Bohm, D. (1980) *Wholeness and the Implicate Order* (London: Routledge).

Bolden, R. (2005) 'The true face of leadership', *European Business Forum*, 21, pp. 54–57.

Brundrett, M. (2000) 'The question of competence; the origins, strengths and inadequacies of a leadership training paradigm', *School Leadership and Management*, 20(3), pp. 353–69.

Burns, J. M. (1978) *Leadership* (New York: Harper & Row).

CEML (2002) – *see* Council for Excellence in Management and Leadership.

Conger, J. and Kanungo, K. N. (1998) *Charismatic Leadership in Organisations* (Thousand Oaks, CA: Sage Publications).

Council for Excellence in Management and Leadership (2002) *Managers and Leaders: Raising Our Game* (London: Council for Excellence in Management and Leadership).

Cullen, E. (1992) 'A vital way to manage change', *Education*, 13(Nov), pp. 3–17.

De Ville, O. (1986), *The Review of Vocational Qualifications in England and Wales* (London: HMSO).

DfES (2002) – *see* UK Department for Education and Skills (2002).

DoH (2000) – *see* UK Department of Health (2000).

Dreyfus, H. L. and Rabinow, P. (1982) *Michael Foucault: Beyond Structuralism and Hermeneutics* (Chicago: University of Chicago Press).

Ecclestone, K. (1997) 'Energising or enervating: implications of National Vocational Qualifications in professional development.', *Journal of Vocational Education and Training*, 49, pp. 65–79.

Fiedler, F. E. (1967) *A Theory of Leadership Effectiveness* (NewYork: McGraw-Hill).

Foucault, M. (1972) *The Archaeology of Knowledge*, trans. A. M. Sheridan Smith (London: Routledge).

Foucault, M. (1980) *Power-Knowledge: Selected Interviews and Other Writings 1972–1977* (Hassocks: Harvester Press).

Goleman, D., Boyatzis, R. and McKee, A. (2002) *Primal Leadership: Realizing the Power of Emotional Intelligence* (Boston: Harvard Business School Press).

Grugulis, I. (1997) 'The Consequences of Competence: a critical assessment of the Management NVQ', *Personnel Review*, 26(6), pp. 428–44.

Grugulis, I. (1998) ' "Real" Managers Don't Do NVQs: a review of the new management "standards" ', *Employee Relations*, 20, pp. 383–403.

Hersey, P. and Blanchard, K. H. (1977) *Management of Organizational Behaviour* (Englewood Cliffs, NJ: Prentice Hall).

Holman, D. and Hall, L. (1997) 'Competence in management development: rites and wrongs' *British Journal of Management*, 7, pp. 191–202.

IiP (2003) – *see* Investors in People UK.

Investors in People UK (2003) *Leadership and Management Model* (London: Investors in People UK).

Lester, S. (1994) 'Management standards: a critical approach', *Competency*, 2(1), pp. 28–31.

Maccoby, M. (2000) 'Narcissistic leaders: the incredible pros, the inevitable cons', *Harvard Business Review*, 78(1), pp. 69–77.

Management Standards Centre (2004) *National Occupational Standards in Management and Leadership* (London: Management Standards Centre), accessed 2005-07-22, http://www.management-standards.org.

Marx, K. (1973) *Grundrisse*, trans. Martin Nicolaus (London: Penguin).

McGregor, D. (1960) *The Human Side of Enterprise* (New York: McGraw Hill).

Mintzberg, H. (1973) *The Nature of Managerial Work* (New York: Harper & Row).

Mintzberg, H. (1975) 'The manager's job: folklore and fact', *Harvard Business Review*, 55(4), pp. 49–61.

Mintzberg, H. (2004) 'Enough leadership', *Harvard Business Review*, 82(11), p. 22.

MSC (2004) – *see* Management Standards Centre (2004).

NHS Leadership Centre (2002) *NHS Leadership Qualities Framework* (London: NHS Leadership Centre), accessed 2005-07-22, http://www.nhsleadershipqualities.nhs.uk.

NHS Leadership Centre (2003) *NHS Leadership Qualities Framework: Full Technical Research Paper* (London: NHS Leadership Centre), accessed 2005-07-22, http://www.nhsleadershipqualities.nhs.uk.

NHS Leadership Centre (2005) *About the Framework*, accessed 2005-11-05, http://www.leadershipqualities.nhs.uk.

PIU (2001) – *see* UK Prime Minister's Strategy Unit (2001).

Richards, S. (2003) *Leadership: An Exploration of Issues Relating to Leadership in the Public Domain*. Paper for the Northern Ireland Review of Public Administration, (Birmingham: University of Birmingham). http://www.rpani.gov.uk/leadership.pdf.

Rickards, T. (1999) *Creativity and the Management of Change* (Oxford: Blackwell).

Salaman, G. (2004) 'Competences of managers, competences of leaders', in J. Storey (ed.), *Leadership in Organizations: Current Issues and Key Trends* (London: Routledge).

Sandberg, J. (2000) 'Understanding human competence at work: an interpretative approach', *Academy of Management Journal*, 43(1), pp. 9–25.

Sanderson, I. (2002) 'Evaluation, policy learning and evidence based policy making', *Public Administration*, 80(1), pp. 1–22.

Stogdill, R. M. (1950) 'Leadership, membership and organization', *Psychological Bulletin*, 47, pp. 1–14.

Swailes, S. and Roodhouse, S. (2003) 'Structural barriers to the take-up of Higher Level NVQs', *Journal of Vocational Education and Training*, 55(1), pp. 85–110.

Tolstoy, L. N. (1997) *War and Peace* (London: Penguin).

Tomlinson, M. (2004) *14–19 Curriculum and Qualifications Reform: Final Report of the Working Group on 14–19 Reform* (Annesley: UK Department for Education and Skills) [ref: DfE-0976-2004].

UK Department for Education and Skills (2002) *Government Response to the Report of the Council for Excellence in Management and Leadership* (Nottingham: UK Department for Education and Skills).

UK Department of Health (2000) *The NHS Plan* (London: HMSO), accessed 2005-07-21 http://www.dh.gov.uk/assetRoot/04/05/57/83/04055783.pdf.

UK Prime Minister's Strategy Unit (2001) *Strengthening Leadership in the Public Sector* (London: Cabinet Office Strategy Unit), accessed 2005-07-22, http://www.number-10.gov.uk/su/leadership/00/default.htm.

Wood, M. (2003) 'Leadership identity beyond relations of appearance to reality', Paper presented at the Studying Leadership: 2nd International Workshop, University of Lancaster.

Wood, M. (2005) 'The fallacy of misplaced leadership', *Journal of Management Studies*.

Yukl, G. A. (2002) *Leadership in Organizations*, 5th edn (Upper Saddle River, NJ: Prentice-Hall).

# 3
# Researching Practice or Practising Research: Innovating Methods in Health Care – The Contribution of Cynefin

*Annabelle L. Mark and David Snowden*

## Introduction

Innovation in health care for many is what medical progress is about and is the subject of many scientific articles in learned journals. However, the majority of these relate to the innovation of treatment and treatment regimes for patients rather than the organizations that deliver them. Increasing awareness of the need to enable the organizations to keep pace with developments in technology in the UK was at the heart of the UK government's work across all departments in the early 1990s. This can be seen both in the setting up of the Performance and Innovation Unit in the Cabinet Office in 1998 and the subsequent paper, *Modernising Government* (UK Cabinet Office, 1999). These developments gave clear indications of the strategies that would be important and were at the heart of the government's intention to improve public services. This has been described as a move away from the staged school to the process, or management of innovation school confirming the complex and often idiosyncratic nature of innovation in organizations (Walker, 2003).

The set of assumptions set out by government is also at the heart of the *Science and Innovation Strategy* issued by the Department of Health in 2001 (UK Department of Health, 2001) and many of these had implications for the organization of health care. For example, it has resulted in new organizational forms such as NHS Direct. This is a 24/7 computerized evidence based decision support system to provide information to patients at all times and increasingly to provide access to appropriate care out of normal working hours (Mark and Shepherd, 2001). As part of this ongoing response to the need for strategic innovation in health and its organization in the UK, the *Science and Innovation Strategy* has set a number of goals:

- To ensure that science and innovation lead to improved interventions for health and social care.

- To ensure that they work with partners to sustain and develop the science base in health and social care.
- To ensure that policy and practice in health and social care are based wherever possible on sound science and research.
- To ensure that the rights, health and safety of the public and patients are protected, and their interests served.

The specific focus within the strategy is on genetics, pharmaceuticals, technology transfer, strategic innovation and information and communication technologies, and this focus is reinforced by the current Economic and Social Research Council (ESRC) program on Innovative Health Technologies (HYPERLINK http://www.esrc.ac.uk/esrccontent/ourresearch/health_technologies.asp, accessed 31st March 2004) where the central objective is to advance understanding of the current and future implications of innovative health technologies together with the mediating effects of the wider processes of social change. This program has, therefore, developed a range of research projects also incorporating pharmaceuticals, genetics, technology and IT.

## International contexts

Deficits in the innovation of health care organization in the USA have been highlighted in a report from the Institute of Medicine (Institute of Medicine (IOM), 2002) which found that health care organizations have not innovated at the rate of medicine. However, US health organizations are not alone in this, as deficits also exist in respect of even the most innovative areas of health technology, for example the pharmaceutical industry (Wechsler, 2004), according to a recent report from the National Institute of Healthcare Management Foundation. This has meant that far from expenditure being focused on developing new drugs, the majority of resources are directed to modifying existing products rather than developing new ones. In pharmaceuticals this may be because of the pressures of taking new products to market. The impact on health systems across the world, however, cannot be underestimated in this lack of development of new drugs. Furthermore, innovation in the organization of pharmaceutical care is not ever seen as part of the equation, although this may influence the single biggest cost of pharmaceuticals to society; that is, the failure by patients to take the drugs, estimated as 50 per cent of all those prescribed according to WHO (Sabate, 2003). This example demonstrates that what is seen as important depends on whose perspective is adopted. Investing in drug innovation is important, but the industry must ensure effectiveness through patient compliance, rather than just efficiency as a revenue earner through sales, if it wishes to be more socially responsible.

## Innovating epistemologies

Innovation in Anglo-American healthcare is, as this pharmaceutical example demonstrates, focused largely on what might be termed the things that are known, be they people or processes. The issue of concern in both UK and US contexts is perhaps further entrenched by implied assumptions about ways of assessing innovations which are based on what the UK Innovation Strategy describes as 'sound science and research' rather than questioning the efficacy of the existing ways of looking at innovations. Innovation in the epistemologies themselves may now not only be required but may be becoming essential if such distortions as demonstrated in our pharmaceutical example are not to increase.

The cultural dominance of such epistemologies in what Cartwright and Cooper (Cartwright, Cooper and Earley, 2001) describe as the Anglo-US model can be seen as somewhat narrow. This may well have its roots in what Flynn and Chatman (Cartright, Cooper and Earley, 2001) describe in their chapter heading as 'Strong Cultures and Innovation – oxymoron or opportunity' because health care is littered with strong cultures be they professional or organizational and their existing epistemologies can be inimical to innovation.

The problems centre around not just the types of methods which have dominated but the hierarchy of methods led by scientific rationality (Baker and Kirk, 1998) with a gold standard headed by the randomized control trial. Even within medicine itself this hierarchy is increasingly questioned as the reality of the complex world in which health care operates is better understood (Sweeney and Kernick, 2002), where as Sweeney and Kernick suggest it may often be better to be vaguely right than precisely wrong. The construction of this world however is deeply embedded, as Foucault demonstrated (Foucault, 2003) in his 1970s seminal text *The Birth of the Clinic* where he suggests that a critical perspective towards specific historical events will uncover new layers of significance. By analyzing the methods of observation that underpinned the origins of modern medical techniques, he challenges assumptions not only about history, but also about the nature of language and reason, even of truth. However, attempts to say that such methods are no longer appropriate are unlikely to succeed unless their role and relevance to date can be shown as appropriate to at least some aspects of health care. What appears as a series of conflicting approaches vying for dominance may in reality be a failure to appreciate alternative perspectives that could incorporate these issues in ways which would enable the appropriate ones to be operationalized but only within the right context. In this way, the notion of a hierarchy is replaced by a nuanced appreciation of difference which is both more acceptable and appropriate.

A wider perspective on these issues of innovation (Snowden, 2003), which has looked at differences across countries and industries, has been undertaken within the Cynefin Centre, www.cynefin.net. At its heart is a set of ideas which was developed to improve understanding of both what is done and how it is done. It rests upon a conceptualization which was first published in the academic literature in 2002 (Snowden, 2002). Associated with it are a further series of ideas that can help in both contextualizing past and current activities as well as providing new strategies for research.

## Cynefin

The word Cynefin (pronounced kun-ev'in) itself is a Welsh word with no direct equivalent in English. As a noun it is translated as 'habitat', as an adjective 'acquainted' or 'familiar', but dictionary definitions fail to do it justice. A more poetic definition comes from the introduction to a collection of paintings by Kyffin Williams: 'It describes that relationship: the place of your birth and of your upbringing, the environment in which you live and to which you are naturally acclimatised' (Sinclair, 2004). It differs from Nonaka's concept of Ba (Nonaka and Konno, 1998), as a shared physical, virtual or mental space for emerging relationships that provides a platform for advancing individual and/or collective knowledge, in that it links a community into its shared history – or histories – in a way that paradoxically both limits the perception of that community, while enabling an instinctive and intuitive ability to adapt to conditions of profound uncertainty. A simplistic two-dimensional representation of these domains is Known, Knowable, Complex, Chaotic.

Disorder is the central point between the domains shown in grey in Figure 3.1.

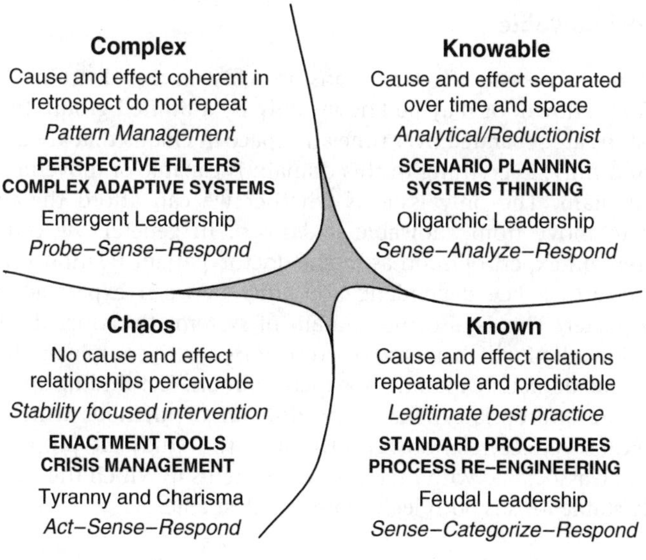

**Complex**
Cause and effect coherent in retrospect do not repeat
*Pattern Management*
**PERSPECTIVE FILTERS
COMPLEX ADAPTIVE SYSTEMS**
Emergent Leadership
*Probe–Sense–Respond*

**Knowable**
Cause and effect separated over time and space
*Analytical/Reductionist*
**SCENARIO PLANNING
SYSTEMS THINKING**
Oligarchic Leadership
*Sense–Analyze–Respond*

**Chaos**
No cause and effect relationships perceivable
*Stability focused intervention*
**ENACTMENT TOOLS
CRISIS MANAGEMENT**
Tyranny and Charisma
*Act–Sense–Respond*

**Known**
Cause and effect relations repeatable and predictable
*Legitimate best practice*
**STANDARD PROCEDURES
PROCESS RE-ENGINEERING**
Feudal Leadership
*Sense–Categorize–Respond*

**Figure 3.1** Cynefin model

## Ordered: known

Here cause and effect relationships are generally linear, empirical in nature and not open to dispute. This domain repeatability allows for predictive models to be created and the objectivity is such that any reasonable person would accept the constraints of best practice that can be found here. This is the domain of process re-engineering, in which knowledge is captured and embedded in structured processes to ensure constancy. The focus is on efficiency. Single point forecasting, field manuals and operational procedures are legitimate and effective practices in this domain.

The decision model here is to sense incoming data, categorize that data and then respond in accordance with predetermined practice. Structured techniques are not only desirable but also mandatory. In research this is the domain of known cause and effect often demonstrated through quantitative techniques such as randomized control trials and statistical models which attempt to quantify human behaviour sometimes erroneously (Mark, 2003). More recently in health care we have seen the use of regression analysis to link good practice in human resource management to patient death rates (West et al., 2002). While this use of regression, for which the authors of that study make no specific causal relation claims, may also appear appropriate to the known domain, it may, however, be more appropriate to the knowable. This is because as Amrit suggests (Amrit, 2002) it is a post hoc attempt to identify a restricted closed system because the gist of successful regression analysis is not being able to offer a law-like statement, but to bring forth evidence of an otherwise hidden mechanism.

## Ordered: knowable

While stable cause and effect relationships exist in this domain, they may not be fully known, or may be known only by a limited group. In general, relationships are separated over time and space in chains that are difficult to understand fully. Everything in this domain is capable of movement to the known domain. The only issue is whether we can afford the time and resource to move from knowable to known. In general, we cannot and instead rely on expert opinion as in the doctor–patient relationship, which in turn creates a key dependency on trust between expert advisor and decision maker. This is also the domain of systems thinking, the learning organization, all of which are too often confused with complexity theory. In the knowable domain, experiment, expert opinion, fact-finding and scenario planning are appropriate. This is the domain of methods which seek to identify cause–effect relationships through the study of properties that appear to be associated with qualities. For systems in which the patterns are relatively stable, this is both legitimate and desirable.

The decision model here is to sense incoming data, analyze that data and then respond in accordance with expert advice or interpretation of that analysis. Structured techniques are desirable, but assumptions must be open to examination and challenge. This is the domain in which what are termed 'entrained' patterns are at their most dangerous as a simple error in an assumption can lead to a false conclusion that is difficult to isolate and may not be seen. In health care such errors are often only demonstrated through the accumulation of error on a large scale as took place in the UK in Bristol, where a high volume of inappropriate childhood deaths took place before questions were asked of the experts involved (Kennedy, 2001). More recently, problems arose over the expert diagnosis in the UK of a psychiatric condition known as Munchausen's syndrome by proxy in which parents use their children's problems (often seen as parentally induced) to draw attention to themselves. The problem was compounded by the systematic and exclusive use by the UK courts of the expert opinion (Meadow, 1977) that originally identified this syndrome. The subsequent impact on hundreds of families, after a series of errors, was drawn to the attention of the public through court proceedings, providing evidence to show that the diagnosis was flawed. As a syndrome it has, however, already been a cause for reflection in other parts of the world (Jureidini, Shafer and Donald, 2003) where it is acknowledged that the social pressure on the medical profession may distort such expert opinions and even the concepts which underpin the syndrome itself.

The known and knowable domains are not based on individuals; one does not move from the known to the knowable domain on learning something. Rather, it means that something is known to society or the organization, whichever collective identity is of interest at the time, and this collectivity of itself maintains the power and credibility of such shared perceptions.

## Un-ordered: complex

This is the domain of complexity theory, a science that arose in chemistry and biology and which is gaining increasing attention in economics and management. Complex systems comprise many constantly interacting agents. Bird flocking behaviour can be simulated on a computer through three simple rules; termites produce elegant nests through the operation of simple rules triggered by chemical traces; snowflakes are unique because of patterns arising from the interactions of water particles during freezing. The patterns are not controlled by a directing intelligence; they are self-organizing systems. There are cause and effect relationships between the agents, but both the number of agents and the number of relationships defy categorization or analytic techniques. There are, however, patterns.

The patterns that emerge through the interactions of many agents can be perceived but not predicted. Within Cynefin this phenomenon is called retrospective coherence and is similar to the notion of post hoc rationality (Weick, 1995) in organizations. In this space, structured methods that seize upon such retrospectively coherent patterns and codify them into procedures will only confront new and different patterns for which they are ill-prepared when future patterns emerge. Once a pattern has stabilized, its path appears logical, but it is only one of many that could have stabilized, each of which would have also appeared logical in retrospect. Therefore, relying on expert opinions based on historically stable patterns of meaning will insufficiently prepare us to recognize and act upon unexpected patterns that emerge. The philosopher Kierkegaard in 1844 identified this in relation to life in general when he said, 'life must be understood backwards. But then one forgets the other principle: that it must be lived forwards' (Journals, IV A 164). (Kierkegaard, 1844).

The decision model in this space is to create probes to make the patterns or potential patterns more visible before taking any action. It is necessary to sense those patterns and respond by stabilizing those patterns that are found to be desirable, and also destabilizing those that are not desirable, and seeding the space so that patterns required are more likely to emerge. Understanding this space requires multiple perspectives on the nature of the system. An example of this within the pharmaceutical services in the UK emerged through the development of the innovative new role of primary care pharmacists (Silcock, Raynor and Petty, 2004). Primary care pharmacists carry out clinical and administrative work directly for family doctors and primary care organizations and their role is still developing. The economic liberalization of the NHS in the 1990s seems to have provided a major stimulus for the growth of primary care pharmacy and effectively acted to seed the space. This is because the establishment of the new professional group was not linked to a deliberate plan or change in health policy with respect to pharmacist development. The pattern, which emerged to enable their development, was perceived but not predicted and emerged as a self-organizing system. Primary care pharmacy practice is much more varied and flexible than traditional pharmacy practice in the community and hospitals. The standards and professional organization for primary care pharmacy are slowly emerging and the modernization of the NHS is providing many new opportunities, which primary care pharmacists are well placed to take advantage of, but the precise nature of future services and providers remains uncertain, allowing future patterns to emerge through self-organization. As a group, their emergence fits with Utterbuck's description of innovators as outsiders with nothing to lose (Utterbuck, 1994), who are set against existing players (hospital and retail pharmacists), who are concerned to maintain the status quo and their roles and reputations. In so doing they fail to take advantage of opportunities while the innovators (primary care pharmacists) persevere in spite of opposition. This description fits within the complex Cynefin domain because, at this point of emergence, the UK health care policy domain has understood that it is the time to stand still (but pay attention) and gain new perspective on the situation rather than relying on the 'entrained' patterns of past experience to determine response. The methods, tools and techniques of the known and knowable domains do not work here. Narrative techniques are particularly powerful in this space and Cynefin has developed a range of interventions designed to stimulate emergence in complex knowledge interactions (Snowden, 2004). These have already been used, coincidentally, elsewhere in the marketing strategies for the pharmaceutical industry to gain a better understanding of reasons for variable adoption of products by culture and also internally within the companies to replace employee satisfaction surveys with the more sophisticated representation of cultural differences provided by these narrative techniques. Within health care there is an emerging interest in the role of narrative both in the UK and the USA as a way of understanding, for example, the chaos presented to both patients and staff by critical illness and death (Crossley, 2003; Del Vecchio Good et al., 2004). However, this acknowledgement of the role played by narrative in such research has yet to gain acceptance as having a place in scientific research as a way of accessing the complex space.

## Un-ordered: chaos

In the first three domains, there are readily visible relationships between cause and effect. In the chaotic domain there are no such perceivable relations. The system is turbulent and the response time to investigate change is not available. Applying best practice inappropriately is probably what precipitated chaos in the first place; there is nothing to analyze; and waiting for patterns to emerge is a waste of time.

The decision model in this space is therefore to act, quickly and decisively, to reduce the turbulence, and then to sense immediately the reaction to that intervention so that we can respond accordingly. The trajectory of our intervention will differ according to the nature of the space. We may use an authoritarian intervention to control the space and make it knowable or known. This would be appropriate in symmetric threat where the parameters of acceptable behaviour are known and intention can be determined. However, in asymmetric threat we need to focus on multiple interventions to create patterns and thereby move the situation into the complex space where new patterns can emerge. In health care treatments this is the domain of the accident and emergency specialist responding to multiple failures in individuals, but also major accidents themselves where the extent and effects are largely unknowable until they present requiring immediate action. Scenario planning is often used from the knowable domain as a predictive tool for future action. Key heuristics around the principal rules which guide such actions, often from the professional rather than the organizational domain, will come into play when the situation itself presents, enabling a shared response to context.

## The domain of disorder

The central area of disorder outlined is key to understanding some of the conflicts that exist amongst decision makers in reaching agreement on the nature of a situation. As a result of this, individuals compete to interpret the central space on the basis of their preference for action. Those most comfortable with stable order will seek to create or enforce rules through control. In health care this is most often managers and or politicians. From the knowable, experts will seek investment to conduct research to determine the 'right' answer. In health care this may be clinical professionals or managers. In the complex, politicians will increase the number and range of their contacts to increase communication and stimulate the emergence of a new solution, as they intuitively understand the problems presented by the complex space. Finally, in the chaotic, the dictators, who can be from any area of expertise but who seek power often without the responsibility that follows, will determine that a crisis has occurred pushing the situation into chaos from which action and not thought is required, allowing their absolute control of the situation.

The reduction in size of the domain of disorder is a consensual act of collaboration and a significant move to the achievement of consensus as to the nature of the situation, removing the conflict otherwise implied. It depends on an understanding and acknowledgement of the differing perspectives and their appropriate utilization to the situation in question, as demonstrated in any emergency situation where clinical teams are required to work together; most recently, for example, in the response to the suicide bombers on the London Transport system in July 2005.

In health care, the domain of disorder is perhaps where much of the existing disagreement exists not least because of the failure to engage with the differential research methods that might be appropriate to each domain. While there is an appreciation of the role of complexity theory in the development of organizational systems like clinical governance (Sweeney and Mannion, 2002), it is not understood as a key issue for research methods themselves. This often results in a resort to more simplistic reductive interpretations, or unique qualitative descriptors of situations which are often not transferable. New concepts require development to overcome such deficits.

The assumption that health care knows about innovation is a fallacy disproved by the many innovations which have not succeeded or have succeeded only in part or in certain contexts. For example, the implementation of evidence based medicine (EBM) is a case in point (Fitzgerald et al., 1999). This attempt to apply a systematic approach to the evidence for health care interventions on the assumption that this is sufficient to ensure that it will be adopted by those giving treatment was confounded by the failure to predict the low adoption by those in the front line. This was in part because the innovations themselves (Fitzgerald et al., 2002) were often ambiguous because of the contested nature of new scientific knowledge, the highly interactive nature of diffusion and no evidence that adoption can be located within any one single decision or moment in time. Science is socially mediated and context and actors interlock to influence diffusion.

## Conclusions

Innovation contests both order and certainty. Any attempts to constrain it to the known or knowable will damage both the emergence of new patterns and innovations.

Health care is distinguished by a search for certainties in an uncertain world – what is wrong and how can we change this? It is a search for causality that will lead to the potential to identify successful intervention. When this is not achieved the purpose is often lost and alternative approaches or indeed alternative problems are sought. It is not, therefore, surprising that this perspective underpins assumption not only about the business of health care but also its organization. When we add to this the vested interests of international organizations like pharmaceutical industries, professions like medicine, governments and their agents like the NHS, it is not surprising that innovation may be misinterpreted and misconstrued. What is required is a way of making such contested domains not competitive but complementary, enabling the appropriate identification of the issues and the appropriate but different responses to be employed. Cynefin is one way of enabling this to happen that does not deny the role and validity of existing perspectives but shows both the relationships and potential interactions between these differing domains. As such, it is at the very least one way forward in understanding the nature and context of health care and how different epistemologies need to be applied as we both research practice and improve the practice of research.

## References

Amrit, R. (2002) 'Regression analysis and the philosophy of Social Science: a critical realist view', *Journal of Critical Realism*, 1(1), pp. 119–42.

Baker, M. and Kirk, S. (1998) *Research and Development for the NHS* (Oxford: Radcliffe Medical Press).

Cartwright, S., Cooper, C., and Earley, C. (eds) (2001) *International Handbook of Organizational Culture and Climate* (Chichester: John Wiley).

Crossley, M. L. (2003) 'Let me explain: narrative emplotment and one patient's experience of oral cancer', *Social Science & Medicine*, 56(3), pp. 439–48.

Del Vecchio Good, M. J., Gadmer, N. M., Ruopp, P., Lakoma, M., Sullivan, A. M., Redinbaugh, E., Arnold, R. M. and Block, S. D. (2004) 'Narrative nuances on good and bad deaths: internists' tales from high-technology work places', *Social Science & Medicine*, 58(5), pp. 939–53.

Fitzgerald, L., Ferlie, E., Wood, M. and Hawkins, C. (1999) 'Evidence into practice? An exploratory analysis of the interpretation of evidence', in S. D. Annabelle and L. Mark (eds), *Organisational Behaviour in Health Care: The Research Agenda* (Basingstoke: Macmillan).

Fitzgerald, L., Ferlie, E., Wood, M. and Hawkins, C. (2002) 'Interlocking interactions: the diffusion of innovations in healthcare', *Human Relations*, 55(12), pp. 1429–50.

Foucault, M. (2003) *The Birth of the Clinic* (London: Routledge).

Institute of Medicine (2002) *Medical Innovation in the Changing Healthcare Marketplace* (Washington DC: National Academy Press).

Jureidini, J. N., Shafer, A. T. and Donald, T. G. (2003) 'Munchausen by proxy syndrome: not only pathological parenting but also problematic doctoring?', *Medical Journal of Australia*, 178(3), pp. 130–32.

Kennedy, I. (2001) *Learning from Bristol: The Report of the Public Inquiry into Children's Heart Surgery at the Bristol Royal Infirmary 1984–95*, CM5207(1) (Norwich, England: The Stationery Office).

Kierkegaard, S. (1844) *Journals*, Volume VI: *Philosophical Fragments* (Princeton: Princeton University Press).

Mark, A. (2003) 'Demand-a rejoinder', *British Journal of Healthcare Management*, 9(2), pp. 67–71.

Mark, A. L. and Shepherd, I. D. H. (2001) *'Don't Shoot the Messenger': An Evaluation of the Transition from HARMONI to NHS Direct in West London* (London: Middlesex University).

Meadow, R. (1977) 'Munchausen by proxy: the hinterland of child abuse', *Lancet*, 2, pp. 343–5.

Nonaka, I. and Konno, N. (1998) 'The concept of "Ba": Building a Foundation for Knowledge Creation', *California Management Review*, 40(3), pp. 40–54.

Sabate, E. (2003) *Adherence to Long term Therapies: Evidence for Action* (Geneva: World Health Organization).

Silcock, J., Raynor, T. D. K. and Petty, D. (2004) 'The organization and development of primary care pharmacy in the United Kingdom', *Health Policy*, 67(2), pp. 207–15.

Sinclair, N. (2004) 'Preface', in K. Williams (ed.), *The Land and the Sea* (Llandysul, Wales: Gomer Press).

Snowden, D. (2002) 'Complex acts of knowing: paradox and descriptive self awareness', *Journal of Knowledge Management*, 6(2), pp. 100–10.

Snowden, D. (2003) 'Innovation as an object of knowledge management: Part 1: The landscape of management', *Knowledge Management Research and Practice*, 1(2), pp. 113–19.

Snowden, D. (2004) 'Narrative patterns: the perils and possibilities of using story in organizations', in E. Lesser and L. Prusak (eds), *Creating Value with Knowledge* (Oxford: Oxford University Press).

Sweeney, K. and Kernick, D. (2002) 'Clinical evaluation: constructing a new model for post-normal medicine', *Journal of Evaluation in Clinical Practice*, 8(2), pp. 131–8.

Sweeney, K. and Mannion, R. (2002) 'Complexity and clinical governance: using the insights to develop the strategy', *British Journal of General Practice*, 52, pp. S4–S9.

UK. Cabinet Office (1999) *Modernising Government* (London: Stationery Office).

UK. Department of Health (2001) *Science and Innovation Strategy* (London: Department of Health).

Utterbuck, J. M. (1994) *Mastering the Dynamics of Innovation* (Boston: Harvard Business School Press).

Walker, R. M. (2003) 'Evidence on the management of public service innovation', *Public Money and Management*, 23(2), pp. 93–102.

Wechsler, J. (2004) 'Blues attack pharma innovation', *Managed Healthcare Executive*, 12(7), pp. 8–10.

Weick, K. (1995) *Sensemaking in Organisations* (Thousand Oaks, CA: Sage).

West, M. A., Borrill, C. S., Dawson, J. F., Scully, J., Carter, M. and Anelay, S. (2002) 'The link between the management of employees and patient mortality in acute hospitals', *International Journal of Human Resource Management*, 12(8), pp. 1299–310.

# 4

# Increasing the Impact of Research on Practice: Dissemination and Implementation Research at the National Institute of Mental Health

*David Chambers*

## Introduction

In recent decades, a veritable 'explosion' of new interventions for medicine and behavioural health has created viable treatments for most clinical conditions. New pharmaceuticals enter the market; new devices become available; new surgical procedures are learned. There have been unparalleled advances in technology, but their transport to front line clinical settings does not always occur.

The process of developing clinical treatments remains linear. Scientific investigation begins with basic science; researchers apply this knowledge toward creating intervention models; and then test the interventions in controlled efficacy and effectiveness trials. At the end of this process, studies test whether interventions integrate within real world service settings. Research indicates that about 14 per cent of scientific results are used in clinical practice – after an average of 17 years (Clancy, 2003). As reviews of changing clinical practice have taught us, 'there are no magic bullets' that will cause practice to change (Oxman et al., 1995); influencing practice is extremely complex (Bero et al., 1998; Davis et al., 1995; NHS Centre for Reviews and Dissemination, 1999; Chambers and Dopson, 2003).

Many systematic reviews have demonstrated the difficulty of changing practice, and millions of dollars and pounds have been devoted to efforts to translate research into practice with limited success. Much of the knowledge base around getting evidence into practice has been largely anecdotal, either through general evaluations on the management of change or through 'lessons learned' during intervention trials, and while this information has been helpful, it does not offer the scientific rigour needed to move the field. In order for research really to 'make a difference', concerted and sustained efforts are required. This chapter outlines work undertaken by the National

Institute for Mental Health in the United States targeted at ensuring that learnings from dissemination and implementation research are integrated into mental health research that can then begin 'making more of a difference' to mental health practice and outcomes.

## Dissemination and implementation research

Dissemination and implementation research intends to bridge the gap between clinical research and practice by building a knowledge base about how mental health care information and new practices are transmitted and translated for health care service use in specific settings. Falling under the general term of 'research to practice', dissemination and implementation research offers to unpack the complexity around using evidence to influence practice. Unfortunately, there continues to be great variation in how these terms are used. Dissemination and implementation have both been used to represent the complete process of bringing 'evidence' into practice, originally defined as 'diffusion'. While using the terms of dissemination and implementation to cover such a wide area can be very helpful in enabling discussion, it does not allow for the division of this very complex diffusion process into smaller, more easily addressed research questions that can develop a robust knowledge base.

In addition, the confusion over the usage of each term has had negative implications on research, practice and policy. For research, the definitions have resulted in theoretical models and studies that have limited applicability to the complex world of everyday clinical practice. For example, assuming dissemination to represent the use of an intervention in practice has limited understanding of how and why the intervention became used. Studies following up on an effort to introduce a particular practice into a system will choose the outcome to be 'any instance where a practice was used'. This creates a problem because the research cannot determine whether a new instance of practice use was related to the effort. It might be that a clinician chose to use the practice after speaking with a colleague, and never actually was impacted by the effort.

For practice, the confusion has led to assumptions that practice will change merely by presenting information to a clinician, in the form of a guideline, as part of continuing medical education, or through a presentation at grand rounds. Numerous reviews of these efforts have shown limited or non-existent change of practice (for example, Davis et al., 1995; Oxman et al., 1995).

For policy, the confusion has limited understanding of how to 'translate evidence into practice'. Public and private initiatives around evidence based medicine have historically been limited in their impact on practice. Large amounts of money have gone toward these initiatives, with minimal discernible results (for example, Dopson et al., 2001; Locock et al., 2001; Chambers and Dopson, 2003; Ferlie et al., 1999).

This chapter does not review all interpretations of dissemination and implementation, but rather lays out working definitions for the terms that can then be used to assess previous research and identify promising new areas. (A brief summary of the key findings that previous studies have brought to the science base of dissemination and implementation is appended.) The definitions presented are adapted from Lomas (1993), whose paper sought to distinguish between dissemination, diffusion and implementation, with specific application to knowledge based interventions. Lomas sets out definitions for three distinct types of knowledge translation activities:

> **Diffusion:** These include activities that are passive and where the actual 'translation' effort is relatively unplanned. The objective is simply to promote awareness. Examples include journal or newsletter publications, information on a website, or in the mass media.
>
> **Dissemination:** Interventions here include more intentional strategies, such as direct mailings of results to intended audiences, workshops, and conferences. The goal is both awareness creation and attitude change.
>
> **Implementation:** Here the interventions are even more active, with the intent of adding behavior change to awareness and attitude change. Efforts are directed to systematically identifying and overcoming barriers. Examples include specific meetings with opinion leaders, audit and feedback or reminder procedures, and administrative or economic interventions. (Lomas, 1993)

The basic message of Lomas' article is that more intense knowledge translation activities will more likely impact behaviour change. In addition, the wider spread the 'diffusion and dissemination', the more likely they are to develop understanding. Lomas' contribution should not be underestimated; it has spread throughout the literature and through discourse on 'research into practice' activities, demonstrating that its own 'diffusion' has been quite successful. However, whether the message, according to Lomas' typography, has achieved the goals of dissemination – awareness and attitude change – is more difficult to assess. Has the Lomas typography been effectively disseminated, so that understanding of the terminology and their implications are widespread?

A clear distinction is made between diffusion and dissemination in the Lomas typography – that of passive versus active spread of knowledge. However, many authors use the two interchangeably. For example, Donald Berwick (2003) alternates between the terms diffusion and dissemination: 'This article examines the theory and research on the dissemination of innovations and suggests applications of that theory to health care. It explores in detail three clusters of influence on the rate of diffusion of innovations within an organization...' Berwick's article does not distinguish between diffusion and dissemination, yet if we accept Lomas' definitions, this has large implications on our understanding of whether we can influence diffusion at all, or whether more intense interventions are needed – dissemination and implementation activities – to elicit change. Other authors use diffusion and dissemination in tandem, more closely aligning with the differences between active and passive interventions, and often leave out 'implementation' as a separate phase, which Lomas indicates as the only process that has behaviour change as an outcome.

## An alternative typology

As the use of a practice in a clinical setting can require more than information (for example, offering angioplasty for cardiac revascularization requires knowledge of the procedure, equipment for the procedure, resources to pay for the procedure), Lomas' terms are not a perfect fit. In order to address this, and in an attempt to open the 'black box' processes of dissemination and implementation, the National Institute of Mental Health distinguishes the two processes.

*Dissemination* is defined as the 'targeted distribution of a well-defined set of information (for example, information about a health treatment)' (NIMH, 2002). As Bauchner and Simpson (1998) state, 'Dissemination is the active process of making information available to the target audience. It is the process by which knowledge is made accessible or available to a particular audience.' Information is most commonly used as an object of dissemination, because one can easily follow the path through which information is transmitted and check on each side of the transmission to see whether the information was consistent.

*Implementation*, in contrast, is the 'process of introducing or changing practice into a specific local setting' (NIMH, 2002). Implementation focuses on the specific effort to fit a program, treatment, device, or procedure within a specific care context. It is distinguished from dissemination by its focus on the relationship of the 'practice' with its ultimate 'host'.

We distinguish between dissemination and implementation to move the field beyond the assumption that the reporting of scientific findings through journal publication and guideline distribution will satisfactorily change clinical practice. Research shows (for example, Wood et al., 1998) that interventions developed in the context of efficacy and effectiveness trials are rarely transferable without adaptations to specific settings. Therefore, we need a framework that acknowledges the process of transferring interventions into local settings, settings often very different from those in which interventions are developed and tested.

## Services research at NIMH

Dissemination and implementation research is located at the National Institute of Mental Health within the Services Research and Clinical Epidemiology

Branch, which plans, supports and administers programs of research, research training and research infrastructure development across the lifespan on all mental health services research issues, including but not limited to:

- Services organization, delivery (process and receipt of care) and related health.
- Economics at the individual, clinical, program, community and systems levels in specialty.
- Mental health, general health and other delivery settings (such as the workplace).
- Interventions to improve the quality and outcomes of care, including diagnostic, treatment, preventive and rehabilitation services.
- Enhanced capacity for conducting services research.
- The clinical epidemiology of mental disorders across all clinical and service settings.
- The dissemination and implementation of evidence based interventions into service settings.

The Services Research Branch is focused on bridging the gap between interventions deemed effective in randomized clinical trials and the use of those interventions in 'real world' clinical settings. The Branch, which houses 11 research programs, has 255 active grants in its portfolio (as of January 2005). Ongoing studies focus on research in all settings in which mental health care is delivered, including schools, primary care, correctional institutions, child welfare, specialty clinics, nursing homes and hospitals, and cover the entire lifespan. Grants funded within the Branch receive money for individual career development, exploratory and developmental research, infrastructure development awards, institutional training programs, conference grants, and large-scale research studies (NIMH, 2004a).

## The NIMH dissemination and implementation research program

In July 2002, the National Institute of Mental Health (NIMH) released a program announcement to share research priorities around a major priority within the Services Research Branch–research on the dissemination and implementation of mental health information and treatments into practice. The document entitled 'Dissemination and Implementation Research in Mental Health' (NIMH, 2002) was created to invite:

> grant applications for research that will build knowledge on methods, structures, and processes to disseminate and implement mental health information and treatments into practice settings...Invited research on dissemination will address how information about mental health care interventions is created, packaged, transmitted, and interpreted

among a variety of important stakeholder groups. Research on implement-ation will address the level to which mental health interventions can fit within real-world mental health service systems. The goals of this PA are to encourage mental health researchers to work with interdisciplinary scientists and practice stakeholders to develop conceptualizations of dissemination and implementation that are applicable across diverse practice settings, and design studies that will accurately assess the outcomes of dissemination and implementation efforts. (NIMH, 2002)

Topics of research funded under the announcement include studies of:

- Factors impacting implementation of suicide prevention programs in schools.
- Influencing uptake of clinical guidelines by psychiatrists.
- Organizational intervention to assist with implementation of therapy programs in rural communities.
- Web based support/recovery for schizophrenia patients.
- Computer based decision support for depression treatment.
- Implementation of a website to test quality of patient-centred care.
- Implementation of screening programs in emergency rooms for intimate partner violence detection.

In addition to grants focusing on local implementation, two NIMH initiatives are assisting state agencies with planning for implementation of evidence based practices at the statewide system level. The first initiative funded nine states (Texas, North Carolina, Ohio, New York, Maine, Michigan, Arkansas, Washington and Maryland) in the fall of 2003 to develop research and service development agendas to improve the uptake of evidence based practices within their state system. A second initiative, announced in the summer of 2004, enables another cohort of states to develop plans for service and science agendas, while additional funds will enable states to conduct exploratory/developmental implementation research to answer questions not currently addressed in academic research (NIMH, 2004).

In October 2004, an NIMH workshop entitled 'Advancing the Science of Implementation' brought together key researchers in the fields of interventions research, organizational research and research methodology, along with clini-cians and 'real world implementers' of evidence based practices, to stimulate implementation research. Over the course of the two-day meeting, five priorities for advancing implementation research were agreed as set out in Table 4.1.

These priorities have strongly informed the development of the next program announcement on Dissemination and Implementation Research, due to be released in the summer of 2005. They have also been disseminated

**Table 4.1** Priorities for advancing implementation research

| |
|---|
| Conceptual frameworks/models for implementation must be proposed and tested. |
| Organizational measures from other industries can be considered for use in the mental health field, but should not be assumed to be appropriate. |
| Constructs related to implementation (for example, training, levels of resources, leadership, culture/climate) can be integrated within intervention research. |
| Implementation research will require a partnership between researchers and practitioners from inception of research idea through completion of the study. |
| More researchers with systems expertise are needed to conduct implementation research. |

at scientific meetings, technical assistance workshops for researchers and through publications.

## Key dissemination and implementation research questions

Several key questions have emerged from NIMH's concentrated efforts to link research efforts to practice improvement, as set out in Table 4.2. These questions are identified and discussed in order to guide the way for answers that can help decrease the gap and increase the fit between scientific discovery and real-world practice.

### How do providers gather information?

Rather than assuming that providers are going to use the information that is sent directly to them, or published in places where they are known to look, it would be helpful to find out more about how different providers gather the information that they use to work with their patients. Different providers may have very different ways of gathering evidence, and learning more about the natural ways that information spreads to providers would help to design dissemination strategies that would fit better to the providers.

**Table 4.2** Key dissemination and implementation research questions

| |
|---|
| How do providers gather information? |
| What information is needed to help different stakeholder groups? |
| How can that information best be transmitted? |
| How can messages created for dissemination be analyzed? |
| How can target audiences (ideal vs actual) be defined? |
| How does fidelity of implementation affect success of a practice within a specific setting? |
| What are the most appropriate outcomes to assess dissemination strategies? |
| How can practice changes be sustained over time? |
| How can the capacity of specific practice settings be enhanced to enable implementation of effective practices? |

## What information is needed to help different stakeholder groups?

Often, we assume as researchers that the evidence we are gathering is helpful to stakeholders in the field. However, we seldom ask people in the field what information they would like to have or in what form. Research that asks questions about the needs of different stakeholders can help to bridge the larger evidence to practice gap.

### How can that information best be transmitted?

A central question of dissemination is how best to transmit information to the field. This remains an area of research that has been underexplored. As discussed above, the field would benefit from studies that will focus on the information being transmitted, as opposed to the eventual goal of practice change and differential health outcomes. Studies that test how different strategies have fared in ensuring that different stakeholders have received the information would be very valuable.

### How can methodologies used to study dissemination be improved?

Another important area within dissemination research is methodological. Are the analytical strategies for testing the effectiveness of dissemination efforts adequate to assess the quality of the efforts? Are the theoretical models for dissemination helpful for researchers and policy makers to improve the flow of information? Are the results from dissemination trials generalizable? These issues have rarely been explored and can contribute heavily to the success of dissemination research.

### How can messages created for dissemination be analyzed?

Studies of evidence based attempts to change practice have continually reinforced the message that evidence is subjective. Therefore, the effectiveness of the evidence to impact its audience may be related to the way in which the evidence is created. An investigation of this issue may not only lead to the creation of better evidence, but can better inform the audiences how the evidence is created. Studies have shown that when the stakeholders know more about the creation of the evidence (for example, the use of local data to convince physicians to change practice), they are more likely to trust it (Bero et al., 1998).

### How can target audiences (ideal vs actual) be defined?

People involved in dissemination often assume that they know the audience to whom they are disseminating. However, few attempts have been made to define the target audience, either from the standpoint of what would be ideal or who the specific people in real world settings are. Research helping to define the ideal audience for which the disseminators are aiming, and the actual audience that will receive the messages, may improve the 'fit' between the evidence and the context.

### How can the effectiveness of implementation efforts best be tested?

So many attempts to implement changes in clinical practice are designed within project teams without necessarily examining research about how best to implement, or documenting the processes through which the implementation plans are made. Much could be learned from studying efforts to implement treatments or clinical procedures of demonstrated efficacy into existing care systems, especially if studies measure the extent to which new practices are utilized, and adhered to, by providers and consumers.

## How does fidelity of implementation affect success of a practice within a specific setting?

Within health services research, much has been written about the importance of implementing interventions with high fidelity to a model. Many fidelity measures have been developed to assess this, but often with the assumption that 100 per cent fidelity is ideal. With much written about the importance of adapting interventions to specific settings, there is a need to better understand the components of interventions that must be held faithful, and how implementation can allow adaptation without negative consequence. New measures are needed that will enable fidelity to be assessed meaningfully.

## What are the most appropriate outcomes to assess dissemination strategies?

Many studies focusing on dissemination strategies have chosen patient outcomes as indicators of whether dissemination was successful. There is a need for experimental studies, testing the effectiveness of individual and systemic dissemination strategies, to focus on outcomes related to the direct outcomes of the strategies (for example, acquisition of new knowledge, maintenance of knowledge, attitudes about the dissemination strategies, use of knowledge in practice decision making).

## How can practice changes be sustained over time?

Many of the implementation studies have followed the attempts to change practice through to the end of the implementation phase, but have not necessarily addressed whether changes will be sustained over time. There is a great need for studies to investigate whether sustainability can be enhanced, and what facilitators and barriers exist that will likely influence sustainability.

## How can the capacity of specific practice settings be enhanced to enable implementation of effective practices?

Many care delivery settings have expressed concern about their ability to incorporate evidence based interventions into their local practice. Theory-driven research on the capacity of specific care delivery settings (primary care, schools, community mental health settings, and so on) to incorporate dissemination or implementation efforts within current organizational forms would greatly benefit the field.

Each question presents an opportunity for researchers to understand more of the 'hows' and 'whys' of moving science into practice, though important additional questions can and should be added to this list. Currently, too many of the 'science to practice' research studies focus on consumer outcomes and may neglect the examination of process variables that will elucidate the reasons behind those outcomes. Knowing more about the link between these processes and intended patient outcomes will increase the likelihood that the desired outcomes can be replicated in complex, real world settings.

## Expanding perspectives of dissemination and implementation

As we have seen from the many studies that have tried to determine effective dissemination and implementation strategies, both processes are incredibly complex, including individual, professional, organizational, informational, cultural, financial and other factors of influence. Thus, our understanding of these processes is likely to be aided by inclusion of these and other related fields. The processes underlying attempts to bring scientific evidence into health services will involve many different stakeholders from unique perspectives; the next wave of research should be as multidisciplinary as the processes themselves. In particular, the NIMH has a shortage of organizational researchers among our pool of grant applicants and awardees. As a result, many of the questions discussed earlier do not appear central in the grant proposals. Previous research has talked about the many barriers that an organization faces in trying to influence clinical practice. The mental health services research field desperately needs the expertise of organizational and management researchers to improve the knowledge base around dissemination and implementation.

Multiple methods of gathering data will also likely be necessary in the next wave of dissemination and implementation research. This may require including researchers with different methodological expertise, and may include the use of several of the following: surveys, interviews, focus groups, case studies, ethnographies, diagnostic tests, epidemiological datasets, and so on.

Much of the NIMH-funded research testing interventions focuses on clinical outcomes. The assumption is that if you can achieve a desired reduction in physical or psychological symptoms, you ought to be able to replicate that reduction in the real world. While this may be true, it tends to neglect the important organizational outcomes that will guarantee that a treatment can be sustained in a real world setting. When determining whether empirically supported treatments can be used by clinicians, research must also contend with the barriers preventing the treatments from being implemented (for example, financial, organizational, training issues).

Outcomes may exist on the individual level (for example, clinical outcomes, stakeholder needs and influences, individual decision making), the treatment program level (for example, fidelity of implementation, sustainability), the organizational level (for example, structural, financial, culture/climate outcomes), or the societal level (for example, technological change, stigma, policy, national/global trends). Researchers will need a theoretical framework that accommodates multiple levels of outcomes in order to address questions concerning the complex nature of dissemination and implementation. Without a population of researchers to develop and test theoretical constructs and address the important questions around the dissemination and implementation of health information and interventions, the gulf between research and practice will remain.

## Appendix: Key findings from previous research

The following appendix provides a brief summary of some of the key findings that previous studies have brought to the science base of dissemination and implementation. This summary is meant to be suggestive rather than comprehensive, providing a starting point for further understanding of what is known about research dissemination and use.

### Dissemination of information

As discussed earlier, dissemination is the process of transmitting information from one individual or group to another. Dissemination does not assume that clinical change will occur as its result, but merely is 'trying to have [the target audience] reach the recognition/identification stage of change. Awareness of better practices would hopefully predispose [the audience] to change but for change to actually occur, generally one would also require enabling and/or reinforcing interventions.' (Hogan et al., 2001)

Dissemination includes the creation of the information, its packaging, its transmission to a target audience and its reception by that audience. Each stage of the process has research behind it, though seldom has all that we know found its way into most dissemination efforts in health services. This section will briefly summarize some key findings about various stages of the dissemination process.

### Creation of information

- Knowledge is based on the context in which it was created, and can be interpreted in different ways by different people (Berger and Luckmann, 1966; Mulkay, 1979; Mannheim, 1936). This subjectivity of knowledge has been specifically discussed within health services research (Wood et al., 1998; Bauchner and Simpson, 1998; Huby and Fairhurst, 1998; Fitzgerald et al., 1999).
- The process of gathering information will greatly influence the final set of information created (Bauchner and Simpson, 1998). This is very important to consider, in light of the assumption that randomized controlled trials are the 'gold standard' of scientific evidence, and experiential evidence is less valuable (Sackett et al., 1996).
- The production of scientific trial data is influenced by social processes and, to some degree, subjective (Huby and Fairhurst, 1998; Fitzgerald et al., 1999). 'Similar, experience-based practice is supported by socially

constructed knowledge produced through interaction between trial data and the context in which it is used. Thus it is more objective than is often recognized.' (Huby and Fairhurst, 1998, pp.11–12)

## Packaging of information

- How information is framed has a profound influence on whether or not it can influence the target of the message that contains it (Rothman and Salovey, 1997). For example, when an intervention is described to people in terms of how many lives it will save, it is more likely to make an impression than if it is framed in terms of how many lives will be lost (Rothman and Salovey, 1997).
- Information should be packaged in a way so that it is not seen as a threat to audiences (Wood et al., 1998).
- Specific criteria may indicate the likelihood that dissemination of that evidence will lead to practice change. These criteria include: Relevance, Timeliness, Clarity, Credibility, Replicability and Acceptability. Different audiences may operationalize these concepts differently (Schoenwald and Henggeler, 2002). Leeds (1979) offers similar criteria for effective communication, consisting of Comprehensiveness, Rapid Access and Reliability.
- The packaging of evidence in journals may be extremely influential in how it is received by readers. Haynes (1990) notes that many journals tend to mix rigorous studies with many preliminary investigations, offering a confusing picture of what is so and what appears to be so. McColl et al. (1998) add that more systematic reviews of evidence can be quite helpful to clinicians, who often are unaware of many sources of evidence.
- It is important to 'package' the evidence based on how clinicians assess evidence (Huby and Fairhurst, 1998). Scientists often present evidence that convinces them of a need to change practice without considering whether clinicians assess evidence in the same way.

## Transmission of information

- Active methods of dissemination, especially those involving interpersonal contact, are more likely to be effective than passive methods, like research journals and conference presentation (Bero et al., 1998; Bauchner and Simpson, 1998; Backer, Liberman and Kuehnel, 1986).
- Passive methods of dissemination are often limited in their timeliness. For example, when information is published in a scientific journal, it often undergoes a time lag of at least a year before it gets to the target audience (Leeds, 1979).

- Rapid publication, via the Internet, for example, may have little or no control over the accuracy and usefulness of the information (Bauchner and Simpson, 1998).
- Online help groups may be able effectively to transmit health information to people, protecting members from stigmatization and discrimination (Hsiung, 2000).
- Research conferences have generally little impact on clinical change, while more systematic attempts to engage local practices were effective, but rarely used (Davis et al., 1995).
- The presenter of the evidence can have a significant impact on its success in dissemination (Ferlie et al., 1999).
- This use of opinion leaders to transmit the evidence is questionable in its effectiveness (Oxman et al., 1995).
- The 'vehicle' to transmit information may likely depend on the audience to whom it is targeted. In a study of the impact of research on policy, Sorian and Baugh (2002) argue that older policy makers are more likely to favour printed materials, while younger officials will tend toward electronic resources.
- Researchers may find scientific journals to be a preferred method of obtaining new information, but practitioners may be less likely to see these journals (Liberman and Eckman, 1989; Prescott et al., 1997).

### Different reception of information

- Audiences view evidence in different ways, according to their 'most valued outcomes' (Hatgis et al., 2001; Leeds, 1979; Allery et al., 1997). For example, clients of health services might value therapeutic relationships and increased knowledge about health problems highest, while administrators might place more emphasis on employee satisfaction and financial health of their organization (Hatgis et al., 2001).
- Some decision makers are only interested in cost/benefit analysis information (Lorenzen and Braskamp, 1978).
- Barriers to receiving information may come in the form of language problems, insufficient access to technologies and insufficient training to understand the information (Leeds, 1979).
- If the information is judged not to be 'user-friendly' to the target audience, it is less likely to be influential (Corrigan, 1998).
- Furthermore, if an organization is not receptive to dissemination, the individuals within that organization may be barred from receiving information (Backer et al., 1986).
- Evidence is always evolving (Dawson et al., 1998). 'Many in our sample whatever their clinical role, commented on the confusing and evolving state of the evidence ... [The bulletin on evidence used to influence

practice] has not proved to be particularly helpful for our group of interviewees in clarifying appropriate practice... Clinical practice is very subtly shaped by a variety of influences... Experience (69% of our respondents rated this of high importance) of the condition built up over time is the most significant influence on practice.' (Dawson et al., 1998, p.18)

Dissemination of evidence is extremely complex. Even with the strongest evidence, there is no guarantee that clinicians who could ultimately benefit from having the evidence will ever see it. Effective dissemination is a challenge. However, disseminating the evidence to relevant stakeholders does not guarantee that change will occur. As Lomas (1993) states, 'change is more likely to occur through working within a specific setting'. Previous research around implementation has given further orientation to the complexity of clinical practice change.

## Implementing change in clinical practice

### Systematic reviews

Within previous research on efforts to implement new practices into real world settings, much of the literature has been aimed at determining the effectiveness of a single implementation strategy (for example, guideline, audit, opinion leaders), or a particular clinical practice (for example, warfarin to help prevent stroke, assertive community treatment for severe mental illness). We have depended largely on systematic reviews for more general information on implementation, to somewhat small benefit. Several of these reviews have been widely disseminated and quoted from, specifically reviews authored by Oxman et al. (1995), Davis and Howden-Chapman (1996), and the NHS Centre for Reviews and Dissemination (1999). Here are a few key findings:

- 'The use of opinion leaders [to change clinical practice] has been shown to have anywhere from a non-significant effect to a substantial effect.' (Oxman et al., 1995, p. 26)
- 'There is a wide range of interventions available that, if used appropriately, can lead to substantial improvements in the application of research.' (Oxman et al., 1995, p. 29)
- 'The process [of translating research into practice] was more one of incremental adjustment to competing pressures than the rational formulation and pursuit of a single goal.' (Davis and Howden-Chapman, 1996)
- 'Any attempt to change should use a systematic approach and involve strategic planning. Any proposed change – for example, the implementation of a clinical guideline – would first involve a period of "information and

diagnostic analysis" to inform the development of an appropriate dissemination and implementation strategy.' (NHS Centre for Reviews and Dissemination, 1999)

- Most interventions are effective under some circumstances; none is effective under all circumstances (NHS Centre for Reviews and Dissemination, 1999).

- Interventions based on assessment of potential barriers are more likely to be effective (NHS Centre for Reviews and Dissemination, 1999).

- Multi-faceted interventions targeting different barriers to change are more likely to be effective than single interventions; and audit and feedback (NHS Centre for Reviews and Dissemination, 1999).

The several reviews of implementation discussed here, as well as other systematic reviews (for example, Davis et al., 1995; Bero et al., 1998; Huby and Fairhurst, 1998) point out how few general lessons have been learned about the implementation process. Most of the evidence contained in these reviews is suggestive rather than definitive, and each review concludes that far more research is needed.

## Implementation studies

A number of additional studies have been conducted, often looking at reasons for changes in clinical practice, or specifically exploring an individual implementation effort.

- Change is not a simple step; it requires the integration of a number of different stages, united in one cohesive process (Grol, 1997).
- 'Implementing changes is usually not a single action but involves a well planned stepwise process, including a combination of interventions, linked to specific obstacles to change.' (Grol, 1997, p. 420)
- Little attention has been paid on the process of translating evidence into practice; high value has been placed on developing basic science, less so on applying that science to practice (Eddy, 1982).
- More intensive efforts to alter practice are generally more successful (Bero et al., 1998, p. 9).
- Implementation must be understood from multiple perspectives, including manager, practitioner and patient for any clinical topic and resulting intervention. (This Howitt and Armstrong, 1999 study discussed the need to understand implementation in the context of both practitioner and patient for any clinical topic and resulting intervention.)
- Common methods of improving implementation success can include use of opinion leaders (Ellrodt et al., 1997; Ferlie et al., 1999; Rubenstein et al., 2000; Wood et al., 1998) – called 'project champions' by Ferlie et al. (1999) – management and clinician commitment to change (Ferlie et al., 1999; Holloway et al., 2000; Mant et al., 1997), attention to local contexts,

professionally credible 'change agents' and involvement of professional groups (Eve et al., 1997; Ferlie et al., 1999).

- Other factors can also increase the likelihood of effective implementation, including (1) early involvement of potential end users in the planning, research and development of an intervention; (2) use of an outside consultant to advise of the development of the implementation strategy and help carry out implementation; (3) personal contact between intervention developers and target users; and, (4) methods to reward adoption of the intervention (Liberman and Eckman, 1989).

- Less effective influences on project implementation include audit (Berger, 1998; Black and Thompson, 1993; Briggs and Gray, 1999), clinical guidelines (Alderson and Roberts, 2000; Cook et al., 1997; Huby and Fairhurst, 1998; Jadad et al., 1998; Miller and Petrie, 2000; Stross, 1999), antagonistic stakeholders, methods which necessitated changes in professional roles and change driven by external forces (Ferlie et al., 2000).

## References

Alderson, P. and Roberts, I. (2000) 'Should journals publish systematic reviews that find no evidence to guide practice? Examples from injury research', *British Medical Journal*, 320(7231), pp. 376–7.

Allery, L. A. et al. (1997) 'Why general practitioners and consultants change their clinical practice: a critical incident study', *British Medical Journal*, 314, pp. 870–4.

Backer, T. E., Liberman, R. P. and Kuehnel, T. G. (1986) 'Dissemination and adoption of innovative psychosocial interventions', *Journal of Consulting and Clinical Psychology*, 54(1), pp. 111–18.

Bauchner, H. and Simpson, L. (1998) 'Specific issues related to developing, disseminating, and implementing pediatric practice guidelines for physicians, patients, families, and other stakeholders', *Health Services Research*, 33(4), pp. 1161–77.

Berger, A. (1998) 'Why doesn't audit work?', *British Medical Journal*, 7135(316), pp. 875–6.

Berger, P. L. and Luckmann, T. (1966) *The Social Construction of Reality: A Treatise in the Sociology of Knowledge* (Harmondsworth: Penguin Books).

Bero, L., Grilli, R., Grimshaw, J, Harvey, E., Oxman, A. and Thomson, M. A (1998) 'Closing the gap between research and practice: an overview of systematic reviews of interventions to promote implementation of research findings by health professionals', in A. Haines and A. Donald (eds), *Getting Research Findings into Practice* (London: BMJ Books).

Berwick, D. M. (2003) 'Disseminating innovations in health care', *Journal of the American Medical Association*, 289(15), pp. 1969–75.

Black, N. and Thompson, E. (1993) 'Obstacles to medical audit: British doctors speak', *Social Science & Medicine*, 36(7), pp. 849–56.

Briggs, A. H. and Gray, A. M. (1999) 'Methods in health service research: handling uncertainty in economic evaluations of healthcare interventions', *British Medical Journal*, 319(7210), pp. 635–8.

Chambers, D. and Dopson, S. (2003) 'Leading clinical practice change: evidence based medicine (EBM) in the United States and United Kingdom', in S. Dopson and A. Mark (eds), *Leading Health Care Organizations*. (London: Palgrave).

Clancy, C. M. (2003) 'Health services research: from galvanizing attention to creating action', *Health Services Research*, 38(3), pp. 777–82.

Cook, D. J. et al. (1997) 'The relation between systematic reviews and practice guidelines', *Annals of Internal Medicine*, 127(3), pp. 210–16.

Corrigan, P. W. (1998) 'Building teams and programs for effective rehabilitation', *Psychiatric Quarterly*, 69(3), pp. 193–209.

Davis, D. A. et al. (1995) 'Changing physician performance: a systematic review of the effect of continuing medical education strategies', *Journal of the American Medical Association*, 274(9), pp. 700–05.

Davis, P. and Howden-Chapman, P. (1996) 'Translating research findings into health policy', *Social Science & Medicine*, 43(5), pp. 865–72.

Dawson, S., Sutherland, K., Dopson, S., Miller, R. in association with Law, S. (1998) *The Relationship between R&D and Clinical Practice in Primary and Secondary Care: Cases of Adult Asthma and Glue Ear in Children. Final report* (Cambridge: Judge Institute of Management Studies, University of Cambridge; Oxford: Said Business School, University of Oxford).

Dopson, S. et al. (2001) 'Implementation of evidence based medicine: evaluation of the Promoting Action on Clinical Effectiveness programme', *Journal of Health Services Research & Policy*, 6(1), pp. 23–31.

Eddy, D. M. (1982) 'Clinical policies and the quality of clinical practice', *New England Journal of Medicine*, 307, pp. 343–7.

Ellrodt, G. et al. (1997) 'Evidence based disease management', *Journal of the American Medical Association*, 278(20), pp. 1687–92.

Eve, R. et al. (1997) *Learning from FACTS: Lessons from the Framework for Appropriate Care Throughout Sheffield (FACTS) Project* (Sheffield: School of Health and Related Research, University of Sheffield).

Ferlie, E., Wood, M. and Fitzgerald, L. (1999) 'Some limits to evidence based medicine: a case study from elective orthopedics', *Quality in Health Care*, 8(2), pp. 99–107.

Ferlie, E., FitzGerald, L. and Wood, M. (2000) 'Getting Evidence into Clinical Practice? An Organisational Behaviour Perspective', *Journal of Health Services Research and Policy*, 5(2), pp. 92–102.

Fitzgerald, L., Ferlie, E., Wood, M. and Hawkins, C. (1999) 'Evidence into practice? An exploratory analysis of the interpretation of evidence', in A. Mark and S. Dopson (eds), *Organisational Behaviour in Health Care* (London: Macmillan).

Grol, R. (1997) 'Beliefs and evidence in changing clinical practice', *British Medical Journal*, 315, pp. 418–21.

Hatgis, C. et al. (2001) 'Cross-fertilization versus transmission: recommendations for developing a bidirectional approach to psychotherapy dissemination research', *Applied & Preventive Psychology*, 10, pp. 37–49.

Haynes, R. B. (1990) 'Loose connections between peer-reviewed clinical journals and clinical practice', *Annals of Internal Medicine*, 113(9), pp. 724–8.

Hogan, D. B. et al. (2001) 'Recommendations of the Canadian consensus conference on dementia: dissemination, implementation, and evaluation of impact', *Canadian Journal of Neurological Sciences*, 28(Suppl. 1), pp. S115–21.

Holloway, R. G., Benesch, C. and Rush, S. R. (2000) 'Stroke prevention: Narrowing the evidence – practice gap', *Neurology*, 54(10), pp.1899–1906.

Howitt, A. and Armstrong, D. (1999) 'Implementing evidence based medicine in general practice: audit and qualitative study of antithrombotic treatment for atrial fibrillation', *British Medical Journal*, 318(7194), pp. 1324–7.

Hsiung, R. C. (2000) 'The best of both worlds: an online self-help group hosted by a mental health professional', *Cyberpsychology & Behavior*, 3(6), pp. 935–50.

Huby, G. and Fairhurst, K. (1998) *How Do General Practitioners Use Evidence? A Study in the Context of Lothian Health Policy and Practitioners' Use of Statin Drugs. Final Report* (Edinburgh: Primary Care Research Group, Department of General Practice, University of Edinburgh).

Jadad, A. R. et al. (1998) 'Methodology and reports of systematic reviews and meta-analyses: a comparison of Cochrane reviews with articles based in paper-based journals', *Journal of the American Medical Association*, 280(3), pp. 278–80.

Leeds, A. A. (1979) 'The future of communication in psychopharmacology', *Neuro-Psychopharmacology*, 3, pp. 125–31.

Liberman, R. P. and Eckman, T. A. (1989) 'Dissemination of skills training modules to psychiatric facilities: overcoming obstacles to the utilisation of a rehabilitation innovation', *British Journal of Psychiatry*, 155(Suppl. 5), pp. 117–22.

Locock, L. et al. (2001) 'Understanding the role of opinion leaders in improving clinical effectiveness', *Social Science and Medicine*, 53, pp. 745–57.

Lomas, J. (1993) 'Diffusion, dissemination, and implementation: Who should do what?', *Annals of the New York Academy of Sciences*, 703, pp. 226–37.

Lorenzen, G. L. and Braskamp, L. A. (1978) 'Comparative influence of political, cost/benefit, and statistical information on administrative decision making', *Evaluation and Program Planning*, 1, pp. 235–8.

Mannheim, K. (1936) *Ideology and Utopia: An Introduction to the Sociology of Knowledge*. L. Wirth and E. Shils (trans) (London: Routledge & Kegan Paul).

Mant, J., Hicks, N., Dopson, S. and Hurley, P. (1997) *Uptake of Research Findings into Clinical Practice: A Controlled Study of a Brief External Intervention on the Use of Corticosteroids in Pre-term Labour* (Oxford: Division of Public Health and Primary Care).

McColl, A., Smith, H., White, P. and Field, J. (1998) 'General practitioners' perceptions of the route to evidence based medicine: a questionnaire survey', *British Medical Journal*, 316(7128), pp. 361–5.

Miller, J. and Petrie, J. (2000) 'Development of practice guidelines', *Lancet*, 355(9198), pp. 82–3.

Mulkay, M. J. (1979) *Science and the Sociology of Knowledge* (London: George Allen & Unwin).

NHS Centre for Reviews and Dissemination – *see* University of York NHS Centre for Reviews and Dissemination.

NIMH – *see* US National Institute of Mental Health

Oxman, A. D., Thomson, M. A., Davis, D. A. et al. (1995) 'No magic bullets: a systematic review of 102 trials of interventions to improve professional practice', *Canadian Medical Association Journal*, 153, pp. 1423–31.

Prescott, K. et al. (1997) 'Promoting clinically effective practice: general practitioners' awareness of sources of research evidence', *Family Practice*, 14(4), pp. 320–3.

Rothman, A. J. and Salovey, P. (1997) 'Shaping perceptions to motivate healthy behavior: the role of message framing', *Psychological Bulletin*, 121(1), pp. 3–19.

Rubenstein, L. V., Mittman, B. S., Yano, E. M. and Mulrow, C. D. (2000) 'From understanding health care provider behavior to improving health care: The QUERI framework for quality improvement', *Medical Care*, 38(6 Suppl 1), pp. I129–41.

Sackett, D. L., Rosenberg, W. M. C., Gray, J. A. M., Haynes, R. B. and Richardson, W. S. (1996) 'Evidence based medicine: What it is and what it isn't', *British Medical Journal*, 312, pp. 71–2.

Schoenwald, S. K. and Henggeler, S. W. (2002) 'Services research and family based treatment,' in H. Liddle, G. Diamond, R. Levant, J. Bray, and D. Santisteban (eds),

*Family Psychology Intervention Science* (Washington, DC: American Psychological Association).

Sorian, R. and Baugh, T. (2002) 'Power of information: closing the gap between research and policy', *Health Affairs*, 21(2), pp. 264–73.

Stross, J. K. (1999) 'Guidelines have their limits', *Annals of Internal Medicine*, 131(4), pp. 304–6.

University of York. NHS Centre for Reviews and Dissemination (1999) 'Getting evidence into practice', *Effective Health Care*, 5(1), pp. 1–16.

US National Institute of Mental Health (2002) Dissemination and Implementation Research in Mental Health – Addendum to PA-02-131, accessed 2005-07-25, http://grants.nih.gov/grants/guide/notice-files/NOT-MH-02-009.html

US National Institute of Mental Health (2004) State Implementation of Evidence based Practices II – Bridging Science and Service, accessed 2005-07-25, http://grants2.nih.gov/grants/guide/rfa-files/RFA-MH-05-004.html.

US National Institute of Mental Health (2004a) *Information for Researchers: Grants*, accessed 2005-07-25, http://www.nimh.nih.gov/researchfunding/grants.cfm.

Wood, M., Ferlie, E. and FitzGerald, L. (1998) *Achieving Change in Clinical Practice: Scientific, Organisational and Behavioural Processes* (Warwick, England: University of Warwick).

# Part II

# When Does Practice Lead the Way?

# 5
# The Limits of Restructuring: A Decade of Health Reforms in New Zealand

*Pauline Barnett, Michael Powell and Jacqueline Cumming*

## Introduction

The last decade of the twentieth century could well be characterized as the decade of health reforms, with many countries, New Zealand included, reinventing their health systems in order to improve performance (Docteur and Oxley, 2003). In this zest for large scale system reform we may have failed to ask whether we have lost opportunities along the way to achieve smaller, more incremental change in the practices and processes that may be significant to the enhancement of health care delivery. Furthermore, the costs of major reform and frequent restructurings have been high in financial and human terms, including low morale, dissatisfaction and high staff turnover.

This chapter draws on analyzes of four sets of structural reforms of the New Zealand health system since the late 1980s to assess their contribution to actual changes in the health care delivery system and to improvements in the delivery of health care services. The first set of reforms, under a Labour Government that introduced many economic and policy reforms during its term, involved, during the 1980s, the establishment of elected Area Health Boards (AHBs) and the introduction of general management to replace the traditional doctor–nurse–administrator management approach (Laugesen and Salmond, 1994; Ashton, 2002). The second set involved a radical shift towards a competitive, market based model in 1993 driven by a neo-liberal government intent on gaining increased efficiencies in the health system through a process of corporatization (Upton, 1991). A 'quasi'-market was created through the separation of the purchasing and provision of health care, with the intention that providers, both public and private, compete for contracts with purchasing agencies. Hospitals were reconstituted as Crown Health Enterprises (CHEs), converted into limited liability companies with the Crown as sole shareholder, governed by appointed boards of business and financial experts and run by CEOs largely recruited from the non-health private sector (Barnett and Barnett, 2005; Gauld, 2001). From their inception, the new competitive, corporate structures lacked support from either the public or health professionals (Cumming and Salmond, 1998). By 1996, there was little evidence of the significant hoped for efficiency gains (Ashby, 1996; Contract Monitoring Group, 1996; Easton, 2002; Ashton, 1999; Barnett et al., 2001) and the government lost considerable ground in the 1996 election. A third set of reforms was introduced following the formation of a coalition government. In 1996, the competitive model was modified to a more co-operative approach (Coalition Agreement on Health, 1997). Symbolically, the Crown Health Enterprises were restructured and renamed more neutrally as Hospital and Health Services, although certain central elements of the competitive model were retained, such as the purchaser–provider split and appointed governing boards. In 2001, following the election of a Labour-led government in late 1999, there was a fourth set of reforms and a second radical reversal of direction. The new government was strongly opposed to market models in the public health system. In a 'back to the future' move, the new government re-introduced elected governing boards, created 21 population based District Health Boards (DHBs), re-integrated purchasing and provision within DHBs, and signalled the progressive devolution of funding to these local boards within the constraints of national strategies and health priorities (Ashton, 2002; Cumming and Mays, 2002).

The introduction of AHBs in 1989 was a significant event denoting the first important change in the health system since 1938 and the introduction of a population based approach to health. The most radical of reforms and, arguably, the most consequential for organizational structure and behaviour were the corporate, market based reforms of 1993 and the shift back to a more traditional public sector, democratic model in 2001. This chapter focuses on these two more radical reforms of 1993 and 2001, both of them attempts at transformational changes driven by strong ideological commitments. The first set of reforms was derived from the neo-liberal conviction that markets and competition drive efficiency and that customer demands, given the ability to choose among providers, will drive improvements in quality and service. The second set of radical reforms in 2001 was equally driven by political commitments and ideology, in this case to the removal of market forces and terminology, the reintroduction of democratic governance, local consultation, engagement and control, and a focus on population health, including health promotion, disease prevention and primary health care. In each set of reforms, both the symbolism and language of reform and consequent structural changes were important. Each set of reforms resulted in the formation of new organizational entities with new names and involved the appointment, by and large, of new leadership at senior management and governance levels. The costs of these reforms were considerable in terms of funding diverted to pay for the restructuring and associated costs, organizational disruption, staff redundancies and health sector morale. A central task of this chapter is to consider whether the benefits of the successive reforms outweighed their considerable costs and to discuss what we might learn from research regarding the relative contributions of structural change and professional practice in achieving such benefits.

## Change and continuity

The first lesson is about change and continuity or the difference between rhetoric and the actuality of change. Ashton et al. (2005) suggest that the extent of actual change is somewhat less than the rhetoric of reform would lead one to believe. They argue that while the organizational structures and legal frameworks may have changed with each set of reforms, 'many of the underlying features of the system have remained untouched' and that 'there has been a continuous contrast between formal structures and political rhetoric, and the reality of day-to-day health system behaviour' (Ashton et al., 2005).

There are classic examples from both sets of radical reform. In the 1993 reforms the rhetoric was largely about the new market for health care services, competition among providers and the development of new contracts that would specify volumes, prices and quality. However, in reality there was minimal competition especially among the providers of hospital services with only a very small fraction of total services moving to the private sector (Cumming and Salmond, 1998; Ashton et al., 2005). While there was a clear perception that increased competition would follow the reforms, there is little evidence that the CEOs of the publicly-owned health care providers were very concerned about competition (Barnett and Malcolm, 1997). Most public hospitals enjoyed a continuation of their pre-existing natural monopoly (Ashton et al., 2005). Typically purchasers were reluctant to move funding from a public to a private provider as there were definite political risks in undermining public institutions. In addition, relatively few private providers actively sought public contracts, not wishing to disrupt the status quo and regarding the price offered as insufficient.

In more vulnerable sectors (that is, less capital intensive areas with opportunities for the entry of alternative providers), such as public health and mental health, the impact of the competitive model was more strongly felt. While there was increased privatization as funding moved from public to private (largely non-profit) providers, this was not inappropriate given the strong community orientation of services. However, in both public health (Malcolm et al., 1996; Fear and Barnett, 2003) and mental health (Barnett and Newberry, 2002) some agencies reported competition as inimical to the goals of service provision, undermining information sharing and service collaboration.

In the second major set of reforms, in 2001, the rhetoric was of decentralization and local control with the introduction of locally elected District Health Boards (DHBs). The DHBs were required to undertake a needs analysis of their regions and to develop locally informed strategic plans. But the Boards soon discovered that their decision making autonomy was relatively constrained. The Ministry of Health appeared reluctant to relinquish control over all funding decisions. Both national health strategies and priorities and the political imperatives of the government have significantly limited the strategic planning freedom of the DHBs (Cumming et al., 2003), particularly DHB efforts to rationalize services because of the political 'fall-out' that might ensue. For instance, attempts by some DHBs to exit the provision of certain services that they have viewed as not being core to publicly provided health care, such as fertility services, have been vetoed by the government, effectively ensuring the continuity of the service status quo.

Another indication of significant continuity, in the face of a rhetoric of change, is evident in the constraints imposed by the population funding formula. For many DHBs, large-scale changes in structures were accompanied by constrained financial allocations and budget deficits. Concern over the ever-increasing fiscal demands of the health sector was a major motivator of the first wave of radical reform in 1993 (Gibbs et al., 1988; Upton, 1991). Competition and market forces were expected to lead to greater efficiencies and thereby reduce fiscal pressure. However, there was initial disappointment with the performance of the CHEs (Barnett et al., 2001), with many continuing to operate deficits and being subject to a high level of financial monitoring. A briefing to the government in 1996 acknowledged that 'the pace of performance improvement seems, if anything, to have weakened since the reforms' (Barnett et al., 2001, p. 145). Towards the end of that reform period, however, many of these entities had actually improved their financial position first through a so-called 'deficit switch' that re-allocated deficit funding to purchasers in order for purchasers to increase the prices they could offer for services (Gauld, 2001), and second through strict monitoring and governance. Once the new set of reforms arrived in 2001 the deficits quickly returned. Consequently, although there had been some progress, some DHBs have taken several years to move from a deficit mode, which has limited their scope to develop existing services or introduce new ones.

## The extent of change

Across all sets of reforms there has been debate about 'depth of change'; that is, the extent to which change has, in fact, permeated the organization as a whole or been quite superficial. For example, reform at one level in the organization – for instance, introducing new governance arrangements and new structures – may have little impact at other levels. Indeed, many health professionals, particularly hospital doctors, while concerned about restructuring and the uncertainty that brings, operate very much as before. As one senior surgeon in a public hospital noted when asked about the impact of the reforms on his practice:

Personally I have worked under 11 different notations of health management. The impact is, this is the issue – the issue is the work goes on. The surgical diseases don't change. The demography changes, people are now older and sicker and the morbidity is higher but...actually the operations and the management of them has not changed in any particular way since 1993 when the reforms really started to happen in a major way. The main impact that reforms have had on our work is that we have had to be involved in the education of managers and board members.

This suggests that many patients would be unaware of the changes that have excited so much controversy, such is the degree of continuity in how patients experience and access services. One area, however, where the impact of reform is now being felt by patients is in primary health care. Here, there have been important changes to the patient experience, including the development of new services, service improvements and changes in clinical practice and quality assurance (Kerr et al., 1996; Malcolm, Barnett and Wright, 2000). These resulted in part from the formation of independent practitioner associations, involving major change in organizational and governance arrangements made possible, but not mandated, by the 1993 reforms (Barnett, Barnett and Kearns, 1998). Gains in access to primary care have become more notable following the 2001 reforms. These, however, are not necessarily attributed to changes in structure alone but to the significant infusion of new funds by the government to reduce the cost barriers New Zealand patients have historically faced in accessing primary health care (Barnett and Barnett, 2004).

## Unplanned consequences of reform

Another lesson from analysis of the New Zealand health reforms is that implementation is often uneven and there are frequently significant unintended consequences of reform policies. A classical rationalist or linear view of policy making and implementation suggests that if policy is soundly based, and structures and resources in place, then the desired outcomes should eventuate. However, modern policy theory acknowledges that unforeseen consequences might be anticipated although the actual form that they take may be unexpected. Experience in the human services policy arena suggests that a range of actors with variable levels of discretion and power will seek to modify policy as it is implemented (Parsons, 1995). In the recent history of health reform in New Zealand, such unplanned consequences have emerged from two particular sources – gaps in policy detail and resistance to stated policy.

## Response to policy 'gaps'

Where gaps occur in policy detail, deliberate or otherwise, these may be filled in by those outside the formal policy process, sometimes in unexpected ways. In New Zealand, in two instances, this has involved the formation of new organizations that then had a significant impact on the system as a whole. The 1993 reforms, for example, failed to specify how the funding of general practice would be addressed although there was a clear indication that the government intended to move from a legislated fee-for-service model to a contractual arrangement, a concern to independent general practitioners who largely operated on a reimbursable fee-for-service model. A preoccupation with restructuring hospitals, and a desire not to antagonize general practice any earlier than necessary, meant that for several years (from the announcement of the reforms in 1991 to mid-1995) there was no clear national policy view on how the relationship between GPs and the purchasing agencies should develop. In that time, general practitioners organized themselves into independent practitioner associations (IPAs), usually with a company structure of some kind, to negotiate contracts with purchasers. In doing so, they created a number of new, collective organizations with significant bargaining power and the capacity to develop and shape their own services and influence the wider system (Barnett et al., 1998; Barnett, 2003). The IPAs have subsequently provided the infrastructure for many of the more comprehensive primary health organizations (PHOs) established by the Labour government since 2001.

The Labour-led 2001 reforms provide another example of an organization forming to fill a gap. The legislation established a contractual relationship between the Ministry of Health and 21 individual DHBs, but DHBs apparently felt the need for a more organized and collective approach. Consequently, the DHBs got together and formed District Health Boards New Zealand (DHBNZ) to represent their interests collectively to government, to co-ordinate industrial relations negotiations, to provide leadership development, and to assist their members in technical areas of planning and development. In response to perceived collective needs a new and important actor has entered the sector, providing an additional dynamic in the formal legislated relationships.

## Resistance to policy

Where there has been strong resistance to policy from among community or sector groups, sometimes unexpected outcomes have occurred. One such outcome is the incomplete implementation of policy, of which there are a number of examples. In the case of the 1993 reforms, tentative proposals were included for radical changes to the financing of health services through social insurance and managed competition between managed care organizations. Strong opposition from both within the health sector and from the general public precluded further progress to implementation, and these plans were quietly abandoned (Cumming and

Salmond, 1998; Ashton et al., 2005; Cumming, 2003). Similarly, a project to develop a 'list' of service entitlements, or core services for public funding, was abandoned after considerable consultation and work because of political sensitivities and the complexity of the task (Cumming, 1994). Other unforeseen consequences have included reversal of policy already implemented, most notably a particularly public 'turnaround' related to hospital user charges. In 1993, the government implemented a $50 per night charge for public hospital stays, but community opposition and refusal to pay created an unsustainable political climate and the charges were soon dropped (Ashton, 1999). Similarly, the differential targeting according to income of primary care fees for children under 6 years of age also proved sufficiently unpopular that it became an election issue in 1996, with the incoming Coalition government introducing a higher, and universal, subsidy. Removal of community representation in governance (a strongly held value in New Zealand) from 1991 was politically unpopular, leading to partial retreat by the Coalition government in 1997 and its subsequent reinstatement in 2001.

On occasion, reforming governments have misjudged the organizational as well as the political environment and implementation did not occur as planned or wished. For example, the formation of IPAs throughout the 1990s created a strong general practice infrastructure that had not existed previously. The incoming Labour-led government, in promulgating its new Primary Health Care Strategy in 2000, chose to ignore these developments in their efforts to create new primary care structures. They expected that, with the formation of the new Primary Health Organizations (PHOs), the IPAs would, in the words of a government official, 'quietly go away'. In fact, IPAs remained a significant force in challenging the detail of government policy and in many cases controlling PHO development notwithstanding an apparent earlier government attempt to exclude them from the process.

## Macro-restructuring or micro-change to delivery systems?

If there have been real changes and improvements in the New Zealand health system (that is, improved planning and management systems, improved service performance, changes at point of delivery, better access), the question is whether these have emerged from controversial system-wide reforms and restructurings, or as a consequence of micro-level attempts at incremental reform and improvement (Hinings et al., 2003). It is arguable that micro-level attempts to deal with specific problems might have had a more significant impact on actual behaviour and performance in the health system, independent of reform strategies. Two key areas where there have been such important micro-changes and service developments are those of waiting lists for elective surgery, a problem that has vexed successive governments since the 1980s, and integrated or co-ordinated care.

## Waiting list management

During the 1980s the numbers of people waiting for surgery rose by 25 per cent, with considerable regional variation in waiting times (Gibbs, Fraser and Scott, 1988, pp. 6–7). Under the 1993 health reforms it was expected that regionalization of purchasing within a competitive market would lead to greater levels of efficiency in elective services through competition and increased privatization of surgical services. Surgical waiting lists, however, continued to grow throughout the 1990s. While some privatization of publicly funded elective surgical services occurred, for reasons discussed above, growth was slow. Nevertheless, some new investor-owned providers entered the scene, but, for the most part, their success has depended on developing private niche markets for their services, and accepting public contracts only for selected procedures (Kearns and Barnett, 2003) and without making much impact on public waiting lists.

From the mid-1990s successive governments attempted to develop rational approaches to setting surgical priorities. Despite the substantial reservations expressed by surgeons, governments pressed ahead with the implementation of a booking system, with cash injections to stimulate the implementation of a criteria based, points system for access to surgery (Gauld and Derrett, 2000). This process has intensified under the most recent set of reforms (2001), with the requirement that all DHBs reduce their waiting lists, with a focus on waiting times for first assessment for surgery, rather than the numbers on lists, for most conditions. Although progress towards reduced waiting lists has been variable, with access to elective surgery continuing to be a political issue, the booking system introduced in the mid-1990s appears to have had a direct impact on provider behaviour, particularly in auditing waiting lists and giving certainty to patients, although there continues to be variability in the use of standard tools and some lack of confidence by surgeons in the system (McLeod, Morgan et al., 2004).

This experience suggests that the introduction of competition and partial privatization did not help the management of waiting lists. However, a rational, government-led approach has provided the tools for more effective prioritization. Progress towards successful implementation depended on the support, or at least compliance, of clinicians and the wider sector assisted by additional targeted funding. Contribution to the better management of waiting times has been halting, but generally in a consistent direction under three different reform regimes suggesting that the broader reform environment might be less important than a well-designed intervention at a more micro level, strongly supported by the government and endorsed by funding incentives or sanctions as may be appropriate.

## Integrated care developments

A further area of importance to all reforming governments has been the issue of a more integrated approach to such issues as the management of specific diseases and the continuum of care across primary and secondary boundaries. In the 1993 reforms it was anticipated that integration of funding in a competitive environment would promote 'better co-ordination in the management of total health care across general practice, other community-based services and hospital services' (Upton, 1991, p. 41). As noted above, competition appears to undermine co-ordination, with the result that the 1997 Coalition government explicitly limited competition and provided stronger political leadership to promote co-ordination, introducing targeted funding for pilot integrated care projects to incentivize such developments (Health Funding Authority, 1998; Davis, 1999). The Labour-led government, in office since 1999, has relied on a decentralized funding model and targeted resources to promote local co-ordination and integrated care.

Effective service integration and disease management rely on good information systems, good working relationships between professionals and organizations, adequate incentives and strong leadership (Shortell et al., 2000). From the mid-1990s, as interest in a more collaborative approach developed (Health Funding Authority, 1998; Davis, 1999), there emerged some early work on integration across the primary-secondary interface, including disease management initiatives and the development of clinical pathways (Keeling et al., 2004; Malcolm, 1998). Following a tentative start in some regions, hospital based services and IPAs in the primary care arena have actively pursued co-ordinated care strategies with the aim of reducing hospital re-admissions through better integration across the sectors (Malcolm et al., 2000; Moriarty et al., 2001).

The development of more sophisticated information systems in both primary and secondary care has made connections between primary care and secondary services possible. A good example is the diabetes disease management project developed in one DHB. This project integrated data from primary and secondary providers and drew on recently developed national guidelines and pilot project work to provide a co-ordinated pathway of care for diabetes patients. The project has developed an effective decision support tool for both primary and secondary care (Brimacombe, 2003, p. 89). Macro-level restructuring from 1997 onwards may have contributed by creating a more supportive environment for local integration, but progress on integrated care and disease management derives largely from the development of good working relationships between local providers, the existence of evidence based guidelines for practice that point to the benefits of co-ordinated care, increasing confidence in collaborative processes and incentives to providers to move in this direction.

The experience of both waiting list management and integrated care programs suggests that the 1993 structural reforms themselves made little contribution and, in fact, may have inhibited development in these important areas. However, the reforms did sweep away many of the institutional barriers to change and permitted the emergence of new sets of relationships. These, when associated with new technology and ideas and, after 1996, with a more collaborative mode of working, encouraged incremental progress on these micro-level matters with direct impact on health care delivery processes.

## Have the reforms improved system performance?

It is uncertain whether successive reforms have improved performance of the system as a whole. Some things have definitely improved. There is a better understanding of the real costs of services and therefore better pricing; there have been advances in contracting for services; and there is also evidence of productivity improvements in terms of increased throughput and reduced length of stay in the hospital sector (Cumming and Salmond, 1998; Devlin and O'Dea, 1998). The latest set of reforms (2001) has established a district level infrastructure for planning and decision making which a recent review suggests has the potential to be responsive to local needs and effective in priority setting (Cumming et al., 2003).

A significant area of performance improvement has been in primary care. There the IPAs provided the basis for local developments by becoming contracted providers and budget holders for general practice consultation, pharmaceuticals and laboratory services, and developing programs for quality improvement (Houston, 2001; Malcolm et al., 1999). Many of the recently established PHOs could not have progressed to the same extent without the existing IPA infrastructure, and the establishment of IPAs would have been impossible without a wider reform environment.

In addition to providing new structures, the reform context encouraged review and reorganization of governance, management and delivery systems (Barnett and Newberry, 2002). Many health providers went through the experience of business process reform that encouraged greater efficiencies in areas such as admission and discharge arrangements. While it could be argued that these 'processual' changes could have been achieved without large-scale, system-wide change through a process of continuous improvement and incremental reform, it is uncertain that this would, in fact, have occurred.

## Conclusion

To any commentator in the 1980s, New Zealand's health system was in need of reform. However, the first attempt at system-wide reform in the late 1980s was short-lived and considered not sufficiently radical by a new government in the early 1990s. The market reforms that followed introduced the language and symbolism of the market if not the reality of competition.

But embracing the internal market as a driver for change, in the absence of evidence based research to justify such a move, was politically risky and led to substantial political discontent particularly as there was little evidence of clear health status or health service gains. It is not surprising, then, that the late 1990s saw a retreat from the neo-liberal agenda although certain elements of the 1993 reforms persisted to the end of the 1990s only to be swept aside in the second wave of radical restructuring in 2001.

This second wave of reform has only been in place for four years as most of the implementation did not occur until 2001, and is still being fine-tuned. However, there are signs that the government has learned from previous reform failures, showing greater willingness to accept a slow pace of reform when faced with obstacles and to negotiate the steps and the specifics of the reform model while holding on to the overall direction. For instance, the government modified the PHO strategy to facilitate involvement of the IPAs in response to considerable lobbying by the IPA movement. Not only did it demonstrate a degree of flexibility, but it also provided significant financial incentives to encourage existing primary health care organizations to make the transition to PHO status. In other words, it was prepared to adopt incremental implementation tactics, along with positive incentives, to achieve its wider reform strategy.

The radical reforms of 1993 and 2001 have had impacts, both positive and negative, beyond macro-structural changes. They have created (for better or worse) changes in system-wide climate, relationships and power relations. For instance, the 1993 reforms engendered a competitive and contentious climate both between purchaser and provider entities and among the providers themselves who were competing for contracts. Power shifted from the medical professionals, especially doctors, to management and business leaders in a governance role. The 2001 reforms reversed the market direction and rhetoric, replacing it with the rhetoric of improved access, local democratic control and population health. With its focus on population health and improvements in the delivery of primary health services, it has also changed the climate and putative power relations in the system.

As policy is frequently modified as it goes through the process of implementation, the service and organizational consequences of these reforms can only be observed over time. In our view, the radical market based reform of the New Zealand health system in 1993 was not sustainable due to lack of popular support and inherent structural flaws, in particular arising from a lack of competition between providers in a small country. However, it created opportunities for incremental change that would otherwise have proceeded at a more glacial pace, if at all. Our research thus far demonstrates that the 2001 reforms have been more palatable to both consumers and health professionals (Cumming et al., 2003), have required adaptation as they have proceeded and may therefore be more likely to be sustainable.

Despite the significant costs of almost continuous health reforms in New Zealand, and the undoubted existence of widespread 'reform fatigue', there appears to be increased capacity to respond to persistent problems in the system, such as waiting lists and the lack of integration of care. The reform environment has encouraged a degree of experimentation and innovation in the system although we lack the ability to determine whether this might have occurred anyway in the absence of system-wide reform. Certainly, the need for integration had become an international issue in the mid-1990s, and there was an urgent political need to deal with the waiting lists issue in some way. However, the New Zealand experience would seem to suggest that micro-reforms in service delivery have occurred alongside, or within, the macro-, system-wide restructurings that have occurred every three or four years and that these restructurings have created a climate, not always comfortable, in which these can occur.

## References

Ashby, M. (1996) *Performance Improvement in the New Zealand Health Sector* (Auckland: New Zealand Institute of Health Management).

Ashton, T. (1999) 'The health reforms: to market and back?', in J. Boston, P. Dalziel and S. St John (eds), *Redesigning the Welfare State: Problems, Policies and Prospects* (Auckland: Oxford University Press).

Ashton, T. (2002) 'Running on the spot: lessons from a decade of health reform in New Zealand', *Applied Health Economics and Health Policy*, 1(2), pp. 97–106.

Ashton, T., Mays, N. and Devlin, N. (2005) 'Continuity through change: the rhetoric and reality of health reform in New Zealand', *Social Science & Medicine*, 61(2), pp. 253–62.

Barnett, J. R. and Barnett, P. (2004) 'Primary health care in New Zealand: problems and policy approaches', *Social Policy Journal of New Zealand*, 21, pp. 49–66.

Barnett, J. R., Barnett, P. and Kearns, R. A. (1998) 'Declining professional dominance? Trends in the proletarianisation of primary care in New Zealand', *Social Science & Medicine*, 46, pp. 193–207.

Barnett, P. (2003) 'Into the unknown: the anticipation of membership of independent practitioner associations', *New Zealand Medical Journal*, 116, p. 1171.

Barnett, P. and Barnett, J. R. (2005) 'Reform and change in health service provision', in K. Dew and P. Davis (eds), *Health and Society in Aotearoa New Zealand*, 2nd edn, (Melbourne: Oxford University Press).

Barnett, P. and Malcolm, L. (1997) 'Beyond ideology: The emerging roles of New Zealand's Crown health enterprises', *International Journal of Health Services*, 27, pp. 89–108.

Barnett, P. and Newberry, S. (2002) 'Reshaping community mental health services in a restructured state: New Zealand 1984–97', *Public Management Review*, 4, pp. 187–208.

Barnett, P., Perkins, R. and Powell, M. (2001) 'On a hiding to nothing? Assessing the corporate governance of hospital and health services in New Zealand 1993–98', *International Journal of Health Planning and Management*, 16, pp. 139–54.

Brimacombe, P. (2003) 'Health care information systems: the Counties Manukau District Health Board experience', in R. Gauld (ed.), *Continuity Amid Chaos: Health Care Management and Delivery in New Zealand* (Dunedin: Otago University Press).

Coalition Agreement on Health (1997) *Implementing the Coalition Agreement: Report of the Taskforce* (Wellington NZ: Wellington Ministry of Health).

Contract Monitoring Group (1996) *Purchasing for Your Health: 1994/5* (Wellington NZ: Wellington Ministry of Health).

Cumming, J. (1994) 'Core services and priority setting: the New Zealand experience', *Health Policy*, 29, pp. 41–60.

Cumming, J. (2003) *Health Service Coverages Regulation: An Evaluation of Policy Options for New Zealand*, PhD Thesis, University of Wellington, Victoria.

Cumming, J. et al. (2003) *Interim Report on the Health Reforms 2001 Research Project* (Wellington NZ: Health Services Research Centre, Victoria University of Wellington).

Cumming, J. and Mays, N. (2002) 'Reform and Counter-reform: how sustainable is New Zealand's latest health system restructuring?', *Journal of Health Services Research and Policy*, 7 (Supp 1), pp. 46–55.

Cumming, J. and Salmond, G. (1998) 'Reforming New Zealand health care', in W. Ranade (ed.), *Markets and Health Care: A Comparative Analysis* (New York: Addison Wesley Longman).

Davis, P. (1999) 'Making sense of integrated care in New Zealand', *Australian Health Review*, 22, pp. 25–42.

Davis, P. and Ashton, T. (2001) *Health and Public Policy in New Zealand* (Auckland: Oxford University Press).

Devlin, N. and O'Dea, D. (1998) 'Hospitals', in M. Pickford and A. Bollard (eds), *The Structure and Dynamics of New Zealand Industries* (Palmerston North: Dunmore Press).

Docteur, E., and Oxley, H. (2003) *Health Care Systems: Lessons from the Reform Experience* (Paris: OECD Health Working Papers).

Easton, B. (2002) 'The New Zealand health reforms in context', *Applied Health Economics and Health Policy*, 1(2), pp. 106–12.

Fear, H. and Barnett, P. (2003) 'Holding fast: the experience of collaboration in a competitive environment', *Health Promotion International*, 18, pp. 5–14.

Gauld, R. (2001) *Revolving Doors: New Zealand's Health Reforms* (Wellington: Institute of Policy Studies).

Gauld, R. and Derrett, S. (2000) 'Solving the surgical waiting list problem? New Zealand's "booking system"', *International Journal of Health Planning and Management*, 15, pp. 259–72.

Gibbs, A., Fraser, D. and Scott, J. (1988) *Unshackling the Hospitals (The Gibbs Report)* (Wellington NZ: Hospital and Health Services Task Force).

Health Funding Authority (1998) *Integrated Care: Glossary of Terms* (Wellington NZ: Health Funding Authority).

Hinings, C. R., Casebeer, A., Reay, T., Golden-Biddle, K., Pablo, A., and Greenwood, R. (2003) 'Regionalizing Healthcare in Alberta: Legislated Change: Uncertainty and Loose Coupling', *British Journal of Management*, 4, pp. S15–30.

Houston, N. (2001) 'Quality improvement with independent practitioner associations: lessons from New Zealand', *New Zealand Medical Journal*, 114, pp. 304–6.

Kearns, R. A. and Barnett, J. R. (2003) 'Reading the Landscapes of private medicine: Ascot's place in Millennial Auckland', *Social Science& Medicine*, 51, pp. 2303–15.

Keeling, S. et al. (2004) 'Integrating care over time: older service users record stability and change', Paper presented at the Inter-Congress Conference Ageing Societies and Ageing Sociology, Roehampton, University of Surrey.

Kerr, D., Malcolm, L. Schousboe, J. and Pimm, F. (1996) 'Successful implementation of laboratory budget holding by Pegasus Medical Group', *New Zealand Medical Journal*, 109, pp. 354–7.

Laugesen, M. and Salmond, G. (1994) 'New Zealand health care: a background', *Health Policy*, 29, pp. 11–23.

McLeod, D., Morgan, S., McKinlay, E., Dew, K., Cumming, J., Dowell, T. and Love, T. (2004) 'Use of, and attitudes to, clinical priority assessment criteria in elective surgery in New Zealand', *Journal of Health Services Research and Policy*, 9(2), pp. 91–9.

Malcolm, L. (1998) 'Towards general practice led integrated care in New Zealand', *Medical Journal of Australia*, 169, pp. 147–51.

Malcolm, L., Barnett, P. and Nuthall, J. (1996) 'Lost in the market: A survey of senior public health managers in New Zealand's reforming health system', *Australian and New Zealand Journal of Public Health*, 20, pp. 567–73.

Malcolm, L., Barnett, P and Wright, L. (2000) 'Emerging clinical governance: developments in independent practitioner associations in New Zealand', *New Zealand Medical Journal*, 113, pp. 33–5.

Malcolm, L., Wright, L., Seers, M. and Guthrie, J. (1999) 'The evaluation of pharmaceutical management and budget holding in Pegasus Medical Group', *New Zealand Medical Journal*, 112, pp. 162–4.

Moriarty, H. et al. (2001) 'Hepatitis services at an injecting drug user outreach clinic' *New Zealand Medical Journal*, 114, pp. 105–6.

Parsons, W. (1995) *Public Policy: An Introduction to the Theory and Practice of Policy Analysis* (Aldershot, UK: Edward Elgar).

Shortell, S. M., Gillies, R. R. and Anderson, D. A. (2000) *Remaking Health Care in America* (San Francisco: Jossey-Bass).

Upton, S. (1991) *Your Health and the Public Health* (Wellington, NZ: New Zealand Government).

# 6
# Reconstructing Continuity of Care in a Local Health Authority in Italy: Putting Humpty Dumpty Back Together Again

*Jennifer Landau, Costanza Ceda and Francesco Ripa di Meana*

## Introduction

The Italian health system is a national public system financed and almost entirely delivered by the state. The Italian national system is tax funded and provides care to the entire population free of charge. It is organized in three levels: Central Government; Regional Government (21 Administrations); and, 200 Local Health Authorities (LHAs), along with 100 independent hospitals. Each LHA is responsible for its population's health. The independent hospitals (IHs) are similar to British NHS trusts (Anessi Pessina, Cantù and Jommi, 2004).

In 1992, the sustainability of the Italian health system as a whole was a critical issue, and legislators introduced a major reform based on introducing new managerial principles. This reform began a long change process to which hospitals and Local Health Authorities are still adapting (Del Vecchio, 2000). This change process introduced new management principles across Italy's health system. These principles included managerialism, regionalization, and quasi-markets (Fattore, 1999). Management tools were drawn from the US health system including using Diagnostic Related Groups (DRGs), departmental management and budgeting (Bergamaschi and Lega, 2000). 'Managerialism gave LHAs and the newly formed IHs considerable direction over their affairs, but required them to improve their performance and encouraged them to adopt private sector management techniques.' (Anessi Pessina, Cantù and Jommi, 2004, p. 309)

Twelve years later, hospital systems have changed in recognizable ways. For example, the results have allowed for a greater transparency in how health system resources for acute care are consumed. However, primary care delivery was less actively involved in this change process as the management tools and approaches developed for use in hospitals were not particularly adaptable to primary care objectives and operating structures. As a result, far less change occurred within the primary care sector.

This chapter delineates a collaborative effort motivated by and situated in practice and incorporating research to support and create organizational change. The process involved continuous interaction between the Chief Executive Officer (CEO) and the research team in developing a model for change that would be both effective and replicable. A change management process that took place in the Piacenza Local Health Authority in northern Italy is presented where positive change has occurred and resulted in enhanced continuity of care delivered outside of hospital. Prior to the change management initiative, there were four health districts in the LHA that were structured and divided into many offices and professionals working in little groups. The continuum of care was like 'humpty dumpty' after he fell off the wall; it just couldn't seem to get 'put together again'. The objective of the new change management process (Pettigrew, 1992) was to reconstruct organizational integration (Longo, 2001). Previously, the introduction of more structured tools such as budgets, contracts and organizational charts had failed to create continuity of care. This case study illustrates the value of introducing implicit marketing and concentrating on working relationships (Argyris, 1970, 1978; Crozier, 1977) in order positively to impact organizational culture and in improving continuity of primary care services within a geographical area. The change management process used five process-oriented tools for change:

1. Focus groups (Schein, 1985; Davis, 2000)
2. The strategic team (Longo, 2000; Hersey et al., 1979)
3. The model of care (Schein, 1988)
4. Communication workshops (Watzlawick et al., 1974)
5. Change laboratories (Mintzberg, 1973; Blau and Allen, 1982)

The idea of linking organizational research to this change initiative began with the strategic plan elaborated by the Local Health Authority's (LHA) new CEO whose specific aim was to use the identified strategies and management tools to improve continuity of care for the non-acute patient and who identified the need to include an evaluative research component to the change process. This chapter draws on research findings captured during the change in practice. It describes the introduction of the model of change management into the LHA's way of doing business and demonstrates how the five tools contributed to organizational integration and continuity of care.

## The case study

The Piacenza LHA in the north of Italy serves 267,164 citizens. The LHA manages three hospitals and four health districts. These districts serve very different needs. One district is the City of Piacenza and is an urban context. Other contexts include peripheral regions of the city, the mountainous region and the country region. The patients served include all residents without acute needs. Some examples which give an idea of the plethora of services that the districts provide are: control of the food chain (for example, controlling food standards in schools), day centres for the elderly and the handicapped, parenthood facilities, homecare, management of general practitioners, ambulatory care, drug and alcohol abuse rehabilitation, nutrition, health promotion, occupational health, and physical rehabilitation.

The LHA employs 3750 people, of whom 550 are MD specialists and 250 General Practitioners. The LHA in Piacenza is responsible for both acute and primary care. The principal form of financing of the LHA is a pro capita contribution for each resident. The health authority spends 410 million euros a year for these services which is 1525 euros per capita. The budget process then defines the division of resources between acute and primary care. In the period 2000 to 2002, hospital spending was reduced by 2 per cent. However, primary care spending had increased by 2 per cent and represented 55 per cent of overall LHA spending.

The CEO asked a critical question that began the change process: 'Is 55 per cent of the overall budget well spent?' The answer was very clearly 'no' as the following issues indicate:

• There were organizational charts but they did not reflect the organizational structure.
• The budget process measured numbers of activities not care processes.
• Services were duplicated in various departments. For example, a pregnancy could be monitored in the hospital or in the parenthood centre.
• The continuity of care was managed by the patient him/herself.
• Primary care was not subject to the same degree of technological innovation as was acute care.
• The management process tools developed for the hospital setting found little 'useful application' in the primary care setting. For example, DRGs could not be applied in primary care.

Lastly, and significantly, morale was low. The CEO's perception was that many professionals working in primary care felt both heroic and lonely. On the basis of this perception, the CEO mandate formulated the following change management goals:

• Analyze organizational culture.
• Create a working organization.
• Connect people and their identity and motivation to the organizational structure.
• Make management tools useful in primary care.

These goals were used to frame the overall purpose of the change model introduced.

## The model for change

The model for change introduced a variation of Normann's principle of internal marketing and also concentrated on improving working relationships. Internal marketing suggested that, in order to market a product or service to consumers, the organization had to make systematic changes internally. For example, Normann (1984) cites the case of a customer who forgets his airline ticket and passport in his hotel. The check-in counter employee at the airport calls the hotel and pays for the taxi to deliver his documents to the airport in time for his flight. The employee, therefore, has enough autonomy in his role to meet the airline's standards of customer service as they are advertised to the public. The authors have used this idea that the message given outside of the organization has to reflect the structure inside the organization. Reasoning backwards – it is impossible to hide the nature of relationships within the organization. We will call this 'implicit marketing'. For example, if you are invited to dinner to a couple's house and their relationship is 'on the rocks', despite the delicious food they have prepared and the fact that the couple is trying hard to hide their crisis, you will nonetheless feel uncomfortable and leave early. In simple terms, this new principle of 'implicit' marketing suggests that customers can read how organizations function and will behave according to the nature of the relationships present within the organization. If we know our relationships are transparent to others and influence the behaviour of others, then we can work to become more able to read our relationships within organizations. This enhanced awareness of relationships and their impact allows us to adjust problems in them and produce more successful interactions and improved customer services. On the basis of this theory of 'implicit' marketing, derived from Normann's internal marketing, an entire process of change management was implemented in the Piacenza Local Health Authority, Italy, in order to enhance health services delivered to the client population.

## Working relationship

In describing the organization, Taylor determined that an organization needed to be characterized by its continuity and had to be replicable. A fundamental tenet of his theory of the organization, unchallenged over the years, is that a person in an organization must be replaceable. In Italy, the personalization of roles, both in private and public service organizations, is very prominent and therefore merits an attempt to model what happens when people are indispensable in the organization. The authors have developed a relationship map to analyze the case of Piacenza, and this can be applied to most organizations in the Italian context. As can be observed in Figure 6.1, three kinds of relationships seem to characterize horizontal

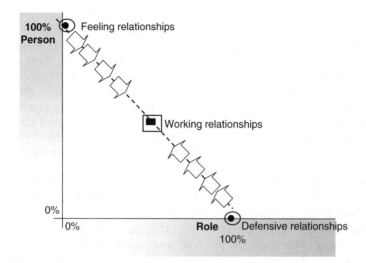

**Figure 6.1**   A relationship map for organizations

integration in the Italian organization: feeling relationships, defensive rela-tionships and working relationships. Feeling relationships take place between one person and another. They position the person at 100 per cent person and 0 per cent professional role.

According to mood and to feeling, the same employees will either produce common sense results or retreat into a definition of role that is so limited to what is formally requested as to appear that the role exists but no human being is present inside that role (100 per cent professional role, 0 per cent person). Responses such as 'Sorry I cannot help you, 'It is not my department' or 'I do not know who can help you' are all examples of this. In these cases, the internal or external client 'hits a wall' and it is not possible to resolve their problem or meet their needs.

When a citizen asks for services and falls into a 'feeling network' the answer to a complex or to an inappropriate question will be given in a miraculously short time. The 'feeling network' is the network with a 'common sense' answer and often bypasses the organization and the organizational competence of its roles. The formal organizational requirements are handled by the 'network' ex-post so that nothing appears out of place. Feeling networks circumvent organ-izational obstacles and find the solutions that make sense. They also leave the people in them with the idea that organizations create obstacles to work around, not tools to work with. Since organizational issues are 'obstacles' they can be both worked around or used to create obstacles for others as a personal defence. When framing an organization in this way, patient care is a product of personal relationships and not of organizational design.

The 'feeling relationship' and the idea that 'organization is an obstacle to work around' is something that the user of public services learns about very quickly. With the introduction of 'implicit marketing', users realize that 'anything is possible if you find the right people to help you'. Many users of the Italian health system do not take no for an answer and treat the organizational response as 'an obstacle to work around'. In organizations with these relationship characteristics it is extremely difficult to introduce management tools; budget processes, quality processes, planning and control efforts are all either worked around (seen as an obstacle) or become the opposite of what they were intended to be (used as a personal defence to say 'no' or 'I don't know').

The 'relationship map' illustrates that what may be missing in many organizations today is the concept of a 'working relationship'. A working relationship involves being a person inside the role you are asked to play in the organization. A box is evidenced in the 'relationship map' to allow for some leeway. There are people who will always be more person than profession, and others more profession than person. Building working relationships involves becoming a person in an organizational role. This is another way to guarantee 'patient care'. Working relationships place the 'care' function in the équipe (team) rather than in the personal relationship.

The premise for the change management process was the following – feeling relationships were creating the problems that the 'population' was experiencing in the Local Health Authority. If these could be transformed into working relationships, the relationship with the 'population' would benefit from the consequences. A series of tools were consequently identified which, when used all together on the basis of the hypothesis of 'implicit marketing', proved that it is possible to produce change management in the health authority and to respond to 'needs of the population' by responding to needs of the organization. The tools are focus groups, the strategic team, the model of care, communication workshops and change laboratories.

## The tools

### Focus groups: 'all the king's men'

In order to construct the perception of the organization, focus groups were used. Focus groups were created using heterogeneous criteria both in terms of the health district and in terms of profession. Therefore, five focus groups were formed; two of them contained managerial profiles and three professional ones. Each of the five focus groups represented the management of, or the work of, a variety of professions from general practitioners, nurses, administrators, nutritionists, physiotherapists, front office, and so on, from all four health districts. Each focus group met once for two hours. Focus groups were composed of 12 to 14 members and involved 60 participants in total.

Focus groups were asked to discuss how multi-need patients were managed geographically, from an operational perspective and from a cultural one. Common to the five focus groups was the organizational culture. It was a 'feeling' culture, multi-need patients were not handled by the organization but by 'willing' individuals and their 'friends' in other offices and functions. The multi-need user had to search for the person who felt like helping on a variety of issues. There were no organizational pathways and the outcomes of each interaction were 'personalized'. There were no data on multi-need patients or on outcomes. The only way to collect this 'history' was by listening to many different 'stories'. This culture went by the 'unwritten rule of the game' – 'the organization is an obstacle, but a nice person knows how to get around even the most difficult obstacles'. From an organizational perspective all formal attempts to achieve an organizational response to integration were seen as 'another obstacle'. Therefore, the best practice of organizational integration had little to do with the organization and everything to do with how people got along with one another. Results were produced primarily through feeling relationships.

From an operational perspective, while the geographical area was differentiated along some clear lines, the services offered were indeed differentiated but not in accordance with the geographical/social ones. In fact, operational differences depended on who worked in the district. This made it impossible to transfer innovation from one district to another. Each operational solution was very 'personal'. Any changes or innovations in formal organizational integration were described by the focus groups as 'a new sign on the old door'. This expression captures how 'superficial' organizational integration was perceived by the culture.

The management focus groups had their version of the same situation. In fact, district managers were often problem solvers for cases that could not find a friendly 'ear'. They described themselves as 'firemen'. Results were achieved through their personal involvement on many single cases which never found time or space to be managed systemically rather than singly. Therefore, while they were given tools for creating organizational integration such as the budget, contracts through negotiated agreements with other institutions, quality processes and certification, and changes in organizational structure, each one of these tools was perceived as taking away time from creating results. To produce results, management worked on problems one at a time. Tools for integration were experimented with in small doses around marginal issues so as not to disturb the functioning of the district. For example, while women's health services offered many pathways to women to help them prevent illness and stay healthy, the quality accreditation process took place around a rarely used sophisticated diagnostic exam.

Another example revolved around the issue of 'protected discharges'. 'Protected discharges' were meant to facilitate hospitalization of acute cases and assure a smooth transition from hospital to either homecare, residential facilities, day centres, or rehabilitation. These agreements took place between different institutions and any number of possible combinations of these responses had been negotiated. The project was managed with contracts in which solutions and competencies were negotiated. A special geriatric evaluation team was created to evaluate a referral to the most appropriate solution. Despite these agreements, what happened in reality? The hospital discharged as soon as the patient was no longer, in their view, acute. Only if the discharging physician knew someone in the health district was the discharge really protected and this, in the view of the management team, covered only 10 per cent of the cases that should have finished in 'protected discharges'. The other 90 per cent were simply discharged. Of these, 50 per cent disappeared and the other 40 per cent took home a gravely ill person and found in short order that the situation was unmanageable. At this point, these families went straight to the district manager asking for the most sophisticated solution (nursing home) regardless of the many other options effectively appropriate for the situation. The anger of the family was such that appropriateness had to be the last priority on the operations manager's list of priorities. Many families went directly to the mayor of the town and this put even more pressure on the district manager to satisfy the family request rather than appropriately direct the case. Formally, everything had been disposed; however, practically, nothing worked.

The strategic team did not consider health district management discharge arrangements adequate because they were not systematic, but random. Operations management considered that they were doing all the work and could not understand why the strategic team was so concerned about management in the districts. Both sides felt the need for organizational integration; however, it was hard to communicate in a language that identified that they were talking about the same problem.

### The strategic team: 'all the king's horses'

The strategic team directed the change management process. Meetings were held twice a month. Initially, the composition of the group was exclusively strategic – the CEO, the medical director, the director of staff, the director of management education and quality, the director of integrated social and health care services. The strategic team began with a request for 'research'. The strategic team was perturbed by the results of the focus group, since there were many tools that were supposed to guarantee organizational integration. The research centred on the management tools that had been introduced; specifically, the budget, the quality process for creating 'standards', the network of integrated social and health care, and the organizational charts. At the end of this process, the strategic team was enlarged to include the four health district directors as they could give a good reading of how true to life the picture had been. These four members were integrated into the strategic team and created no conflict or problems and remained as permanent members.

The issues that were raised put the focus on continuity of care. Just like the problems raised by the focus groups, the tools for organizational integration in fact had not been used together, but separately and had been perceived as bureaucracy and not as organization. Given that these problems had to do with creating experience in integrating different professionals, two new members were added. These were the two directors of dependency (drug and alcohol rehabilitation) that had, by definition, always had to integrate psychological, clinical and social issues.

The strategic team was able to grow, adding new members, without producing conflict. The dimension of the group passed from eight to 16 members in about a year's time, without ever losing sight of its objectives or losing its efficacy. The strategic team addressed different issues and each meeting used all the perspectives of its members. This flexible model for building a strategic team seemed very innovative for managing change and providing support to a new CEO. Its flexibility both in number of participants and professional diversity allowed for a strong strategic direction and control. While 10 to 12 participants is considered the breaking point for group efficiency, this experience demonstrated that in health care management where professional diversity is very high, it can be useful to experiment with larger groups and the membership of the group can be modelled over time without losing efficacy.

## The model of care: 'reconfiguring humpty'

What emerged from the research through focus groups and the study of management tools was a difficulty in putting pieces, both professions and services, together. The issue at hand was offering continuity of care to multi-need patients. The strategic team worked on this issue in two meetings. What emerged was that the LHA theoretically was responsible for a continuum of care which could be described as having the following characteristics:

- Health promotion
- Multidisciplinary integrated clinical projects
- Services to strengthen the family role
- Referral to appropriate institutions in the event that complexity exceeded the capacity of the health authority

However, in fact, many little services made up the big picture. What was missing was the integration between existing services. By creating a table which represented the users of services on the y axis and the characteristics of services on the x axis, it was possible to map the existing ability to integrate services.

In Table 6.1, one example has been illustrated – that of the elderly patient. All four characteristics of the continuum of care were present, but there were evident 'integration gaps' between services. Prevention of illness revolved

Table 6.1   Continuum of care

| Patients | Health promotion | Multi-disciplinary integrated clinical projects | Services to strengthen the family role | Referral to appropriate institutions in the event that complexity exceeded the capacity of the Health Authority |
|---|---|---|---|---|
| Infants | | | | |
| Minors/adolescents | | | | |
| Women | | | | |
| **Elderly people** | Flu vaccination | Multi-disciplinary, negotiated with family | Relief for family, economic, and hospital beds for vacation | Often based on family exasperation, not on appropriate setting |
| Handicapped | | | | |
| Citizens with chronic disease | | | | |
| Citizens with symptoms | | | | |
| Citizens with dependencies | | | | |
| Citizens | | | | |

around flu vaccinations. Multidisciplinary homecare was discussed between health care providers and the family of the elderly patient. Services to the family were based on relief not on sustaining the family with the patient. The referral process was driven by the family rather than by the most appropriate case management. Services were not integrated; they had been developed to handle problems as they arose, not to manage the patient. By looking at the continuum of care it became clear that appropriate management lay in the capacity to integrate the characteristics of services.

Two other problems arose. The first was that some services were present in one box and had no continuum. These were spot activities, like a sophisticated examination for diagnostic purposes that had no precedent and had no consequences. The second had to do with targeting the users of services. For example, a marvellous course for parents of a newborn baby was offered. It explained the importance of roles in the family and the needs of the newborn baby. While this course was well attended it was frequented by parents who knew most of its content already. The group who most needed the course did not attend (that is, immigrants, single mothers, parents with dependencies). What emerged was that the four characteristics of services were in fact a definition of what the multi-need patient needed. However, as can be seen by Table 6.1, the emptiness of the picture lay in the lack of integration between characteristics.

## Communication workshops

The results of the analysis had shown that objectives were constantly enunciated, however they were not comprehended in many cases. In order to create a broader understanding of strategic objectives, communication workshops were developed. That is, the results of the analysis were shared with a group of 100 operators in the organization and work groups were organized to 'clarify' any questions concerning the analysis or the objectives of top management. No invitations were made to 'review' or 'critique' the work that had been concluded. These were half-day sessions in which the managing director and the researchers presented the issues at hand. Work groups then discussed the information they had obtained and formulated questions. These questions were answered by the CEO. These events were very well attended and appreciated and helped create a broad support for strategic initiatives in general. Furthermore, groups were heterogeneous and these work groups contributed to more connectivity between districts and professions.

Two workshops also were created during a year's time. The first explained the results of focus groups and the study of the management tools. The second explained the characteristics of the continuum of care and of case management. Communication workshops validated the work as it proceeded and created consensus. With 100 operators directly involved, relaying messages became much easier.

## Change labs

During the process it became evident that one of the biggest 'holes' in realizing results was middle management's difficulty with the management tools and systematic thinking. Another issue was, now that all the problems were identified and now that a direction had been given and shared, what was to happen next so that things would actually change at an operational level? With these two issues in mind, 30 operators with potential for assuming a middle management position were involved in change labs. There were four encounters in which two specific issues were 'explained' from a systemic perspective. These issues were primary care groups and integrated social and health care services. Each issue was preceded by a 'lecture' which explained what primary groups were and what tools were available for integrated social and health care services.

The groups worked for 12 hours on each topic, with the goal of creating a presentation of their results for their health district and for the Chief Executive

Officer at the end of the experience. In order to guide the work groups some specific questions were raised to help direct the discussion. The group was multidisciplinary and the groups helped each professional see the 'managerial' problems that lay behind the activities that each was used to supplying 'separately'. The results of this experience produced a variety of concrete proposals for change.

One proposal focused on the primary care groups as a multidisciplinary response to multi-need patients. The change lab groups saw the primary care groups as having a physical location, and an approach that went beyond the members of the local health authority to include the police department, court related services, church, schools and other actors in the local area. The CEO was able to use these ideas to develop a plan which involved donating 'physical locations' in exchange for what were then seen by the communities as their own little 'country hospitals'.

Another proposal focused on the tools for integrating social and health care services; the groups worked on understanding what these would be useful for. For example, the health district from the mountainous region identified a typical mismanaged patient – the elderly, alcoholic, isolated patient. This patient was an example of a 'missed target' who escaped from the network of services organized by the health district. Hospitalized for acute symptoms, the patient would go home to no one, drink alcohol in great quantities, accompany heavy drinking with a diet of bread and onions, only to reappear in the emergency room with his symptoms. The group identified the importance of linking local health services with other outside actors, and connecting these with preventive measures and services. This enabled the CEO and his management team to identify principal strategic patients that needed continuity of care and to focus the strategy for the coming year on specific but critical patients.

The laboratory was an experience that created 'stickiness' between strategic problems and operational experience. It also enabled the development of 'working relationships' within the district between professions that were linked in theory but not in fact.

## Conclusions: 'putting humpty back together again'

This change management model organizes change processes based on a model of 'implicit marketing'. By improving continuity within the organization it is possible to improve services, efficacy and efficiency. The model for change management does not allow for 'structured results', as do other tools like management by objectives or budgeting processes, which fix a start and an end point for measuring performance improvement (we need to get from point A to point B).

This is a model for achieving organizational integration and continuity of care, working on the principle of implicit marketing. By correcting relationships within the organization, it is possible to deliver continuous services to patients. By working at various levels on working relationships, it is possible to introduce a new relationship model in the organization. The process directly involved 150 different members of the organization. The strategic team, the communication workshops and the change laboratories all worked on a model of working relationships. These tools allowed the organization to reach a new, improved end state, even though it was not possible to predict a targeted degree of change at the beginning of the change initiative project.

The change management process introduced involves restructuring services to the patient, but, unlike re-engineering, it is not based on a radical 'starting over' model of change that asks how valuable services are to patients, but looks at how the organization can improve continuity of care to manage the patient experience. The challenge now for primary care management is to develop indicators for measuring organizational performance. Continuity of care is the critical management objective introduced in the case study; however, measures of continuity of care and its effects on spending have yet to be developed and employed locally. The use of implicit marketing and working relationships on continuity of care suggest a strategy worth testing in future research for 'putting humpty dumpty back together again'.

## References

Anessi Pessina, E., Cantù, E. and Jommi, C. (2004) 'Phasing out Market Mechanisms in the Italian National Health Service', *Public Money & Management*, 24(5), pp. 309–316.

Argyris, C. (1970) *Intervention Theory and Method: a Behavioral Science View* (Reading, MA: Addison-Wesley).

Argyris, C. (1978) *Organizational Learning: a Theory of Action Perspective* (Reading, MA: Addison-Wesley).

Bergamaschi, M. and Lega, F. (2000) 'L'organizzazione delle strutture ospedaliere: il dipartimento', in M. Bergamaschi (ed.), *L'organizzazione delle Aziende Sanitarie*, (Milan: McGraw-Hill).

Blau, J. and Allen, R. (1982) 'Empowering Nets of Participation', *Administrative Science Quarterly*, 27(3), pp. 363–79.

Crozier, M. and Friedberg, E. (1977) *L'acteur et le système* (Paris: Editions du Seuil).

Davis, P. (2000) 'Use of focus group to assess the educational needs of the Primary Care physician for the management of asthma', *Medical Education*, 34(12), pp. 987–93.

Del Vecchio, M. (2000) 'Evoluzione delle logiche di organizzazione delle aziende sanitarie pubbliche', in E. Anessi Pessina and E. Cantù (eds), *L'aziendalizzazione della sanità in Italia, Rapporto OASI 2000* (Milan: Egea).

Fattore, G. (1999) 'Cost containment and reforms in the Italian N.H.S.', in E. Mossialos and J. Legrand (eds), *Health Care and Cost Containment in the European Union* (Aldershot, VT: Ashgate).

Hersey, P., Blanchard, K. and Natemeyer, W. (1979) *Situational Leadership, Perception and the Impact of Power* ( La Jolla, CA: Center for Leadership Studies, Learning Resources Corp).

Longo, F. (2000) 'Il vertice direzionale nelle Aziende Sanitarie: accentramento e decentramento delle funzioni e schemi organizzativi', in M. Bergamaschi (ed.), *L'organizzazione delle Aziende Sanitarie* (Milan: McGraw-Hill).

Longo, F. (2001) 'Tendenze in atto negli assetti organizzativi: i principali indirizzi regionali', in E. Anessi-Pessina and E. Cantù (eds), *L'aziendalizzazione della sanità in Italia, Rapporto OASI 2001* (Milan: Egea).

Mintzberg, H. (1973) *The Nature of the Managerial Work* (New York: Harper & Row).

Normann, R. (1984) *Service Management: Strategy and Leadership in Services Business* (New York: John Wiley).

Pettigrew, A., Ferlie E. and McKee, L. (1992) *Shaping Strategic Change – the Case of the National Health Service* (London: Sage Publications).

Schein, E. H. (1985) *Organizational Culture and Leadership* (San Francisco, CA: Jossey-Bass).

Schein, E. H. (1988) *Process Consultation*, vol. I (Reading, MA: Addison-Wesley).

Taylor, F. W. (1911) *The Principles of Scientific Management* (New York: Harper).

Watzlawick, P., Weaklund, J. H. and Fish, R. (1974) *Change: Principles and Problem Formulation* (New York: W.W. Norton).

# 7
# Patient Safety Culture in Health Organizations: Whose Culture Is It Anyway?

*Liane Soberman Ginsburg, Deborah Tregunno, Peter G. Norton and Ann L. Casebeer*

This chapter draws on the organizational literature and raises the question of whether it is appropriate to consider patient safety culture as an organizational level variable. First, we draw on findings from the organizational culture literature to demonstrate the presence of an organization's subcultures and professional cultures. Next, we briefly introduce stakeholder theory which suggests organizations are comprised of multiple stakeholders who often hold inconsistent, or even competing, performance priorities. Finally, the question of monolithic safety culture is explored through analysis of patient safety culture data obtained from multiple internal stakeholders in a large Canadian health region. The data suggest that the reality of multiple and complex patient safety subcultures is understood within practice but not yet clear within the existing patient safety literature. Our evidence suggests that this is an area where practice may indeed be 'leading the way'.

There is a growing body of literature on patient safety culture in health care organizations (Singer et al., 2003; Pronovost et al., 2003; Ginsburg et al., 2005). Patient safety culture, in addition to being an important outcome measure, has become a key research priority in its own right (Battles and Lilford, 2003; Battles, 2003). Many have argued that patient safety culture change is the key to reducing error in health care (for example, Ohlhauser and Schurman, 2001). While levers to improve safety, such as training and information technology, are important, it has been suggested that such initiatives cannot be successful in the absence of a culture of safety (Nieva and Sorra, 2003; Firth-Cozens, 2003). A culture of safety, it is argued, is necessary for reducing errors and adverse events (Institute of Medicine, 2003), increasing reporting (Barach and Small, 2000) and improving patient safety more generally. In health care, safety culture has been defined as 'the product of individual and group values, attitudes, perceptions, competencies, and patterns of behaviour that determine the commitment to, and the style and proficiency of, an organization's health and safety management.

Organizations with a positive safety culture are characterized by communications founded on mutual trust, by shared perceptions of the importance of safety, and by confidence in the efficacy of preventive measures' (Sorra and Nieva, 2004).

## Culture in the organizational literature

Definitions of organizational culture emphasize its shared or social nature, and the role that social beliefs, values and assumptions play in defining an organization's character and norms. Much of the work on organizational culture can be traced back to the work of Schein who defined culture as 'the set of shared, taken-for-granted implicit assumptions that a group holds and that determines how it perceives, thinks about, and reacts to its various environments' (Schein, 1996, p. 236). In essence, culture consists of the basic assumptions that a given group has identified and developed, in response to the challenges of external adaptation and internal integration that have worked well enough to be taught to new members as the correct way to perceive, think and feel in relation to these challenges (Schein, 1991).

The interest in the concept of organizational culture owes itself to the idea that culture is a key variable for influencing organizational effectiveness (for example, Kotter and Heskett, 1992; Barney, 1986; Denison, 1990; Denison and Mishra, 1995). The study of organizational culture focuses on the recursive interaction between the individual and their environment. Culture can be strong or weak depending on the pervasiveness of the experiences and assumptions of a group – something which will, in part, be influenced by a group's stability, tenure and intensity of experiences. Culture also exists and is experienced at different levels. Observable artifacts or climate are the tangible things one observes or feels in an organization – the mission statement, whether the CEO leaves his/her door open. Less tangible are the norms and values that exist within groups and in organizations. Norms and values are the manifestation of culture and can be gauged by asking people about how certain things are done in the organization. At the deepest level of culture are the taken-for-granted, often unconscious assumptions that determine how people interpret and respond to events (Schein, 1990).

It is widely recognized that cultures exist and arise in occupational, professional and other communities or subgroups (van Maanen and Barley, 1984) and culture can be studied at the level of the organization, functional department, hierarchical level, profession, and so on (Hofstede, 1998). In his 1996 paper, Schein raises the question of whether organizations are necessarily the appropriate unit of study and analysis for certain constructs such as culture because unique cultures exist and arise in occupational, professional and other communities or subgroups and what is often conceived and described as 'organizational' culture may in some cases actually be a series of different group cultures. Hofstede (1998) suggests that meaningful subgroups are those that have relatively homogeneous (for example, strong) perceptions of culture. Indeed, the notion of a monolithic organizational culture has been called into question (Jermier et al., 1991), and it has been suggested that once developed, professional subcultures are sustained despite the fact that they are often held in check by a dominant organizational culture. The question remains as to whether organizational experience and history will dominate and 'override the prior cultural assumptions of all of their employees' (Schein, 1996, p. 234) to create a true organizational culture.

What contributes to the presence of subcultures in an organization is the fact that in some cases 'parts of organizations are as much a reflection of the occupational backgrounds and experiences of some of their members as they are of their own unique organizational histories' (Schein, 1996, p. 234). If group or organizational culture is created through the history and experiences of its members, then the question is which history and experience will be the most influential and the most enduring. Schein (1996) found that occupational or professional subcultures might be more enduring for certain professionals and for chief executive officers. This has particularly important implications for the study of culture in highly professionalized work environments such as health care. In health care each professional group functions in a highly specialized role with discrete professional competencies and cultures, which often leads to the formation of territories and an emphasis on group differences. In fact, even before individuals become members of professional groups there is evidence in the organizational literature that people select themselves into professions consistent with their own values and interests (Holland, 1985; Schneider, 1987). This means that trainees may come to their programs with preconceived stereotypes that may form the root of strong professional identities and cultures. Training serves to further entrench these values and assumptions and professionals are socialized to view the world and work in a similar manner (these are the kind of normative forces that DiMaggio and Powell (1983) found lead to similarity in certain organizational fields). Whether professional or organizational culture is more dominant may be industry or context specific (Jermier et al., 1991). In any event, questions regarding strength of ties to professions versus organizations have been raised with respect to other important organizational variables (for example, Wallace, 1995).

## Multiple stakeholders

The stakeholder literature further demonstrates the presence of multiple constituencies or subgroups in organizations. Stakeholder theory tends to focus on the firm/organization as the reference point and defines stakeholders in relation to one organization. For instance, Freeman defines stakeholder as 'any group or individual who can affect or is affected by the achievement of the *organization's* objectives' (1984, p. 46). The multiple constituency model of organizational performance assumes that organizations are dependent on various constituency groups for resources and that, unless the interests of such groups are at least minimally satisfied, they will withdraw support, causing potentially detrimental affects on performance (Zammuto, 1984). Zammuto also argues that conceptions of performance are inherently subjective and are based on the personal values and preferences of individuals. Cyert and March (1966) remind us that organizations can be viewed in terms of shifting coalitions of interest groups, and that an organization's performance is influenced by the constant negotiation and renegotiation of the conditions of their participation. Thus, effective organizations are those that have accurate information about the expectations of multiple stakeholders, and that adapt their internal activities, values and goals to satisfy the interests and expectations of one or more of their key constituencies.

Stakeholder theory is often used to understand how managers manage different stakeholders, while acknowledging that 'virtually anyone can affect or be affected by an organization's actions' (Mitchell, Agle and Wood, 1997, p. 854). In health care there are many different stakeholder groups. Health care is co-ordinated and provided by and for multiple groups, including providers and caregivers, managers, patients, community members, regulators, purchasers, payers and, in the United States, shareholders (Malloch, 1999). The health care performance literature tells us that the performance interests and expectations of stakeholder groups vary (McGlynn, 1997; Leatherman and McCarthy, 1999; Jennings and Staggers, 1999) and that the experiences and needs of each stakeholder group are often very different (Oakley Davies and Marshall, 1999). There is the potential for conflict between different constituencies as a result of different perspectives about what different groups value.

The notion that stakeholders have varying expectations and criteria of performance is widely recognized in organizational theory, and there is empirical evidence to suggest that stakeholders tend to set priorities based on their values and interests (Tregunno et al., 2004). The presence of various internal stakeholders with competing interests is consistent with the culture literature showing the presence of professional and occupational communities or subgroups, where these subgroups often provide the basis for conflict (Jermier et al., 1991; van Maanen and Barley, 1984) and disunity (Taft, Hawn, Barber and Bidwell, 1999).

## Patient safety culture

Much of the work on safety culture in health care draws on Weick's (1987) work on high-reliability organizations where he suggests that a culture based on open communication, dependability and integrity is critical for maintaining safety in high risk environments such as the nuclear power industry, on aircraft carriers, and so on. And, as noted, many people have argued that patient safety culture change is the key to reducing error in health care and that safety improvement initiatives cannot be successful in the absence of a culture of safety. Leape and his colleagues argue that we need to move from a 'culture of blame that hides information about risk and error into a culture of safety that flushes information out and enables us to prevent or quickly recover from mistakes before they become patient injuries' (Leape et al., 1998, p. 1447). Indeed, many talk about the need for a culture based on teamwork, tolerance of mistakes, full disclosure of errors and learning rather than a culture of blaming. The safety literature emphasizes a culture which recognizes the high risk, error prone nature of health care activities; encourages reporting of errors and near-misses without fear of punishment; creates expectations of collaboration in order to identify vulnerabilities and seek solutions; and allocates resources to remedy safety concerns. The theory of human error underpinning this approach is based on a systems perspective that accepts human fallibility, avoids individual blame and seeks root causes often latent in the system's operational and cultural assumptions. A culture that is antithetical to what was just described (for example, a culture of secrecy, defensiveness, blaming individuals, and so on) has been identified as contributing to major patient safety failures (Walshe and Shortell, 2004; Weick and Sutcliffe, 2003). Finally, it is acknowledged that 'achieving the culture we need – one of learning, trust, curiosity, systems thinking, and executive responsibility – will be immensely difficult' (Leape and Berwick, 2000, p. 726) and is likely to take years to accomplish (Institute of Medicine, 2003; Ginsburg et al., 2005).

Discussions of patient safety culture, including the most up-to-date work (for example, Stryer and Clancy, 2005) advocate a strong, monolithic safety culture within organizations. Further, it is acknowledged that safety culture is at odds with medicine's long-standing cultural traditions of autonomy and infallibility (Wu, 2000). Overall, the patient safety literature highlights the importance of measuring safety culture, but is silent with respect to the pervasiveness and importance of subcultures (professional or occupational). Empirical work by Singer et al., (2003) and Sexton, Thomas and Helmreich (2000) has shown that different groups have different perceptions of safety culture though results of these studies appear not to have been incorporated into broader theoretical discussions of patient safety culture. Taken together, organizational theory highlights an important question for the measurement of safety culture. If organizations have subcultures (and one might consider stakeholder groups as a proxy for subcultures), then is it reasonable to think of safety culture as an organizational level variable? In other words, given what we know about the existence of professional subcultures in health care, should we think of safety culture as a monolithic variable?

To understand the present state of affairs with respect to safety culture today, data on patient safety culture gathered from a large Canadian health region were examined to see whether perceptions of safety culture are uniform across the organization or whether, consistent with the organizational literature, they vary by professional and occupational group.

## Safety culture in a Canadian health region

### Methods

During fall 2003 and winter 2004 data on patient safety culture were gathered from staff in a large Canadian health region as part of ongoing quality and safety initiatives. All physicians, senior leaders and nurse leaders (patient care managers, directors and clinical educators) in the region's acute care and community sites were surveyed and a sample of registered nurses (RNs), allied health professionals and admin and support staff were surveyed. Surveys were administered anonymously and there was no follow up. Response rates were 28 per cent (459/1630) for physicians, 17 per cent (17/101) for senior leaders, 27 per cent (532/1999) for RNs, 30 per cent (269/909) for allied, and 20 per cent (257/1829) for admin and support staff. Response rates for the nurse leader group were substantially higher (77 per cent) as there was follow up with this group using a modified Dillman (1978) approach.[1] A 32-item patient safety culture questionnaire with Likert response scale was used. The instrument and details of the factor analysis are described elsewhere (Ginsburg et al., 2005). This paper presents data comparing RNs, allied health professionals, nurse leaders and physicians from the four urban acute care sites in the health region.[2]

### Results

Table 7.1 shows the scores on three patient safety culture factors – (1) valuing safety, (2) fear of repercussions and (3) state of safety – by stakeholder group. When we compare subgroup scores on these three patient safety culture factors, we see significant differences between the groups on all three factors ($F = 12.8$ to $28.8$, $p = .000$). Based on post hoc testing using Bonferroni correction for multiple comparisons, Table 7.1 shows that nurse leaders are more positive about the extent to which safety is valued in their organizations (factor 1) and are less fearful of repercussions (factor 2) than their RN, allied health professional and physician counterparts. RNs and allied health professionals score similarly, while physicians score significantly lower than

**Table 7.1**  Factor scores by professional/occupational status

| Patient safety culture factor | RNs (n = 374) | Allied (n = 171) | Nurse leaders (n = 161) | Physicians (n = 453) |
|---|---|---|---|---|
| 1. Valuing safety* | 3.24 | 3.36 | 3.58 | 3.06 |
| 2. Fear of repercussions* | 3.61 | 3.68 | 4.07 | 3.40 |
| 3. Perceived state of safety** | 2.65 | 2.77 | 2.71 | 2.51 |

* Scores are significantly different between all pairs of groups except for between nurses and allied health professionals ($p < .01$).
** Only physicians' scores are significantly lower than the other three groups. All other pairs of scores are not significantly different from one another ($p < .01$).

the other three groups on both of these factors. With respect to the perceived state of safety (factor 3), RNs, allied health professionals and nurse leaders report similar views, while physicians score significantly lower than the other three stakeholder groups. Scores are a mean score out of 5 on a 5-point Likert agree–disagree scale (with negatively worded items recoded so a higher response is always more positive). In terms of the clinical significance of the differences seen in Table 7.1 it is useful to consider that in some cases the differences are a half point on a 5-point scale (for example, between being neutral or agreeing).

Table 7.2 shows the percentage of negative responses, by professional/occupational group, to the 23 individual survey questions that loaded onto

Table 7.2 Percent negative responses by professional/occupational status

| Question | RNs (n = 374) | Allied (n = 171) | Nurse leaders (n = 161) | Physicians (n = 453) |
|---|---|---|---|---|
| **Valuing Safety Factor** | | | | |
| Senior management provides a climate that promotes patient safety (q7) | 28.2% | 14.9% | 11.2% | 28.3% |
| Patient safety decisions are made at the proper level by the most qualified people (q1) | 30.4% | 11.8% | 12.4% | 24.0% |
| Good communication flow exists up the chain of command regarding patient safety issues (q2) | 32.2% | 24.3% | 21.7% | 39.9% |
| Senior management has a clear picture of the risk associated with patient care (q4) | 47.8% | 29.6% | 30.6% | 53.9% |
| My organization effectively balances the need for patient safety and the need for productivity (q29)[ns] | 29.4% | 24.0% | 21.9% | 24.8% |
| My department does a good job managing risks to ensure patient safety (q6)[ns] | 12.0% | 9.5% | 7.5% | 11.9% |
| Senior management considers patient safety when program changes are discussed (q12) | 26.3% | 21.6% | 15.5% | 26.5% |
| I work in an environment where patient safety is a high priority (q30)[ns] | 10.7% | 10.6% | 5.1% | 10.7% |
| My department takes the time to identify and assess risks to patients (q5)[ns] | 12.4% | 15.2% | 8.1% | 13.1% |
| I am rewarded for taking quick action to identify a serious mistake (q18) | 35.9% | 28.1% | 20.6% | 31.7% |

**Table 7.2** (Continued)

| Question | RNs (n = 374) | Allied (n = 171) | Nurse leaders (n = 161) | Physicians (n = 453) |
|---|---|---|---|---|
| **Fear of Repercussions Factor** | | | | |
| I will suffer negative consequences if I report a patient safety problem (q16 reversed) | 8.0% | 6.4% | 3.1% | 9.8% |
| If people find out that I made a mistake, I will be disciplined (q17 reversed) | 19.7% | 11.2% | 6.9% | 13.7% |
| Clinicians who make serious mistakes are usually punished (q23 reversed) | 11.3% | 5.4% | 8.1% | 20.5% |
| Reporting a patient safety problem will not result in negative repercussions for the person reporting it (q3) | 18.8% | 11.2% | 7.5% | 25.6% |
| **Perceived State of Safety Factor** | | | | |
| I am provided with adequate resources (personnel, budget, and equipment) to provide safe patient care (q25) | 51.6% | 35.9% | 39.1% | 48.7% |
| Loss of experienced personnel has negatively affected my ability to provide high quality patient care (q21 reversed) | 54.4% | 43.3% | 33.5% | 61.1% |
| I am less effective at work when I am fatigued (q11)[ns] | 3.5% | 1.8% | 4.4% | 2.4% |
| I have enough time to complete patient care tasks safely (q22) | 43.7% | 32.0% | 25.9% | 29.0% |
| I believe that health care error constitutes a real and significant risk to the patients that we treat (q27 reversed) | 78.3% | 70.2% | 84.9% | 86.3% |
| In the last year, I have witnessed a co-worker do something that appeared to me to be unsafe for the patient in order to save time (q24 reversed)[ns] | 32.8% | 23.1% | 29.6% | 26.0% |
| Personal problems can adversely affect my performance (q13) | 23.3% | 17.5% | 20.0% | 11.7% |
| I believe health care errors often go unreported (q28 reversed) | 66.7% | 59.6% | 80.7% | 81.6% |
| I have made significant errors in my work that I attribute to my own fatigue (q26 reversed) | 10.5% | 15.2% | 10.6% | 29.6% |

[ns] Differences between the groups are not significant.

one of the three patient safety culture factors. Negative responses are the 'disagree' and 'strongly disagree' categories on a 5-point Likert scale and, for negatively worded items, the 'agree' and 'strongly agree' categories (the word 'reversed' follows negatively worded items in Table 7.2). Several aspects of Table 7.2 are worth highlighting. First, there are significant differences in the percentage of negative responses between the stakeholder groups ($\chi^2$ range of 7.82 to 60.26, $p < .05$) on 17 of the 23 questions. The six questions where there are no significant differences between the groups tend to relate to the general environment for patient safety in the department or organization (for example, 'my organization effectively balances the need for patient safety and the need for productivity'). Second, for most questions, and notably those related to communication and senior leadership for safety (q7, q2, q1, q4), nurses and physicians have a higher percentage of negative responses than allied health professionals and nurse leaders. For instance, 48 per cent and 54 per cent of nurses and physicians, respectively, disagreed with the statement 'senior management has a clear picture of the risk associated with patient care' compared to 30 per cent of allied health professionals and nurse leaders. Third, physicians, followed by nurses, seem to have the most serious concerns about aspects of safety culture related to reporting and repercussions (for example, 20 per cent of physicians, compared to 5 to 10 per cent of the other 3 groups agreed that 'Clinicians who make serious mistakes are usually punished'). Finally, nurse leaders tend to have the lowest percentage of negative responses across the question set, and physicians the highest.

## Discussion/conclusions

The goal of this chapter was to gain insight into whether safety culture is a monolithic construct in the context of health care or whether professional and occupational subcultures are a reality. Our results show that different professional groups (physicians, nurses, allied health professionals) and stakeholder groups (direct care providers, mid-level managers) do have different views of the safety culture in the health region we studied. The presence of various subcultures within an organization is entirely consistent with the organizational literature (van Maanen and Barley, 1984; Hofstede, 1998; Jermier et al., 1991; Bloor and Dawson, 1994; Schein, 1996). Our data are also consistent with recent work on patient safety culture showing there are differences between clinician and non-clinician views of safety culture, and between senior leader and non-senior leader views (Singer et al., 2003), as well as between different medical specialties views, and between surgeons and nurses views of safety culture and teamwork (Sexton et al., 2000; Thomas, Sexton and Helmreich, 2003). In particular, our finding that nurse leaders have more positive perceptions of patient safety culture than direct care providers is consistent with findings by Singer et al., (2003) showing that senior leaders are more positive than clinicians about safety culture. Going forward, it would be useful to assess differences in perceptions of safety culture between different levels of management (for example, front-line, mid-level, and senior). Neither our study nor Singer and colleagues (2003) was able to assess this, though such differences have been suggested in the organizational literature (Trice and Beyer, 1991). Finally, our data indicate that professional groups have both divergent and convergent perspectives. Specifically, there is a higher degree of homogeneity with respect to the perceived state of safety and the environment for safety. In contrast, there is greater diversity among professional/occupational groups with respect to their fear of repercussions, with physicians reporting the highest level of concern.

The health care safety literature establishes the importance of a strong safety culture, and the goal of creating and sustaining safety culture in relation to improved safety outcomes. Although much of this discussion recognizes that this is something that has not yet been achieved (Wachter, 2004), it refers to a 'culture of safety' as something that organizations should, nonetheless, be striving for. Despite evidence to the contrary (Singer et al., 2003; Sexton et al., 2000; Thomas, Sexton and Helmreich, 2003), the patient safety culture literature has not yet properly acknowledged or accounted for the reality that organizations are faced with professional and occupational safety subcultures. Our findings provide further empirical support for the presence of professional and occupational patient safety subcultures within health care organizations. To the extent that safety culture is critical to the success of the patient safety movement, recognition of the presence of safety subcultures is also critical to success in this area. We know from the organizational literature that different subgroups often do not have common goals, that subcultures are often in conflict (Jermier et al., 1991; van Maanen and Barley, 1984), and that, unless conflicts between different occupational or professional subcultures are reconciled, learning and moving forward may not be possible (Schein, 1996). An example of subculture conflict can be easily seen in professional views regarding autonomy in clinical decision making. Although this is something that is cherished and protected in the physician subculture, autonomy in clinical decision making is in many respects antithetical to aspects of an organizational safety culture which requires professionals to be vigilant about questioning any clinical decisions that may appear to put patients at risk for adverse events. Discordance or different perceptions of safety culture may mask the true state of safety or concerns about safety making it difficult to 'determine changes needed, and to assess ... attempt[s] to create and maintain a culture of safety' (Singer et al., 2003, p. 117). Sexton and his colleagues also show why different perceptions of culture can be problematic: 'the perception of poor teamwork by one team member, whether actual or perceived, is enough to change the dynamics within that team, causing that team member to withdraw' (2000, p. 748). Indeed, the importance of recognizing different subcultures or stakeholder perspectives has been shown with respect to moving forward in the area of performance improvement (Tregunno et al., 2004).

Despite discussion of one monolithic patient safety culture in the safety literature, it is clear from the organizational literature and from health care safety culture survey data that we lack a strong safety culture in health care thus far. By asking the question, 'Whose culture is it anyway?', we question whether it is meaningful to think in terms of a monolithic patient safety culture. Instead, our data suggest that professionals have differing, often inconsistent, perceptions of the culture of safety in health care organizations. This raises concerns about the present state of our evidence base, suggesting that current literature may be blurring or ignoring the existence and impact of patient safety subcultures actually identifiable and at play in practice. Accordingly, as we measure culture, it is clear that we must seek out the opinions and perspectives of people at all levels in the organization. However, we also need to ensure that some aggregate of these data is not assumed to represent the culture of the organization as a whole. Only if there is sufficient homogeneity of perspective is it reasonable to make such an assertion (Hofstede, 1998). Otherwise, it becomes more meaningful, and indeed more appropriate, to talk about patient safety subcultures.

## Acknowledgements

The authors would like to thank and acknowledge the Quality Improvement and Health Information (QIHI) department of the Calgary Health Region for their role in the data collection process and, in particular, Margaret Sevcik for the lead role she played in this process. We also thank Wendy Spragins for her role in the collection of the nurse leader data. Finally, we would like to acknowledge the support of the Centre for Health and Policy Studies at the University of Calgary where the lead author completed a Canadian Health Services Research Foundation postdoctoral fellowship.

## Notes

1. Data for this group were collected as part of another study that used a more rigorous protocol. However, the data for this group were collected at the same time using the same instrument and should be comparable.
2. Data for administrative and support staff are not presented due to high levels of missing data and data from senior leaders are not presented due to the small number of cases. In addition, data from community are not presented because the instrument has not been validated outside of acute care. Data from the rural organizations are excluded because they were brand new additions to the region at the time of data collection.

# References

Affonso, D. and Doran, D. M. (2002) 'Cultivating discoveries in patient safety research: a framework', *Journal International Nursing Perspectives*, 2(1), pp. 33–47.

Baker, G. R. and Norton, P. G. (2001) 'Making patients safer! Reducing error in Canadian healthcare', *Healthcare Papers*, 2(1), pp. 10–31.

Barach, P. and Small, S. D. (2000) 'Reporting and prevention medical mishaps: lessons from non-medical near miss reporting systems', *British Medical Journal*, 320, pp. 759–63.

Barney, J. B. (1986) 'Organizational culture: can it be a source of sustained competitive advantage?', *Academy of Management Review*, 11, pp. 656–65.

Battles, J. B. (2003) 'Patient safety: research methods for a new field', *Quality and Safety in Health Care*, 12(sup. 2), p. ii1.

Battles, J. B. and Lilford, R. J. (2003) 'Organizing patient safety research to identify risks and hazards', *Quality and Safety in Health Care*, 12(sup. 2), pp. ii2–ii7.

Bloor, G. and Dawson, P. (1994) 'Understanding professional culture in organizational context', *Organization Studies*, 15(2), pp. 275–95.

Cyert, R. M. and March, J. G. (1966) *A Behavioral Theory of the Firm* (Englewood Cliffs, NJ: Prentice-Hall).

Denison, D. R. (1990) *Corporate Culture and Organizational Effectiveness* (New York: Wiley).

Denison, D. R. and Mishra, A. K. (1995) 'Toward a theory of organizational culture and effectiveness', *Organization Science*, 6(2), pp. 204–23.

Dillman, D. A. (1978) *Mail and Telephone Surveys: The Total Design Method* (New York, NY: John Wiley).

DiMaggio, P. J. and Powell, W. W. (1983) 'The iron cage revisited: institutional isomorphism and collective rationality in organization fields', *American Sociological Review*, 48(April), pp. 147–60.

Firth-Cozens, J. (2003) 'Evaluating the culture of safety', *Quality and Safety in Health Care*, 12, p. 401.

Freeman, R. E. (1984) *Strategic Management: A Stakeholder Approach* (Boston: Pitman).

Ginsburg, L., Norton, P. G., Casebeer, A. and Lewis, S. (2005) 'An educational intervention to enhance nurse leaders' perceptions of patient safety culture', *Health Services Research*, 40(4), pp. 997–1020.

Hofstede, G. (1998) 'Identifying organizational subcultures: an empirical approach', *Journal of Management Studies*, 35(1), pp. 2–12.

Holland, J. L. (1985) *Making Vocational Choices: A Theory of Careers* (Englewood Cliffs, NJ: Prentice-Hall).

Institute of Medicine (2003) *Keeping Patients Safe: Transforming the Work Environment of Nurses* (Washington, DC: National Academies Press), accessed 2005-01-05, http://www.nap.edu/books/0309090679/html/

Jennings, B. M. and Staggers, N. (1999) 'A provocative look at performance measurement', *Nursing Administration Quarterly*, 24(1), pp. 17–30.

Jermier, J. M., Slocum, J. W., Fry, L. W. and Gaines, J. (1991) 'Organizational subcultures in a soft bureaucracy: resistance behind the myth and facade of an official culture', *Organization Science*, 2, pp. 170–94.

Kohn, L. T., Corrigan, J. M. and Donaldson, M. S. (eds) (1999) *To Err Is Human: Building a Safer Health System* (Washington: National Academy Press).

Kotter, J. P. and Heskett, J. L. (1992) *Corporate Culture and Performance* (New York: Free Press).

Leape, L. L. and Berwick, D. M. (2000) 'Safe health care: are we up to it?', *British Medical Journal*, 320, pp. 725–6.

Leape, L. L., Woods, D. D., Hatlie, J., Kizer, K. W., Schroeder, S. A. and Lundberg, G. D. (1998) 'Promoting patient safety by preventing medical error', *Journal of the American Medical Association*, 280(16), pp. 1444–7.

Leatherman, S. and McCarthy, D. (1999) 'Public disclosure of health care performance reports: experience, evidence and issues for policy', *International Journal for Quality in Health Care*, 11(2), pp. 93–8.

Malloch, K. (1999) 'The performance measurement matrix: A framework to optimize decision making', *Journal of Nursing Care Quality*, 13(3), pp. 1–12.

McGlynn, E. A. (1997) 'Six challenges in measuring the quality of health care', *Health Affairs*, 16(3), pp. 7–21.

Mitchell, R. K., Agle, B. R. and Wood, D. J. (1997) 'Toward a theory of stakeholder identification and salience: Defining the principle of who and what really counts', *Academy of Management Review*, 22(4), pp. 853–86.

Nieva, V. F. and Sorra, J. (2003) 'Safety culture assessment: a tool for improving patient safety in healthcare organizations', *Quality and Safety in Health Care*, 12, p. ii17.

Oakley Davies, H. T. and Marshall, M. N. (1999) 'Public disclosure of performance data: Does the public get what the public wants?', *The Lancet*, 353(9165), pp. 1639–40.

Ohlhauser, L. and Schurman, D. P. (2001) 'National agenda: local leadership', *Healthcare Papers*, 2(1), pp. 77–8.

Pronovost, P. J., Weast, B., Holzmueller, C. G., Rosenstain, B. J., Kidwell, R. P., Haller, K. B., Feroli, E. R., Sexton, J. B. and Rubin, H. R. (2003) 'Evaluation of the culture of safety: survey of clinicians and managers in an academic medical center', *Quality and Safety in Health Care*, 12, pp. 405–10.

Schein, E. (1991) *Organizational Culture and Leadership* (San Francisco, CA: Jossey-Bass).

Schein, E. (1996) 'Culture: The missing concept in organizational studies', *Administrative Science Quarterly*, 41, pp. 229–40.

Schein, H. E. (1990) 'Organizational culture', *American Psychologist*, 45(2), pp. 109–19.

Schneider, B. (1987) 'The people make the place', Personnel Psychology, 40, pp. 437–53.

Sexton, J. B., Thomas, E. J. and Helmreich, R. L. (2000) 'Error, stress, and teamwork in medicine and aviation: cross sectional surveys', *British Medical Journal*, 320, pp. 745–9.

Singer, S. J., Gaba, D. M., Geppert, J. J., Sinaiko, A. D., Howard, S. K. and Park, K. C. (2003) 'The culture of safety: results of an organization-wide survey in 15 California hospitals', *Quality and Safety in Health Care*, 12, pp. 112–18.

Sorra, J. S. and Nieva, V. F. (2004) *Hospital Survey on Patient Safety Culture*, AHRQ Publication No. 04-0041 (Rockville, MD: Agency for Healthcare Research and Quality).

Stryer, D. and Clancy, C. (2005) 'Patients' safety', *British Medical Journal*, 330, pp. 553–4.

Taft, S., Hawn, K., Barber, J. and Bidwell, J. (1999) 'Fulcrum for the future: The creation of a values-driven culture', *Health Care Management Review*, 24(1), pp. 17–32.

Thomas, E. J., Sexton, J. B. and Helmreich, R. L. (2003) 'Discrepant attitudes about teamwork among critical care nurses and physicians', *Critical Care Medicine*, 31(3), pp. 956–9.

Tregunno, D. T., Baker, G. R., Barnsley, J. and Murray, M. (2004) 'Competing values of emergency department performance: balancing multiple stakeholder perspectives', *Health Services Research*, 39(4 Part1), pp. 771–92.

Trice, H. M. and Beyer, J. M. (1991) 'Cultural leadership in organizations', *Organization Science*, 2, pp. 149–69.

van Maanen, J. and Barley, S. (1984) 'Occupational communities: culture and control in organizations', *Research in Organizational Behavior*, 6, pp. 287–365.

Wachter, R. M. (2004) 'The end of the beginning: patient safety five years after "To Err is Human" ', *Health Affairs*, July–Dec, Web Exclusives Suppl W4, pp. 534–45.

Wallace, J. E. (1995) 'Organizational and professional commitment in professional and nonprofessional organizations', *Administrative Science Quarterly*, 40(2), pp. 228–56.

Walshe, K. and Shortell, S. M. (2004) 'When things go wrong: how health care organizations deal with major failures', *Health Affairs*, 23(3), pp. 103–11.

Weick, K. E. (1987) 'Organizational culture as a source of high reliability', *California Management Review*, 29, pp. 112–27.

Weick, K. E. and Sutcliffe, K. M. (2003) 'Hospitals as cultures of entrapment: A re-analysis of the Bristol Royal Infirmary', *California Management Review*, 45(2), pp. 73–84.

Wu, A. W. (2000) 'Medical error: the second victim', *British Medical Journal*, 320, pp. 726–7.

Zammuto, R. (1984) 'A comparison of multiple constituency models of organizational effectiveness', *Academy of Management Review*, 9(4), pp. 606–16.

## Searching for the optimal structures for health care organizations

Arguably, the ubiquitous problem facing health care services around the world is to provide consistent quality care through organizational arrangements that span professional disciplines, employers and employment conditions, within a constrained budget and across varying geographical contexts. A logical assumption is that there are ways of organizing health resources (people and money, and so on) that will optimally address the needs of the patient population they serve. Believing this starts a quest to identify what these organizing and facilitating systems and structures might look like and how they might operate to address current priorities and maximize quality of health outcomes. This is or should be the role of those that set policy and those who seek to operationalize it.

Whatever the specific recommendations of these areas of searching, one thing seems unavoidable – that whatever solution fits and is adopted now, will be 'time-limited'. Changing demographics and lifespan issues; better educated, more demanding patients; emergent illnesses; volatile world politics and migrant populations; advanced technological treatments; and rising costs constantly provide new challenges to be met. As the context changes what counts as and is defined as effective and efficient service provision alters, forcing change in service provision. What becomes pivotal is the way that the system adapts and responds to changing circumstances and to patient needs. What works now almost certainly will not work forever.

Traditionally, organizing health care services along specialist functional areas (for example, coronary care) and different professions allowed practitioners to develop deep skills, enhancing quality of care. Policy makers and managers were able to deploy resources around tightly defined clinical needs. Yet, the cost of order was rigidity, and strict demarcation and tribalism between staff and ranks resulted (Hunter, 1996); status and pecking orders were guarded jealously (McClure, 1984); departmental silos emerged (Stewart, 2000); and, where tightly defined organizational roles once gave clarity, they began to impede flexibility and innovation (UK Department of Health, 2000). Attempts to address these issues through legislation in the UK (Scottish Executive: Department of Health 1998a, 1998b, 1999a, 1999b, 1999c) has, ironically, not led to change but to 'reform fatigue' (van Eyk et al., 2001), a demoralized workforce and problematic recruitment and retention of skilled staff (UK Department of Health, 2000). Service provision seems unable or unwilling to join up (Hogg, 2000). IT systems across health care organizations do not capture, store or retrieve information in compatible ways and department silos across health, social care and the voluntary sector (Stewart, 2000), fuelled by budgetary and costing constraints, all offer significant barriers. We might conclude that policy aimed at the 'seamless delivery of care' between health care professionals might be difficult to achieve.

## A health care system that can learn

'Clever health care systems' are needed. The 'secret' might be to create a system that allows busy practitioners to identify and effect changes that would make a real difference to their daily practice, creating learning and change that is owned, rises from the ranks and makes an immediate difference (Senge, 1990) and alters service provision to match patient needs closely. Such a system would serve its staff by creating order, but not fossilize service delivery or stifle capacity to respond rapidly, with flexibility and innovation to changing demands.

A way of addressing the issues above is through the theoretical framework of the Learning Organisation (LO) (Senge, 1990), Organisational Learning (OL) (Argyris and Schon, 1978) and Wenger's notion of communities of practice (Wenger, 1998). The LO ideal rests on:

> the intentional use of learning processes at the individual, group and system level to continuously transform the organization in a direction that is increasingly satisfying to its stakeholders. (Dixon, 1994, p. 4)

Professional discretion is prioritized – those who do the job are considered best placed to know how to adapt it to changing circumstances and are charged to effect the changes needed. Thus, the new ways of behaving are 'owned', 'empowering', motivating (Hackman and Oldham, 1980), build individual capacity (Mintzberg et al., 1998), and confidence, commitment and job satisfaction (Hackman and Oldham, 1980). Organizational issues such as low morale and retention problems are potentially addressed simultaneously. However, LOs and OL (Dodgson, 1993) do not simply advocate individually skilling staff, they are more about learning collectively – 'what-we-all-know', knowledge, skills and know-how that is shared and held in common with others (Pedlar and Aspinwall, 1998). What fundamentally underpins a clever system is over-capacity, and duplication of skills. This idea seems to run counter to ideas of efficiency; however, this is not so. Giving staff multiple skills allows them to be more productive in a greater number of places, and increases the flow of patients through the system as 'blockages' (waiting on the availability of key practitioners) are reduced as other staff can carry out their duties if needed.

### Potential benefits

From an operational perspective, OL builds flexibility (Atkinson, 1984) and multiple levels of responsiveness, reducing dependency on key staff and opening systems to further change and adaptability. In these systems, staff themselves tackle the changes they identify as needing to be addressed (Senge,

**Table 8.1**    To illustrate the potential benefits associated with the development of a learning culture or organizational learning (Rushmer et al., 2004a)

| Potential benefit | Empirical evidence base |
| --- | --- |
| Helps practitioners cope with information overload | Skelton-Green (1995) |
| Surfaces otherwise indiscernible information regarding barriers to change | Beer and Eisenstat (1996) |
| Colleagues feel supported, valued and able to make a difference within the collective efforts of the whole practice | Timpson (1998); Chin and McNichol (2000); Deutschman (2001) |
| Brings about sustainable long-term change despite increasing demands; working smarter not harder | Cowley (1995); Chin and McNichol (2000) |
| Allows individuals to grow and develop and to share these experiences with colleagues | Beer and Eisenstat (1996); Deutschman (2001); Milstein (2001) |
| Service provision can be flexible and focused on patients and staff | Timpson (1998) |
| May help practitioners evaluate their own practice and ability to learn | Beer and Eisenstat (1996); Milstein (2001) |
| Builds an enduring capacity to change (although this may prove to be more difficult) | Cowley (1995); Skeleton-Green (1995); Chin and McNichol (2000) Beer and Eisenstat (1996); Coghlan and Casey (2001) |

1990) without the strong push of external requirements or scrutiny – and they are both able and willing to take on the responsibility to do so (Argyris and Schön, 1978). Change is done by staff, not done to them. Practice is not 'stuck-in-a-rut' because of outdated traditions, but change is ongoing, up-to-date and based on what works. The 'buy-in' from practitioners, in theory, enhances the likely success and sustainability of policy and operational changes and decreases stress levels of staff (Kanter, 1983). The move towards a learning culture capable of collective (or organizational learning) in a primary care setting can be all about many things, depending on how the practice chooses to prioritize its developments. Some of these benefits associated with these changes are listed in Table 8.1.

## The critique

These LO ideas have criticisms too. Some claim that LO notions are too idealistic and impractical (Garvin, 1993). Others, researching specifically in health care settings, claim that the ideas will only work if certain conditions are present: strong and visionary leadership (Mallory, 1993); involvement of all staff at all times (Bartkus, 1997); protected times and places to learn (Bohmer and Edmondson, 2001); and thinking reflectively (Greenwood, 1998). Others suggest that the present system provides a poor starting place (restricted organizational roles, status and pecking orders) (Bartkus, 1997), making integrated working and collective learning very difficult (West, 1995). Allowing localized autonomy might destroy the very coherence and consistent quality that policy makers seek (Rushmer et al., 2002a, b).

Clearly, without research evidence we will not know if the ideas could work, what they would look like, under what circumstances they might flourish, how they could be measured or their impact assessed. Moreover, how can we get practitioners to address these issues?

## Investigating organizational learning in primary care – conceptualizing the learning practice

### Primary care in the UK

In the UK, the GP Practice or unit (the GP Surgery, or Health Centre) provides primary health care and is the main gateway to secondary care (and other related services) for a population of patients (usually geographically defined). The staff and skills mix located in each practice will vary, and often be an historical rather than deliberately planned feature. A typical practice would have 'at its core' a GP(s) who will be partner(s) in the practice that acts as a small business, contracted to provide health care services for their population of patients. Employed by the partners will be a number of practice based nurses (running clinics) and administrative and reception staff. Attached to (but employed by a government funded health care trust) will be community nurses who will be based in the practice building, but work delivering community nursing services to the same population of patients. There may also be other 'attached staff'; for example, community midwives, community psychiatric nurses, dieticians, and so on.

### The study – a dual remit

Within the Centre for Public Policy and Management, St Andrews University, and under the auspices of NHS Education for Scotland (NES), a project has been developed to investigate the role that LO attitudes, behaviours and culture might play in facilitating change and enhanced quality in service delivery in primary care (PC). This project has a dual purpose. For researchers within St Andrews University, there is a research focus to 'open-the-black-box' that is PC in the UK and to explore its diversity – in particular to: (i) examine its present capacity to cope with health care reform and to learn (including an examination of the role of a learning culture in this) and (ii) explore helping and hindering factors at individual, team, systems and organizational levels in this process. For colleagues within NES, the remit is wider and has a pragmatic thrust. The research data on present capacity for learning, what helps and what hinders, would inform a change (organization development) program and identify levers to build organizational arrangements that would foster greater capacity to learn and change within PC. Progress on the project is explored briefly below.

### Review of literature and research

An extensive theoretical and empirical literature review was undertaken, looking at OL, LO and the communities of practice literature, concentrating on how these ideas have been applied to, or used in, health care settings (Rushmer et al., 2004a, b, c). This early work informed development of the learning project and followed Pettigrew and Whipp's context, content and process framework for change (Pettigrew and Whipp, 1991). The successes, failings and points for learning that were provided by this material informed the creation of a position paper (Rushmer et al., 2002b). With the production of this piece of work, the evidence base for the project was formed. The scope, opportunities, boundaries and pre-set 'givens' came together in clearer focus to enable the research team to see where 'learning' was likely to be taking place already and what could be done to facilitate and foster further learning developments within PC. Thus envisioned, the project aims to identify the present learning capacity of PC in the UK and to further build the capacity of PC practitioners to learn (and to learn-to-learn) where development could be practitioner-led and aimed at making the lives of patients and staff alike better and easier.

### The learning practice

A deliberate choice was made to locate the focus of the project on the GP practice and its staff as the rationale and ethos behind the bodies of literature examined was grassroots, service-led, practitioner based, owned and empowered development. We contrasted this with developments that might occur at places outside the practice and be imposed (top-down) on the practice, its staff and the patients it serves. We define the learning practice LP as:

> A GP (or similar) unit where individual, collective and organizational learning and development is systematically pursued according to Learning Organization principles, in order to enhance service provision in a way that is increasingly satisfying to its patients, staff and other stakeholders. (Rushmer et al., 2004a, pp. 377–8)

This is a 'guiding star' (Pedlar et al., 1997) definition, it is not prescriptive or uni-directional, but alludes to principles and values that underpin and inform ways of working, behaviour, attitudes and aspirations. The research team are fully aware that this definition may be said to 'fit' many different modes of service provision or varying ways of organizing GP practices, without specifying one form as better than any other – this is deliberate. What works as a learning culture has to work in its own setting and for its members (Garvin, 1993).

One of the leading critiques of OL and LO material is its often nebulous, evangelical nature and its reluctance to specify specific actions, structures or behaviours (Harrison, 2000). From the above it may appear that the research project has fallen into the same trap. This is not so. The looseness in the definition and other material can be taken as a tolerance of diversity, an acknowledgement of complexity and the impact of local contextual conditions on the likelihood of success in developing learning cultures. This does not mean that 'anything goes', as clearly, from the empirical research on organizational learning conducted in health care settings (as scoped out in the position paper), some approaches will work better than others. There appear to be clusters of helping factors, issues and components but no one definitive answer. The way these factors then combine to give dual linkages and then triple linkages (and so on . . . ) makes a simple recommendation for clear-cut routes to progress a problematic concept both difficult to identify and to justify. However, from the literature it is possible to identify 'clusters' of factors that seem to work across a variety of health care settings. It is important to share this information and raise awareness of the evidence base on which the project and its future work would be based.

## Exploring primary care – identifying the diversity and levering change

Given the diversity and dispersal of GP practices, it was a logical assumption that the capacity to learn collectively would vary across practices. In the messy real life contexts of PC (Plsek and Greenhalgh, 2001), it is entirely feasible that some practices might already be able to learn together, making collective decisions about developments and following these through with enhanced service provision. Conversely, finding disjointed, dysfunctional practices is also a possibility.

Given this, what was required was a way of identifying the present learning capacity of a practice. A diagnostic tool was needed that, in practical terms, would identify the characteristics of LP already in place within a certain GP unit and those characteristics which are to date underdeveloped. It would need to reflect the views of all staff in the practice. In turn, this would allow the practice to identify areas of consensus and variety between different groups of practitioners, and so on within the practice.

As part of the organizational development (OD) program to support the development of learning cultures, such a tool would need to be able to feed back the information to all practice members to raise awareness of identifiable strengths and weaknesses, allowing the practice, together as a collective, to identify areas of development they wish to prioritize. It would be very important that the data was suitably anonymized and the feedback session facilitated to allow the development opportunities to be emphasized rather than a witch hunt conducted to investigate who might have given negative feedback on certain issues.

The data generated could form a baseline of data to be collected against which the practice may 'tag' and 'track' the effect of changes and developments through time. Further than this, the methodology and format of the tool could be used to allow the practice to add items to the instrument and use the method to add in issues and questions of their own in their own ongoing development program. These items would not form part of the 'norms' built up as part of the wider data collection but would inform local, personalized development. In this way, the diagnostic tool could become a live methodology in tracking development. This would all help to build capacity amongst primary care staff, empowering them to identify and execute their own development and collect data in evaluation of the changes. The Learning Practice Inventory has been developed to meet these needs.

## The Learning Practice Inventory (LPI)

The LPI uses knowledge identified through the earlier review of literature and synthesis of issues and process of relevance to generate key themes. These themes address the attitudes, behaviours, routines, structural and organizational arrangements and context that might characterize and identify a LP. If the inventory has validity then a practice's score on this inventory will be an indication of their present capacity to learn collectively and illustrate the extent to which they presently exhibit a learning culture. The themes identified were arranged into cognate domains and are listed in Table 8.2.

Table 8.2  To illustrate the domain structure of the learning practice inventory

| Domains in the learning practice inventory |
| --- |
| *Foundations* <br> • Ownership and involvement <br> • Supporting attitudes and beliefs |
| *Support* <br> • Supporting hard structures/organizational arrangements <br> • Supporting behaviours <br> • Supporting systems |
| *Evidence of change* <br> • Evidence of learning routines <br> • Outcomes associated with learning practices |

A series of questions under these themes compile a 60 item self-assessment inventory which uses a modified behaviourally anchored rating scale (BARS) (Smith and Kendall, 1963). The assumption behind the LPI is that practices which are capable of collective learning will answer the questions differently to practices that exhibit less evidence of a learning culture. Within the LPI, questions from the different domains are mixed up and practitioners have a choice to score each item on a 1 to 10 scale. All members of a practice fill in the inventory, identifying themselves (if they wish) by role, gender and length of service. The inventory is scored by the research team and the individual questions reassembled under their domain headings, allowing the practice to gauge their present capacity in each area. The data is fed back using visual markers within a facilitated practice development meeting (survey feedback technique within an OD program). Data and changes can be tracked longitudinally as the practice undertakes change.

The LPI has undergone stringent testing during its development, with iterative testing of the various domains with volunteer practices. Feasibility and ease of use has also been explored as well as the acceptability and accuracy of the language and terminology used (for all the stakeholders). Methods of presenting the feedback, both in terms of format of the data and the process of delivering the feedback, have been investigated with multidisciplinary teams within the volunteer practices. Comments and suggestions made were used to modify and enhance the impact of the LPI. Practitioners who have helped in the development of the inventory, and who are supporting the project and development program more generally, are very positive about the initiative. Practitioners like the inventory, find it revealing, illuminating and instrumental in helping them to understand their own professional practice and how this dovetails with colleagues to deliver a quality service. They also find the LPI useful in helping them to hone their development priorities and plans.

The LPI is presently undergoing further statistical testing to establish its validity, reliability and general statistical characteristics as a psychometric inventory, with all the data collected by the LPI to date being used to support this statistical analysis. In time it may be possible to establish the typical profile of answers provided by urban or rural practice, or those with extended services as opposed to those who offer more limited, modest services, in terms of their capacity for collective learning. It might also be possible to compare a practice's profile with other practices geographically close by, or link groups of responses to a typical GP, nurse or receptionist response, and so on. This would give feedback to the practice on their learning capacity and culture and how this compares to their 'peers' (producing 'norms' tables).

The LPI does not assume that the hard measures scored on the inventory will be the most valuable measures to the practice development. The LPI may offer a much more valuable opportunity than this. It may be the catalyst that prompts 'wise conversations' (MacDonald, 2002; Rushmer and Davies, 2004), to take place within the practice. It can raise understanding of differing perceptions, expectations and experiences of practice life held by the different practice members and make these visible in the feedback. Variation in ratings (without knowing specifically who allocated what score) can begin conversations about how such difference is possible and whether it is important to practice life or services to patients. The practice is able collectively to gauge the overall 'feeling' of the way they operate and use the measures to identify and prioritize changes they may wish to make.

The LPI does not assume that there is one best way to proceed in developing learning capacity in PC. It 'measures' practitioners' learning against the ideas and theories of OL and the empirical findings of issues arising when these ideas are operationalized in health care settings. But, what the practice does with its feedback, their priorities, aspirations, history, context and trade-offs is a decision that rests with the practice and what 'fits' in their context. There may be many ways of actually operationalizing OL ideas in PC, with no one best way to proceed.

The LPI does not assume that learning or change efforts will necessarily be cumulative or progressive. The rating scale of the LPI allows 'scores' on the questions to go down as well as up over time. So a new higher score in one area after a change effort may initiate a knock-on 'fall' in scores in another area. For example, as the practice gets 'better' at providing more complete information to its members, then its scores on the timeliness of information may fall (as getting the full information may take more time and delay communication). In this way, the inventory tries to capture some of the interlinking flows and complexity of an open system highlighting some of the choices and 'trade-offs' to be made when making changes to practice in PC.

The LPI does not assume linearity in change. It makes it clear that great effort may lead to very little change, whereas a small effort may sometimes lead to an unforeseen and unprecedented level of change. Whereas this is not predictable, it will be tracked over time by the LPI. This and the above feedback could fuel practice conversations, creating understanding, ownership and opening choices to view within the practices. Reflective practice (Greenwood, 1998) is encouraged; practitioners engage in their own developments building confidence and further capacity for learning and change. In this way the LPI is both a diagnostic inventory, a survey feedback tool and a potential driver and lever for change as it educates, empowers and skills those who use it.

## Implications and next steps

Once the full development of the LPI is in place, planned work includes a larger epidemiological study to measure the scores of practices (across the UK) on the LPI (as a measure of learning capacity) with their development (over time) on identified clinical priority areas as imposed by government (as a measure of achieving desired quality services). Data collected would be supported and complemented by in-depth case studies exploring the particular actions within a few of the practices to see what is actually happening on-the-ground behind the figures collected. Following in parallel with this work will be an educative program to support practices in their attempts to interpret the messages that the feedback from the LPI holds for them.

An important, unanswered question forms the basis upon which the whole project ultimately rests: Do learning cultures matter in primary care? It is the assumption or belief that if a practice is able to learn it will deliver more effective, efficient, quality services to its patients. Also, that it will be more flexible and responsive to changing patients' needs. This is a relatively untested assumption. Additionally perhaps, another hope is that with these developments being practitioner led and owned, they might be sustainable (Chin and McNichol, 2000) and build an enduring capacity to learn and change within PC whatever the circumstances. If so, the transferability of these properties to other health care organizations or areas of health and social care provision (generalizability and transferability) would then be the next highly desirable quest. Many of the issues raised so far in this project suggest that, for change to work, the learning and development must mean something to the people locally, address their concerns and allow them to make visible differences to their professional practices. How many of the factors involved in this will be sufficiently generic (triple-loop learning) to allow them to be uplifted and planted in other places and at other times to work equally well, we do not know. It may not be that these things are either possible or impossible. It might be more sensitive to question and explore under what conditions a learning culture may become possible. Lessons learned may always require adaptation rather than simple adoption. Only further experience of conscious learning in practice situations will inform additional research opportunities.

## References

Argyris, C. and Schön, D. (1978) *Organisational Learning* (London: Addison-Wesley).

Atkinson, J. (1984) 'Manpower strategies for flexible organisations', *Personnel Management*, 16(8), pp. 18–31.

Bartkus, B. (1997) 'Employee ownership as a catalyst for organisational change', *Journal of Organisational Change Management*, 10(4). pp. 331–44.

Beer, M. and Eisenstat, R. A. (1996) 'Developing an organization capable of implementing strategy and learning', *Human Relations*, 49(5), pp. 597–619.

Bohmer, R. M. J. and Edmondson, A. C. (2001) 'Organizational learning in health care: health care leaders need to design structures and processes that enhance collective learning', *Health Forum Journal*, 44(2), pp. 32–5.

Carkhuff, M. H. (1996) 'Reflective learning: work groups as learning groups', *Journal of Continuing Education in Nursing*, 27(5), pp. 209–14.

Chin, H. and McNichol, E. (2000) 'Practice development credentialling in the UK: a unique framework for providing excellence, accountability and quality in nursing and healthcare', *Online Journal of Issues in Nursing*, 5(2), http://www.nursing-world.org/ojin/admin/tocv5n2.htm.

Coghlan, D. and Casey, M. (2001) 'Action research from the inside: issues and challenges in doing action research in your own hospital', *Journal of Advanced Nursing*, 35(5), pp. 674–82.

Cowley, J. (1995) 'The changing pattern of employment in nursing', *Professional Nurse*, 11(3), pp. 163–4.

Deutschman, M. (2001) 'Re-defining quality and excellence in the nursing home culture', *Journal of Gerontological Nursing*, 27(8), pp. 28–36.

Dixon, N. (1994) *The Organisational Learning Cycle* (London: McGraw-Hill).

Dodgson, M (1993) 'Organizational learning: a review of some literature', *Organization Studies*, 14(3), pp. 375–94.

Garvin, D. (1993) 'Building a learning organisation', *Harvard Business Review*, 71(4), pp. 78–91.

Greenwood, J. (1998) 'The role of reflection in single loop learning', *Journal of Advanced Nursing*, 27(5), pp. 1048–53.

Hackman, J. R. and Oldham, G. R. (1980) *Work Redesign* (Reading, MA: Addison-Wesley).

Harrison, R. (2000) *Employee Development*, 2nd edn (London: Institute of Personnel and Development).

Hogg, K. (2000) *Making a Difference: Effective Implementation of Cross-cutting Policy* (Edinburgh: Scottish Executive Policy Unit Review).

Hunter, D. L. (1996) 'The changing roles of health personnel in health and health care management', *Social Science & Medicine*, 43, pp. 799–808.

Kanter, R. M. (1983) *The Change Masters* (London: Routledge).

MacDonald, G. (2002) 'Transformative Unlearning: safety, discernment and communities of learning', *Nursing Inquiry*, 9(3), pp. 170–8.

McClure, L. M. (1984) 'Teamwork, myth or reality: community nurses' experience with general practice attachment', *Journal of Epidemiology and Community Health*, 31, pp. 68–74.

Mallory, G. A. (1993) 'Commentary on management practices in learning organisations', *Nursing Scan in Administrations*, 8(2), p. 1.

Milstein, B. (2001) 'The Collaborative Evaluation Fellows Project (CEFP): building evaluation capacity', *Cancer Practice: A Multi-disciplinary Journal of Cancer Care*, 9(Suppl), pp. S99–102.

Mintzberg, H., Ahlstrand, B. and Lampel, J. (1998) *The Strategy Safari* (New York: Free Press).

Pedlar, M. and Aspinwall, K. (1998) *A Concise Guide to the Learning Organisation* (London: Lemos & Crane).

Pedlar, M. J., Burgoyne, J. G. and Boydell, T. H. (1997) *The Learning Company: A Strategy for Sustainable Development* (Maidenhead: McGraw-Hill).

Pettigrew, A. M. and Whipp, R. (1991) *Managing for Competitive Success* (Oxford: Blackwell).

Plsek, P. E. and Greenhalgh, T. (2001) 'The challenge of complexity in healthcare', *British Medical Journal*, 323, pp. 625–28.

Rushmer, R. K. and Davies, H. T. O. (2004) 'Un-learning: in healthcare', *Quality and Safety in Health Care*, 13(Suppl. 2), pp. 10–15.

Rushmer, R. K., Kelly, D., Lough, M., Wilkinson, J. E. and Davies H. T. O. (2002b) *Learning Organisations in Primary Care. Position Paper*, unpublished (St Andrews, Scotland: Centre for Public Policy and Management, St Andrews University).

Rushmer, R. K., Kelly, D., Lough, M., Wilkinson, J. E. and Davies, H. T. O. (2004a) 'Introducing the learning practice, I. The characteristics of learning organizations in primary care', *Journal of the Evaluation in Clinical Practice*, 10(3), pp. 375–86.

Rushmer, R. K., Kelly, D., Lough, M., Wilkinson, J. E. and Davies, H. T. O. (2004b) 'Introducing the learning practice, II. Becoming a learning practice', *Journal of the Evaluation in Clinical Practice*, 10(3), pp. 387–98.

Rushmer, R. K., Kelly, D., Lough, M., Wilkinson, J. E. and Davies, H. T. O. (2004c) 'Introducing the learning practice, III. Leadership, empowerment, protected time and reflective practice as core contextual conditions', *Journal of the Evaluation in Clinical Practice*, 10(3), pp. 399–405.

Rushmer, R. K., Parker, J. and Phillips, S. (2002a) 'Introducing self-directed primary care teams in the NHS: an overview of initial strategic issues', in R. K. Rushmer, H. T. O. Davies, M. Tavakoli and M. Malek (eds), *Organisation Development in Health Care: Strategic Issues in Health Care Management* (Aldershot, England: Ashgate).

Scottish Executive. Department of Health (1998a) *Designed to Care: Renewing the National Health Service in Scotland*, Cm 3811 (Edinburgh: The Stationery Office).

Scottish Executive. Department of Health (1998b) *Towards a New Way of Working: The Plan for Managing People in the NHS in Scotland* (Edinburgh: The Stationery Office).

Scottish Executive. Department of Health (1999a) *Agenda for Change: Modernising the NHS Pay in Scotland* (Edinburgh: The Stationery Office).

Scottish Executive. Department of Health (1999b) *Towards a Healthier Scotland*, Cm 4269 (Edinburgh: The Stationery Office).

Scottish Executive. Department of Health (1999c) *Learning Together: A Strategy for Education, Training and Life-Long Learning for All Staff in the NHS* (Edinburgh: The Stationery Office).

Senge, P. M. (1990) *The Fifth Discipline: The Art and Practice of the Learning Organization* (New York: Doubleday).

Skelton-Green, J. M. (1995) 'How a better understanding of adult learning can help improve your practice as a nurse administrator', *Canadian Journal of Nursing Administration*, 8(4), pp. 7–22.

Smith, P. C. and Kendall, L. M. (1963) 'Retranslation of expectations: an approach to the construction of unambiguous anchors for rating scales', *Journal of Applied Psychology*, 47, pp. 149–55.

Smith, R. (1991) 'Where is the wisdom?' *British Medical Journal*, 303(6806), pp. 798–9.

Stewart, M. (2000) 'Collaboration and conflict in the governance of the city region', Paper presented at the seventh International conference on Multi-Organisational Partnerships, Leuven, Belgium.

Timpson, J. (1998) 'The NHS as a learning organization: aspirations beyond the rainbow?', *Journal of Nursing Management*, 6(5), pp. 261–74.

UK. Department of Health. (2000) *The NHS Plan: A Plan for Investment, A Plan for Reform* (London: HMSO), accessed 2005-07-21, http://www.dh.gov.uk/assetRoot/04/05/57/83/04055783.pdf.

van Eyk, H., Baum, F. and Houghton, G. (2001) 'Coping with Health Care Reform', *Australian Health Review*, 24(2), pp. 202–06.

Wenger, E. (1998) *Communities of Practice: Learning, Meaning and Identity* (Cambridge: Cambridge University Press).

West, M. A. (1995) *The Effectiveness of Teamworking in Primary Care. A Report to the Health Education Authority* (Sheffield: Institute of Work Psychology).

# Part III
# What is Evidence Based Management?

# 9
# What Works and What Works Well?
## Levels of Evidence in Clinical Governance

*David Rea*

## Introduction

'Evidence based medicine' (EBM) and 'evidence based management' are terms suggesting that neither clinical practice nor the management of health care has been sufficiently evidence based to date. Moreover, it is suggested that good evidence is insufficiently disseminated (Sackett and Rosenberg, 1995) and that good evidence of poor outcomes is insufficiently investigated (Kennedy, 2001). It is argued that greater reliance on an evidence basis for decisions will result in significant and beneficial change (Starey, 2001).

Despite the central importance of evidence in current attempts to improve health care quality, the extent to which evidence should form a basis for decisions and policies is potentially ambiguous. As a 'basis', evidence is promoted as fundamental to good clinical practice. But it is also argued that evidence should never be used alone; evidence should be used alongside resources and values (Muir Gray, 2004; Sackett et al., 1996).

The extent to which evidence of effectiveness should be weighed against resources and values is equally of concern for evidence based management. Frequently there is insufficient time or resources to gather and assess evidence (Ansoff, 1994; Mintzberg, 1994). Evidence, and its associates 'knowledge' and 'information', lie at the centre of many models of rational decision making (Simon, 1982) and strategic change (Graetz, 2000) and also underpin government health care strategies (DoH, 2001; NHS Management Executive, 1998). Nevertheless, organizational decision processes are characterized as open to political bargaining between competing interests (Hunter, 1979; Wildavsky, 1964); irrational (Brunsson, 1985; Cohen, March and Olsen, 1972); or based on habitual practice, tradition and precedent (Bevir, Rhodes and Weller, 2003).

An evidence basis for medicine and management is offered as a stimulus for change and as a counter to any anticipated resistance to change. Resistance to change is anticipated in many change management models (Ackerman, Anderson and Anderson, 2001; Conner and Clutterbuck, 1997; Kotter, 1996;

ProSci, 2004). In health care, resistance from a variety of sources is expected because there is a context of conflicting goals and objectives, and an organizational culture described variously as too bureaucratic, too risk-averse and too prone to blame individuals (Audit Commission for Local Authorities, 2001; DoH, 2000a). Within this context, professional interests maintain considerable autonomy that supports professional values that are claimed to be protective of the public. An alternative is sometimes presented where professional values are depicted as reasonable, not self-interested, in an organizational model which recognizes complexity and the legitimacy of differing organizational perspectives (Audit Commission, 2002; DoH, 2002; DoH, 2003; WAG, 2002b).

The relationship between evidence and organizational change (or changes to clinical practice) may not be viewed as straightforward (Locock et al., 2001). However, this chapter is concerned with the necessity to examine the processes by which evidence is acquired because the evidence is presented as factual, neutral, 'above' self-interest and power, and therefore able to serve as the basis for decisions.

For evidence to play any central role in justifying particular actions and strategies for improvement, the manner in which it is obtained must conform to accepted methods of enquiry. At issue here is that some methods are more acceptable than others, producing differing 'levels of evidence' dependent on how closely the accepted methods of enquiry were followed. The acquisition of relevant evidence must be recognized as a social process in which economic and political forces are at work and where differing criteria are deployed to provide validity of evidence.

The chapter examines the differing levels of evidence that are likely to prove acceptable, contrasting the evidence requirements for clinical decisions in psychiatric care with those of effective service delivery of mental health services. The focus for this discussion is the UK policy of 'clinical governance', national strategies for mental health, and the authoritative provision and dissemination of knowledge about treatment (clinical and service) effectiveness.

The first section introduces the policy framework and some of the issues, focusing primarily on the requirement to demonstrate that evidence informs decision making and policy. Some commentators have seen clinical governance as a restriction on clinical autonomy or as a mechanism for rationing the availability of demonstrably effective treatments. This chapter will argue that clinical governance can also be seen as a mechanism for regulating medical and clinical expertise in matters of public concern and where the public has an expertise that must also be recognized. The following sections will then examine the extent to which these various forms of expertise are legitimate in informing decisions. At least in the short term, given the need to proceed with decisions and policies, the legitimacy of expertise will depend on which 'levels of evidence' are accepted, authorized or sanctioned.

## Clinical governance

'Clinical governance' is a term that may be alien to many outside the UK where it is used to combine organizational and clinical aspects of health care delivery (Giraud, 2001). While the term has spread elsewhere, its use does not always correspond closely to its use in the UK (Berti and Grilli, 2004; Eeckloo et al., 2004; Eno and Spiegelman, 2000; Glazebrook and Buchanan, 2001; Panå and Muzzi, 2004). Nevertheless, clinical governance will be of interest to any health care system committed to improving quality and performance. Its use originated with the 'New Labour' government and publication of plans for *The New NHS* (DoH, 1997). Later, clinical governance was set out as:

a framework through which NHS organizations are accountable for continuously improving the quality of their services and safeguarding high standards of care by creating an environment in which excellence in clinical care will flourish. (NHS Executive, 1999)

Clinical governance was established as a statutory responsibility to demonstrate local accountability for quality of care, including parameters of self-regulation performance, audit studies and demonstration of effective risk-management procedures (Golding, 2000). These new responsibilities were supported by two initiatives, the National Institute for Clinical Excellence (NICE) and the Commission for Health Improvement (CHI). NICE was established to provide an authoritative source of technological appraisal, clinical guidelines and information on intervention procedures. CHI was to be an independent inspection body and inspection of services was to be set against criteria developed for certain areas of service designated as National Service Frameworks (NSFs).[1] The public was given a right to have local standards and information about compliance to audit made available. Services were also developed to monitor patient experience and maintain early detection of poor performance and problem areas. The relationship between national and local elements of this quality framework is illustrated in Figure 9.1.

As has frequently been pointed out, clinical governance uses nothing new (Starey, 2001), but requires the systematic integration of activities only partially developed: clinical audit, risk management, openness and patient involvement (quality assurance), clinical effectiveness, research and development, and education and training.

This raises a question about what sort of evidence there could be for the systematic integration of all these elements comprising clinical governance when each element is likely to be assessed on differing criteria. For example, there is an established hierarchy for assessing evidence based medicine or clinical effectiveness that places the double blind randomized controlled trial (RCT) at its apogee. Evidence of patient involvement or of risk management will likely be very different.

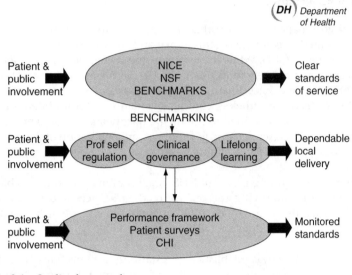

**Figure 9.1**   Quality framework
Source: *Essence of Care* (DoH, 2001)

The need to address quality issues within the NHS was given prominence by a number of high profile scandals (Ferguson, 2002; Kennedy, 2001; Mohammed et al., 2001; Redfern, 2001). These measures were broadly welcomed because both clinical professionals and health care managers would be accountable to both government and the public (Scally and Donaldson, 1998).

Large numbers of clinicians seem to have embraced a recognition for more public accountability and the need to demonstrate that evidence is used to inform and adjust practice (Gomm and Davies, 2000; Hicks, 1997; Knottnerus, van Weel and Muris, 2002; Sackett and Rosenberg, 1995; Sackett et al., 1996). The term 'clinical governance' diverts any anticipated association with managerial change or greater managerial control. 'Clinical' connotes a direct concern with patient care, while 'governance' is open to a variety of differing interpretations, but does not connote management or policy. Used together, 'clinical governance' may imply control and regulation will be centred on patient needs and perhaps thereby minimize any anticipated threat to clinical interests.

Nonetheless, clinical governance was also perceived as a diminution of clinical autonomy, constraining or modifying clinical behaviour (Buetow and Roland, 1999; Harrison and Lim, 2003); as a top-down imposition of rules for rationing health care (Harrison, 2000); likely to fail through under-funding and by measuring the easily measured (Fletcher, 2000; Golding,

2000); likely to reduce patient choice (Onion, 2000); and reliant on a rhetoric of improvement that stressed leadership and the need to define quality without any evidence that these will produce any improvement (Goodman, 2001).

## Levels of evidence and clinical governance

Despite the criticisms, there seems little doubt that the use of evidence in managing health care is increasing and that the organizational and financial costs of not doing so are considerable (Øvretveit, 1999). It is difficult to argue against turning to the evidence and it is to be hoped that decisions will be less affected by expediency, historical precedent or the power of vested interests. The problem is that, in selecting which facts are interesting or relevant, in interpreting what evidence means and in making recommendations, 'turning to the evidence' can render a view of the world limited to scientific or research-based legitimacy. Powerful interests already able to ensure their view of reality prevails will then be able to use evidence consistent with their views to provide greater legitimacy for their views. Evidence is important because it can justify particular actions ostensibly grounded in reality, and criteria for spending decisions, promotion and changes in modes of service delivery. But evidence is also important in that it confirms (or denies) the power of differing views of the world over others.

Evidence will then support actions and decisions that are biased towards those held by powerful interests and consistent with their views. Instead of challenging professional autonomy and increasing accountability to government or the public, as was suggested by some of the critics above (Harrison, 2000; Harrison and Lim, 2003), clinical governance may reinforce clinical autonomy and bolster clinicians in their view of the world.

While research evidence has the appearance of neutrality, medical professions, pharmaceutical companies and health service providers have powerful incentives to produce evidence supportive of their own interests. Thus, the decision to search for evidence is posed within a framework of what defines good medical practice, and the availability of evidence is equally unlikely to be totally free from bias. Indeed, the World Health Organisation has questioned the close links with the pharmaceutical industries that NICE has developed (WHO, 2003). The availability and certainty of medical knowledge outweigh that concerned with management and health service delivery. In any event, evidence of good service delivery rarely matches the 'gold standards' of established medical practice. In short, the search for evidence, its availability, its interpretation and any subsequent use offers a vision of openness, transparency, accountability based on evidence accumulated through scientific endeavour that is only apparently neutral.

This does not result from financial and economic power alone. There is a hierarchical discourse of science that places pure science above applied sciences, biology above psychology and sociology above management studies. It is a pejorative discourse where social sciences are scarcely science at all. As Hudson stated, the experimental scientist looks down on the social, industrial, clinical, or educational – 'the clean look down on the messy' (Hudson, 1972). In the resulting search for higher status, researchers address research problems that are 'promoted' to a level of 'methodological inappropriateness'. In Hudson's argument, the social psychologist may abandon the study of man in social settings to engage in experiments in laboratories using booths and one-way screens.

Social studies of science therefore offer the prospect of upsetting this hierarchical order by offering insights, deconstructing the processes by which scientific knowledge is said to be acquired (Shapin, 1995). The consequence has been the so-called 'science wars' (Brown, 2001; Hacking, 1999; Preston, 1999; Rorty, 1999; Sadar, 2000; Turner, 2003) and questions over the legitimacy and use of scientific evidence in creating public policy (Collins and Evans, 2002; Collins and Evans, 2003; Jasanoff, 2003; Wynne, 2003).

There is a view that science must be independent of politics since science is 'about revealing "the truth" about reality' (Heazle, 2004) and only as such can it serve as an ultimate benchmark. However, the authority of science is increasingly called into question. For instance, Collins and Evans argue that the public legitimacy of science, in which distinctions between experts and the public, between technical and political expertise, has now dissolved (Collins and Evans, 2002). They raise important questions about how the scientific and technical communities should interact with the public over issues (such as BSE, nuclear power, RSI, cloning and so on) that are no longer thought of as 'purely technical issues'. The perception of value-free science becomes difficult to sustain especially once we consider funding arrangements, as important in health care as anywhere. Abandoning the idea that scientific evidence corresponds to 'reality' does not mean we have to move to its opposite where scientific evidence is constructed (Hacking, 1999; Rorty, 1980; Rorty, 1999). But, it requires us to examine the processes by which evidence is produced, classified, examined, verified and validated – whether by scientists or by doctors or managers.

Clinical governance may then be perceived as a framework for regulating the use of science in making decisions affecting the public in which medical, pharmaceutical and economics expertise – and the public as experts – might expect to make a contribution. As such, medical practitioners, pharmacologists, health care managers, politicians and service users will determine which sorts of evidence are legitimate for treatment and service delivery decisions. It is unlikely the contestants will unanimously agree who is suitably qualified to act as judge. This is not to suggest a never-ending free-for-all in which there is no victor, only that, as with any struggle for power, the outcome is not over-determined (Hindess, 1984). Clinical governance will involve the regulation of a number of sometimes wholly incommensurate truth claims, each with differing methods and differing views of which evidence is to be prioritized.

The criteria used to judge evidence is therefore central to managerial practice. The next section examines the evidence criteria for two elements of clinical governance: EBM and patient involvement.

## Evidence criteria

### The evidence criteria in evidence based medicine

Medicine is not precisely concerned with pure science and is lower down Hudson's hierarchy than biology. It uses pragmatic criteria where it is not strictly necessary to understand why a drug introduced in 1899 is now a recommended treatment for prevention of cardiovascular disease (Aspirin®), or why the Atkins diet causes people to lose weight. What matters are effectiveness, side-effects, benefits, dis-benefits (including financial costs) and comparison with alternatives. For example, NICE's recent treatment guidelines for schizophrenia acknowledge 'the aetiology remains poorly understood' (NICE, 2003, p. 3). Moreover, the knowledge required for medical practice includes an understanding that each treatment will take differing courses within differing patients and the population at large, so that the outcomes for differing patients will vary. It also requires an understanding of social behaviour and disease prevalence to aid identification of patient conditions.

Laboratory knowledge is useful only in so far as it is tested in effect and the principal means of testing useful medical knowledge is the RCT, the gold standard of clinical effectiveness (Rogers et al., 2003). It is rooted in the experimental method where an artificial situation is created where the multiple causes of an event can be controlled. They are controlled either by exclusion, or by standardization (neutralizing their effects). Different treatments are provided for similar patients, or similar treatments are provided for differing patients. Differences in outcome are then attributed to differences in treatment or differences in patients (Gomm, 2000).

Without adequate safeguards, there are two major dangers: the differences must be those intended and only those intended; and, similarity of outcomes may result from differing treatments. The RCT attempts to safeguard against these dangers by ensuring comparison groups are selected at random. Each participant should have an equal chance of being allocated to any category. Then, because researcher, patient and practitioner judgements may be biased, placebos are used to prevent them knowing which category is affected by the treatment.

But, results from RCTs vary and sometimes contradict. Moreover, medical diagnosis and treatments are provided without reference to how science is distinguished from non-science, through concepts such as falsifiability

(Kuhn, 1960; Lavor, 1998; Popper, 1972). That said, medical claims to be a scientific endeavour are made and such claims are more secure when the underlying science can be stated and when RCTs can be cited. Even so, because RCTs cannot alone be taken as scientific 'proof', the status of any medical practice can be enhanced by the process of a 'systematic review'. Systematic reviews 'appraise and synthesize evidence from primary studies' (Davies and Crombie, 2001; NHS CRD, 2001).

The security of medical knowledge is also bolstered by high levels of professional organization (Burrage and Torstendahl, 1990; Coburn, 1992). Although the status of professional organization is frequently questioned (Coburn, 1992; Freidson, 1970; Navarro, 1988; Southon and Braithwaite, 1998), professional organization acts to authorize practice and license practitioners, and establish which procedures and treatments are recognized as good practice or not (Drazin, 1990). Within the boundaries of orthodox practice, thus established, new treatment methods and new conditions are accepted. Then, less orthodox understandings of medical knowledge are categorized as:

1. 'dissent' – questions over the facts (that is, the link between HIV and AIDS);
2. 'rebellion' – challenges to the profession's authority structure (that is, women entering the profession, or the use of untested AIDS drugs); or
3. 'heresy' – challenges to central values of the orthodoxy, including how claims are to be evaluated (that is, Szasz's claim that mental illness is a myth, homeopathy, or the holistic health movement) (Martin, 2004; Wolpe, 1994).

While some doctors are suspicious of EBM (Cranney et al., 2001; CRAP, 2002; Straus and McAlister, 2000), the introduction of clinical governance provides a further arena for authorizing the efficacy and cost-effectiveness of medical procedures. The RCT and systematic reviews do not form the sole basis for EBM (Sackett et al., 1996); nevertheless, they are given pre-eminence in hierarchical typologies such as those published by Bandolier (Bandolier, 1995) or in the *Cochrane Handbook* (Oxman, 1994).

The Bandolier article cited here also suggests 'evidence is not just about science or medicine. It is, or should be, also about management.' This view is echoed by Axelson (Axelson, 1998) and Stewart (Stewart, 2002). So, given that clinical governance is supposed to be a systematic framework, we might ask what evidence is expected; for example, in standard 6 of the NSF for adult mental health services in Wales which states:

Services must be responsive, effective and offer high quality, evidence based care in an environment and an atmosphere that provides dignity, privacy and support. (WAG, 2002a) and in standard 7 where it states:

> Effective high quality care based on the best evidence and including provision for the medical, physical, psychological and social needs of service users and carers. (WAG, 2002a)

Standards such as these refer to clinical care and service delivery issues, although there are acknowledged difficulties in detection, diagnosis and treatment of such common disorders as schizophrenia (Kulhara, 1994; Shepherd, Murray and Muijen, 1995; Wray, 1994) or dementia (Bowers et al., 1990; Hofman, Rocca and Brayne, 1991; MRC CFAS, 1998).

The next section examines the criteria for evidence of patient involvement, another element of clinical governance.

### The evidence criteria of patient involvement

Briefly, patient involvement can refer to either an individual's participation in their own care, or it can refer to users (and carers) acting together to affect the delivery of services (policies and management). The NSF for adult mental health in Wales, for instance, requires operational strategies to be developed jointly with service user representatives; actions to reduce stigma; the needs of people with mental health problems to be addressed in all local services and plans; and liaison with the justice system and with local housing agencies (WAG, 2002a). At an individual level, the NSF requires a system of care management in which service users agree with the definition of the problems they face and the methods used to address them (NAW, 2001).

The historical record is not good, particularly so in the area of mental health. For instance, while care management has been practised in the UK for more than a decade (DoH and SSI, 1991) and its effectiveness well documented, its implementation is sporadic (Challis, 1999; Challis et al., 1998; Challis et al., 2001; Ormiston, 1999; Stalker and Campbell, 2002). It is difficult to demonstrate the effectiveness of care management because there is no standard approach to its implementation.

Services have not involved service users for a variety of stated reasons, such as that either their symptoms or their medication interfere with their ability to hold and express their views (Barnes and Wistow, 1994). There are also methodological and conceptual obstacles to surveying user perspectives (Godfrey and Wistow, 1997; Rea, 1999). Principally, these are that vulnerable service users are frequently distrustful of the motives, suspecting no real change will result but that 'kudos' will go to the organization. Surveys may therefore draw on too narrow a number of people to yield reliable and valid results. In addition, service providers do not have the resources to employ sufficiently skilled researchers who can devote sufficient time to ensure empathy. Quantitative research methods are unlikely to be satisfactory to the researcher or acceptable to the researched (Rea, 1999). The attempt to involve service users in processes of service evaluation and planning is ad hoc and superficial (Pickard et al., 2002) but has grown significantly (Anthony and Crawford, 2000; Colombo et al., 2003; Crawford et al., 2003; Lammers and Happell, 2003; Peck, Gulliver and Towel, 2002; Pickard et al., 2002; Rea, 2001; Rea, 2004; Rose, 2001; Rose, 2003; Truman and Raine, 2001; Truman and Raine, 2002). However, some suggest user involvement is cosmetic (Diamond et al., 2003), is problematic for professionals (Crawford et al., 2002; Summers, 2003), and that its purposes have not been clear (Pickard et al., 2002).

An examination of these studies shows that RCTs are not often used for establishing the validity of service evaluations or for testing the effects of user involvement on planning, although there are exceptions (Martin et al., 1998). This raises a question over whether evidence obtained from an RCT has validity when involving service users in assessment and evaluation of services. Their views on clinical trials have not been adequately researched (Rogers et al., 2003). It can be argued that the RCT does not provide sufficient validity when researching people with less power (Best, 2003; Logan and Huntley, 2001; Tétrault, 1996) or when the researcher is an 'outsider' (De Paola and Scoppa, 2003; Hoffman, Snell and Webb, 1976; Logan and Huntley, 2001; McCutcheon, 1999; Thomas, Blacksmith and Reno, 2000). These arguments place greater emphasis on ensuring the research evidence is qualitative and that the methods used are valid from the perspective of the researched.

This difference affects the questions that can be asked. For instance, clinical effectiveness will concern itself with systematic reviews of which RCTs demonstrate greater effectiveness. The NICE guidelines for atypical antipsychotic drugs for treatment of schizophrenia were issued after a review of 172 RCTs (NICE, 2003). Of the 172 RCTs reviewed in producing the NICE guidelines, 31 published economic evaluations. The majority used a cost-minimization approach. Only three used a cost-utility approach, so very few estimated costs per additional unit of clinical effect (for example, Quality Adjusted Light Years). In other words, costs were assessed from the sole perspective of the provider or the exchequer. Few considered the costs and dis-benefits for the patients being treated.

Clinical effectiveness raises questions about whether the desired outcome of treatment is the removal of distress, the imposition of social conformity or quality of life in ordinary communities (Pilgrim, 1999). So, it is important to note that the NICE guidelines are concerned with effects on symptoms (listed as cognitive, emotional and behavioural, and including hallucinations, delusions, flattening of mood, emotional apathy, social withdrawal, lack of motivation and loss of pleasure), and undesirable side effects (weight gain and sexual dysfunction). Undesirable side effects may affect compliance, but perhaps it is important to assess how service users offset them against the benefits of effective treatment for distressing symptoms.

Patient interests were represented in establishing the guidelines and Appendix C provides patient information which says:

> Your doctor should discuss with you which antipsychotic drug you should take. Your doctor should explain the benefits and side effects of the drugs, and if appropriate consult your advocate or carer. (NICE, 2003)

The NICE guidelines look at the issue from the perspective of the provider – the clinician – not the user. While addressing the information needs of patients in the appendices, their main purpose is to provide guidance for doctors.

As shown above, clinical governance, through the NSF and care management processes, requires evidence that service users were involved in decisions over their own care. Evidence is also required that service users are involved in service delivery and planning mechanisms. Both are relatively easy to demonstrate in that patients will sign care plan documents, and that minutes and other documentary evidence are routinely assembled in planning activities. However, this evidence is entirely questionable given that there is little attempt in practice to apply the same rigour as is used in RCTs to the internal validity of this evidence. A patient's signature on a care plan may merely indicate confusion and a desire to end the process of review. Attendance at meetings does not indicate involvement, let alone the possibility that service user representatives are driving the planning and delivery of their services. CHI uses four categories in respect of patient involvement where excellence is defined as 'co-ordinated activity and development across the trust and with partner organizations in the local health economy that is demonstrably leading to improvement' (CHI, 2002b), but has found few examples of excellence (CHI, 2002a).

This sort of evidence is of a very different order to that required for judging treatment efficacy or efficiency, but may be the more appropriate. An RCT could not be used because no placebo could be offered to a randomly selected population to account for the subjective effects of being measured. Alternatively, a quasi-experiment or a natural experiment might be devised to assess whether patient 'involvement' (however defined) resulted in greater satisfaction with services or greater compliance, say, or even reduced symptoms. But, there would still be problems of external validity because there would be no sure way of replication. 'Involvement' would be peculiar to one place and one time.

These difficulties are clear and acknowledged, for instance by CHI (CHI, 2003). In short, validity requires that particular attention be paid to ensuring that service users frame the issues that need to be addressed, that communications are conducted in an environment conducive to trust, and that the consequences of any decisions are clearly communicated and clearly beneficial.

## Discussion

The effort to introduce greater reliance on evidence in medicine and health care delivery through clinical governance in the UK has come at a time when many question the role of science and expertise in public policy. Evidence based medicine, evidence based management and evidence based policy all assert the primacy of using the best available scientific processes. Evidence gained through RCTs and systematic review is presented as authoritative, enabling better decisions affecting treatment regimes or service delivery, and compelling of health care organizations to examine existing practice. This is unlikely to be straightforward given the context of external accountability and government policy and relatively autonomous professional practitioners.

This chapter, however, has highlighted the need to examine how evidence is established as authoritative before reaching any decision making processes. We have to question the processes by which topics are selected for medical research and funding; the degree to which patients were involved; and the degree to which their perspective was considered in evaluating success. Similar questions should be asked about organizational change and service effectiveness.

The issue may be perceived as whether clinical governance can genuinely act as a bridge between clinically defined measures of quality (as with clinical audit and clinical effectiveness) and managerial approaches to quality. Concerns have been expressed that clinical effectiveness and EBM will curtail clinical autonomy, increase rationing and reduce patient choice. Greater external accountability and the requirement to involve patients to a larger extent have also been interpreted as a further curtailment on clinical autonomy. However, EBM defines the clinical task more specifically than previously around measurable outcomes. Because the evidence requirements can be stated as more rigorous than those of other aspects of health care, clinical treatments may be prioritized. Symptom control or reduction is emphasized as clearly more amenable to effective intervention than other elements of clinical governance such as patient involvement.

So, the assertions made that systematic review of RCTs provides higher levels of evidence may prevent the systematic integration requirements of clinical governance. While clinical governance may bring together differing views of what evidence is to be prioritized, it is likely to see disputes (and resolution) over what sorts of evidence can be used to judge or make decisions affecting the delivery of services and an individual's care. Without being over-deterministic, clinical governance may afford greater opportunity for health care issues to be defined as clinical issues, and greater opportunity for evidence of patient wishes to be played down. While the knowledge base for what constitutes effective, evidence based clinical governance remains uncertain, clinical governance does provide a new arena in which the processes developing evidence acquire greater practical urgency.

# Note

1. In April 2004 CHI was replaced by the Healthcare Commission (in England), and the Healthcare Inspectorate Wales.

# References

Ackerman Anderson, L. and Anderson, D. (2001) *The Change Leader's Roadmap: How to Navigate your Organization's Transformation* (Chichester: Pfeiffer).

Ansoff, H. I. (1994) *Milestones in Management* (London: Schaffer Pöschel).

Anthony, P. and Crawford, P. (2000) 'Service user involvement in care planning: the mental health nurses perspective', *Journal of Psychiatric and Mental Health Nursing*, 7, pp. 425–34.

Audit Commission (2002) *Building a Whole System Approach in England: Integrated Services for Older People* (London: Audit Commission).

Audit Commission for Local Authorities (2001) *Change Here! Managing Change to Improve Local Services* (London: Audit Commission for Local Authorities & the National Health Service in England and Wales).

Axelson, R. (1998) 'Towards an evidence based health care management', *International Journal of Health Planning Management*, 13, pp. 307–17.

Bandolier (1995) 'Evidence based everything', *Bandolier*, 12.

Barnes, M. and Wistow, G. (1994) 'Learning to hear voices: listening to users of mental health services', *Journal of Mental Health*, 3, pp. 525–40.

Berti, E. and Grilli, R. (2004) 'Practice guidelines and clinical governance', *Clinical Governance: An International Journal*, 9, pp. 312–17.

Best, A. L. (2003) 'Doing race in the context of feminist interviewing: constructing whiteness through talk', *Qualitative Inquiry*, 9, pp. 895–914.

Bevir, M., Rhodes, A. W. and Weller, P. (2003) 'Traditions of governance: interpreting the changing role of the public sector', *Public Administration*, 81, pp. 1–17.

Bowers, J., Jorm, A., Henderson, C. and Harris, P. (1990) 'General practitioners detection of depression and dementia in elderly patients', *Medical Journal of Australia*, 153, pp. 192–6.

Brown, R. B. (2001) *Who Rules in Science? An Opinionated Guide to the Wars* (Cambridge, MA: Harvard University Press).

Brunsson, N. (1985) *The Irrational Organization: Irrationality as the Basis for Organizational Action and Change* (Chichester: Wiley).

Buetow, S. A. and Roland, M. (1999) 'Clinical governance: bridging the gap between managerial and clinical approaches to quality of care', *Quality in Health Care*, 8, pp. 184–90.

Burrage, M. and Torstendahl, R. (1990) *Professions in Theory and Practice: Rethinking the Study of the Professions* (London: Sage).

Challis, D. (1999) 'Assessment and care management: development since the community care reforms in the UK', in M. Henwood and G. Wistow (eds), *Royal Commission on Long Term Care. With Respect to Old Age: Long-term Care – Rights and Responsibilities, Community Care and Informal Care. Research Volume 3, Part 1: Evaluating the Impact of Caring for People* (London: Stationery Office).

Challis, D., Darton, R., Hughes, J., Stewart, K. and Weiner, K. (1998) *Care Management Study: Report on National Data. Mapping and evaluation of care management arrangements for older people and those with mental health problems* (London: UK Department of Health).

Challis, D., Weiner, K., Darton, R., Hughes, J. and Stewart, K. (2001) 'Emerging patterns of care management: arrangements for older people in England', *Social Policy & Administration*, 35, pp. 672–87.

CHI – *see* Commission for Health Improvement

Clinicians for the Restoration of Autonomous Practice (2002) 'EBM: unmasking the ugly truth', *British Medical Journal*, 325, pp. 1496–8.

Coburn, D. (1992) 'Freidson then and now: an "internalist" critique of Freidson's past and present views of the medical profession', *International Journal of Health Services*, 22(3), pp. 497–512.

Cohen, M. D., March, J. G. and Olsen, J. P. (1972) 'A garbage-can model of organisational choice', *Administrative Science Quarterly*, 17, pp. 1–25.

Collins, H. M. and Evans, R. (2002) 'The Third Wave of science studies: studies of expertise and experience', *Social Studies of Science*, 32, pp. 235–96.

Collins, H. M. and Evans, R. (2003) 'King Canute meets the Beach Boys: responses to the Third Wave', *Social Studies of Science*, 33, pp. 435–52.

Colombo, A., Bendelow, G., Fulford, B. and Williams, S. (2003) 'Evaluating the influence of implicit models of mental disorder on processes of shared decision making within community-based multi-disciplinary teams', *Social Science & Medicine*, 56(7), pp. 1557–70.

Commission for Health Improvement (2002a) *Emerging Themes From 175 Clinical Governance Reviews* (London: Commission for Health Improvement).

Commission for Health Improvement (2002b) *A Guide to Clinical Governance Reviews: Mental Health Services* (London: Commission for Health Improvement).

Commission for Health Improvement (2003) *Nothing About us Without Us: The Patient and the Public Strategy for CHI* (London: Commission for Health Improvement).

Conner, D. R. and Clutterbuck, D. (1997) *Managing at the Speed of Change* (New York: Wiley).

Cranney, M., Warren, E., Barton, S., Gardner, K. and Walley, T. (2001) 'Why do GPs not implement evidence based guidelines? A descriptive study', *Family Practice*, 18, pp. 359–63.

CRAP – *see* Clinicians for the Restoration of Autonomous Practice

Crawford, M. J., Aldridge, T., Bhui, K., Rutter, D., Manley, C., Weaver, T., Tyrer, P. and Fulop, N. (2003) 'User involvement in the planning and delivery of mental health services: a cross-sectional survey of service users and providers', *Acta Psychiatrica Scandinavica*, 107, pp. 410–14.

Crawford, P., Brown, B., Anthony, P. and Hicks, C. (2002) 'Reluctant empiricists: community mental health nurses and the art of evidence based praxis', *Health and Social Care in the Community*, 10(4), pp. 287–98.

Davies, H. T. O. and Crombie, I. K. (2001) 'What is a systematic review?', *Evidence based medicine*, 1(5), pp. 1–6, accessed 2005-08-04, http://www.jr2.ox.ac.uk/bandolier/painres/download/whatis/Syst-review.pdf.

De Paola, M. and Scoppa, V. (2003) 'Family ties and training provision in an insider–outsider framework', *Journal of Socio-Economics*, 32, pp. 197–217.

Diamond, B., Parkin, G., Morris, K., Bettinis, J. and Bettesworth, C. (2003) 'User involvement: substance or spin?', *Journal of Mental Health*, 12, pp. 613–26.

DoH – *see* UK Department of Health

Drazin, R. (1990) 'Professionals and innovation: structural-functional versus radical-structural perspectives', *Journal of Management Studies*, 27(3), pp. 245–63.

Eeckloo, K., Van Herck, G., Van Hulle, C. and Vleugels, A. (2004) 'From corporate governance to hospital governance. authority, transparency and accountability of Belgian non-profit hospitals' board and management', *Health Policy*, 68, pp. 1–15.

Eno, L. M. and Spiegelman, A. D. (2000) 'A survey of surgical audit in Australia: Whither clinical governance?', *Journal of Quality in Clinical Practice*, 20, pp. 2–4.

Ferguson, B. A. (2002) 'Learning from Bristol: reflections from a health economist', *British Journal of Clinical Governance*, 7, pp. 233–41.

Fletcher, I. R. (2000) 'Editorial: Clinical governance', *European Journal of Anaesthesiology*, 17, pp. 471–3.

Freidson, E. (1970) *The Profession of Medicine: A Study of the Sociology of Applied Knowledge* (London: Harper & Row).

Giraud, A. (2001) 'Accreditation and the quality movement in France', *Quality in Health Care*, 10, pp. 111–16.

Glazebrook, S. G. and Buchanan, J. G. (2001) 'Clinical governance and external audit', *Journal of Quality in Clinical Practice*, 21, pp. 30–3.

Godfrey, M. and Wistow, G. (1997) 'The user perspective on managing for health outcomes: the case of mental health', *Health and Social Care in the Community*, 5, pp. 325–32.

Golding, S. J. (2000) 'Clinical governance in the UK: logical conclusion of cost-effectiveness or road to ruin?', *European Journal of Radiology*, 10, pp. S411–12.

Gomm, R. (2000) 'Understanding experimental design', in R. Gomm and C. Davies (eds), *Using Evidence in Health and Social Care* (London: Open University Press in association with Sage).

Gomm, R. and Davies, C. (eds) (2000) *Using Evidence in Health and Social Care* (London: Open University Press in association with Sage).

Goodman, N. W. (2001) 'Clinical governance: vision or mirage?', *Journal of Evaluation in Clinical Practice*, 8, pp. 243–9.

Graetz, F. (2000) 'Strategic change leadership', *Management Decision*, 38, pp. 550–62.

Hacking, I. (1999) *The Social Construction of What?* (London: Harvard University Press).

Harrison, S. (2000) 'NICE, CHI, clinical governance and health care rationing', *Radiography*, 6, pp. 9–10.

Harrison, S. and Lim, J. N. W. (2003) 'The frontier of control: doctors and managers in the NHS 1966 to 1997', *Clinical Governance: An International Journal*, 8, pp. 13–18.

Heazle, M. (2004) 'Scientific uncertainty and the International Whaling Commission: an alternative perspective on the use of science in policy making', *Marine Policy*, 28, pp. 361–74.

Hicks, N. (1997) 'Evidence based health care', *Bandolier*, 39.

Hindess, B. (1984) 'Rational choice theory and the analysis of political action', *Economy and Society*, 13, pp. 255–77.

Hoffman, D. E., Snell, J. C. and Webb, V. J. (1976) 'Insiders and outsiders in criminal justice education', *Journal of Criminal Justice*, 4, pp. 57–61.

Hofman, A., Rocca, W. A. and Brayne, C. (1991) 'The prevalence of dementia in Europe: a collaborative study of 1980–1990 findings', *International Journal of Epidemiology*, 20, pp. 736–48.

Hudson, L. (1972) *The Cult of the Fact* (London: Cape).

Hunter, D. (1979) *Coping with Uncertainty* (Letchworth: Research Press).

Jasanoff, S. (2003) 'Breaking the waves in Science Studies: comment on H.M. Collins and R. Evans' The Third Wave of Science Studies', *Social Studies of Science*, 33, pp. 389–400.

Kennedy, I. (Chair) (2001) *Learning from Bristol: the Report of the Public Inquiry into Children's Heart Surgery at the Bristol Royal Infirmary1984–1995* (London: Bristol Royal Infirmary Inquiry).

Knottnerus, J. A., van Weel, C. and Muris, J. W. M. (2002) 'Evidence base of clinical diagnosis: Evaluation of diagnostic procedures', *British Medical Journal*, 324, pp. 477–80.

Kotter, J. P. (1996) *Leading Change* (Boston: Harvard Business School Press).

Kuhn, T. S. (1960) *The structure of Scientific Revolutions* (Chicago: University of Chicago Press).

Kulhara, P. (1994) 'Outcome of schizophrenia: some transcultural observations with particular reference to developing countries', *European Archives of Psychiatry and Clinical Neuroscience*, 244, pp. 227–35.

Lammers, J. and Happell, B. (2003) 'Consumer participation in mental health services: looking from a consumer perspective', *Journal of Psychiatric and Mental Health Nursing*, 10, pp. 385–92.

Lavor, B. (1998) *Lakatos: An Introduction* (New York: Routledge).

Locock, L., Dopson, S. Chambers, D. and Gabbay, J. (2001) 'Understanding the role of opinion leaders in improving clinical effectiveness', *Social Science & Medicine*, 53(6), pp. 745–57.

Logan, M. E. and Huntley, H. (2001) 'Gender and power in the research process', *Women's Studies International Forum*, 24, pp. 623–35.

Martin, B. (2004) 'Dissent and heresy in medicine: models, methods, and strategies', *Social Science & Medicine*, 58(4), pp. 713–25.

Martin, D. P., Diehr, P., Conrad, D. A., Hunt-Davis, J., Leickly, R. and Perrin, E. B. (1998) 'Randomized trial of a patient-centered hospital unit', *Patient Education and Counseling*, 34(2), pp. 125–33.

McCutcheon, R. T. (ed.) (1999) *The Insider/Outsider Problem in the Study of Religion* (London: Cassell).

Medical Research Council Cognitive Function and Ageing Study (MRC CFAS) (1998) 'Cognitive function and dementia in six areas of England and Wales', *Psychological Medicine*, 28, pp. 319–35.

Mintzberg, H. (1994) *The Rise and Fall of Strategic Planning* (New York: Prentice Hall).

Mohammed, M. A., Cheng, K. K., Rouse, A., and Marshall, T. (2001) 'Bristol, Shipman, and clinical governance: Shewhart's forgotten lessons', *Lancet*, 357, pp. 463–7.

MRC CFAS – *see* Medical Research Council Cognitive Function and Ageing Study.

Muir Gray, J. A. (2004) 'Evidence based policy making', *British Medical Journal*, 329, pp. 988–9.

National Institute for Clinical Excellence (2003) *Guidance on the Use of Newer (atypical) Antipsychotic Drugs for the Treatment of Schizophrenia* (London: National Institute for Clinical Excellence), accessed 2005-07-29, http://www.nice.org.uk/pdf/ANTIPSY-CHOTICfinalguidance.pdf.

Navarro, V. (1988) 'Professional dominance or proletarianisation? Neither', *Milbank Quarterly*, 66(Suppl), pp. 57–75.

NAW – *see* UK National Assembly for Wales.

NHS CRD – *see* University of York Centre for Reviews and Dissemination.

NHS Executive – *see* UK NHS Executive.

NHS Management Executive – *see* UK NHS Management Executive.

NICE – *see* National Institute for Clinical Excellence.

Onion, C. W. R. (2000) 'Principles to govern clinical governance', *Journals of Evaluation in Clinical Practice*, 6, pp. 405–12.

Ormiston, H. (1999) *Still Building Bridges: The Report of a National Inspection of Arrangements for the Inspection of Care Programme Approach with Care Management* (London: Department of Health, Social Services Inspectorate).

Øvretveit, J. (1999) 'Evaluation informed management and clinical governance', *British Journal of Clinical Governance*, 4, pp. 103–8.

Oxman, A. D. (1994) *The Cochrane Collaboration Handbook* (Oxford: Cochrane Collaboration).

Panå, A., and Muzzi, A. (2004) 'Clinical governance and public health', *Igiene e sanita pubblica*, 60(3), pp. 115–20.

Peck, E., Gulliver, P. and Towel, D. (2002) 'Information, consultation or control: User involvement in mental health services in England at the turn of the century', *Journal of Mental Health* 11, pp. 441–51.

Pickard, S., Marshall, M., Rogers, A., Sheaff, R., Sibbald, B., Campbell, S., Halliwell, S., and Roland, R. (2002) 'User involvement in clinical governance', *Health Expectations* 5, pp. 187–98.

Pilgrim, D (1999) 'Editorial: Making the best of clinical governance', *Journal of Mental Health*, 8(1), pp. 1–2.

Popper, K. R (1972) *The Logic of Scientific Discovery* (London: Hutchinson).

Preston, J. (ed.) (1999) *Paul K Feyerabend: Knowledge, Science and Relativism* (Cambridge: Cambridge University Press).

ProSci (2004) *Best Practices in Change Management* (Loveland, CO: ProSci).

Protti, D. (2002) 'A proposal to use a balanced scorecard to evaluate Information for Health: an information strategy for the modern NHS (1998–2005)', *Computers in Biology and Medicine*, 32, pp. 221–36.

PSBS – *see* Public Sector Benchmarking Service.

Public Sector Benchmarking Service (2003) *The Balanced Scorecard* (London: Public Sector Benchmarking Service).

Rea, D. M. (1999) 'Towards routine user assessment of mental health service quality performance', *International Journal of Health Care Quality Assurance*, 12, pp. 169–76.

Rea, D. M. (2001) 'Involving mental health service users in planning service provision', Paper presented at the 3rd International Conference on Social Work in Health and Mental Health, Tampere, Finland.

Rea, D. M. (2004) 'Changing practice: involving mental health service users in planning service provision', *Social Work in Health Care*, 39(3–4), pp. 325–42.

Redfern, M. (2001) *The Royal Liverpool Children's Inquiry Report* (Chaired by Michael Redfern) (London: House of Commons).

Rogers, A., Day, J., Randall, F., and Bentall, R. P. (2003) 'Patients' understanding and participation in a trial designed to improve the management of anti-psychotic medication: a qualitative study', *Social Psychiatry and Psychiatric Epidemiology*, 38, pp. 720–7.

Rorty, R. (1980) *Philosophy and the Mirror of Nature* (Oxford: Blackwell).

Rorty, R. (1999) 'Phoney science wars', *Atlantic Monthly*, 284, pp. 120–2.

Rose, D. (2001) 'User-focused monitoring', *Mental Health Care*, 4, pp. 207–10.

Rose, D. (2003) 'Partnership, co-ordination of care and the place of user involvement', *Journal of Mental Health*, 12, pp. 59–70.

Rose, N. (1999) *Powers of Freedom: Reframing Political Thought* (Cambridge: Cambridge University Press).

Sackett, D. L., and Rosenberg, W. M. C. (1995) 'On the need for evidence based medicine', *Journal of Public Health Medicine*, 17, pp. 330–4.

Sackett, D. L., Rosenberg, W. M. C., Muir-Gray, J. A., Haynes, R. B. and Richardson, W. S. (1996) 'Evidence based medicine: what it is and what it isn't', *British Medical Journal*, 312, pp. 71–2.

Sadar, Z. (2000) *Thomas Kuhn and the Science Wars* (Cambridge: Icon Books).

Scally, G. and Donaldson, L. (1998) 'Clinical governance and the drive for quality improvement in the new NHS in England', *British Medical Journal*, 317, pp. 61–5.

Senge, P. M. (1999) *The Fifth Discipline: The Art & Practice of the Learning Organization* (London: Century).

Shapin, S. (1995) 'Here and everywhere: sociology of scientific knowledge', *Annual Review of Sociology*, 21, pp. 289–321.

Shepherd, G., Murray, A. and Muijen, M. (1995) 'Perspectives on schizophrenia: the views of users, relatives and professionals', *Journal of Mental Health*, 4, pp. 403–22.

Simon, H. A. (1982) *Models of Bounded Rationality* (Cambridge, MA: MIT Press).

Southon, G., and Braithwaite, J. (1998) 'The end of professionalism?', *Social Science & Medicine*,. 46, pp. 23–8.

Stalker, K., and Campbell, I. (2002) *Review of Care Management in Scotland* (Edinburgh: Scottish Executive, Central Research Unit).

Starey, N. (2001) 'What is clinical governance?', *Evidence based Medicine*, 1(12), pp. 1–8, accessed 2005-08-05, http://www.jr2.ox.ac.uk/bandolier/painres/download/whatis/WhatisClinGov.pdf

Stewart, R. (2002) *Evidence based Management: A Practical Guide for Health Professionals* (Oxford: Radcliffe Medical Press).

Straus, S. E., and McAlister, F. A. (2000) 'Evidence based medicine: a commentary on common criticisms', *Canadian Medical Association Journal*, 163, p. 837.

Summers, A. (2003) 'Involving users in the development of mental health services: A study of psychiatrists' views', *Journal of Mental Health*, 12, pp. 161–74.

Tétrault, M. A. (1996) 'Deconstructing the other: teaching the politics of the Middle East', *Political Science and Politics*, 29, pp. 696–700.

Thomas, M. D., Blacksmith, J. A. and Reno, J. (2000) 'Pearls, pith, and provocation: utlizing insider-outsider research teams in qualitative research', *Qualitative Health Research*, 10, pp. 819–28.

Truman, C. and Raine, C. (2001) 'Involving users in evaluation: the social relations of user participation in health research', *Critical Public Health*, 11, pp. 215–29.

Truman, C. and Raine, P. (2002) 'Experience and meaning of user involvement: some explorations from a community mental health project', *Health and Social Care in the Community*, 10(3), pp. 136–43.

Turner, S. (2003) 'The Third Science War', *Social Studies of Science*, 33, pp. 581–611.

UK Department of Health (1997) *The New NHS: Modern, Dependable* (London: Department of Health).

UK Department of Health (1998) *A First Class Service: Quality in the New NHS* (London: Department of Health).

UK Department of Health (2000a) *The NHS Plan: A Plan for Investment, A Plan for Reform* (London: HMSO).

UK Department of Health (2000b) *An Organisation with a Memory: Report of an Expert Group on Learning from Adverse Events in the NHS*, chaired by the Chief Medical Officer (London: Department of Health).

UK Department of Health (2001) *Mental Health Information Strategy* (London: Department of Health).

UK Department of Health (2002) *National Service Framework for Older People: Supporting Implementation – Intermediate Care: Moving Forward* (London: Department of Health).

UK Department of Health and Social Services Inspectorate (1991) *Care Management and Assessment: Managers' Guide* (London: Social Services Inspectorate).

UK Department of Health, Health and Social Care Change Team (2003) *Defining a Whole Systems Approach* (London: Department of Health).

UK National Assembly for Wales (2001) *Assessment and Care Management for Adults: Developing the Single Assessment and Care Management System, including Fair*

*Access: Guidance for Local Authorities and Health Services*, consultation document (Cardiff: National Assembly for Wales).

UK NHS Executive (1999) *Clinical Governance: Quality in the New NHS* (Leeds: Department of Health).

UK NHS Management Executive (1998) *Information for Health: An Information Strategy for the Modern NHS 1998–2005, A National Strategy for Local Implementation* (Leeds: NHS ME).

UK Welsh Assembly Government (2002a) *Adult Mental Health Services: a National Service Framework for Wales* (Cardiff: Welsh Assembly Government).

UK Welsh Assembly Government (2002b) *When I'm 64 and More: The report from the Advisory Group on a Strategy for Older People in Wales* (Cardiff: Welsh Assembly Government).

University of York Centre for Reviews and Dissemination (2001) *Undertaking Systematic Reviews of Research on Effectiveness* (York: Centre for Reviews and Dissemination, University of York).

WAG – *see* UK Welsh Assembly Government.

World Health Organization (2003) *Technology Appraisal Programme of the National Institute for Clinical Excellence* (Geneva: WHO).

Wildavsky, A. (1964) *The Politics of the Budgetary Process* (Boston: Little Brown).

Wolpe, P. R. (1994) 'The dynamics of heresy in a profession', *Social Science & Medicine*, 39, pp. 1133–48.

Wray, S. J. (1994) 'Schizophrenia sufferers and their carers: a survey of understanding of the condition and its treatment, and of satisfaction with services', *Journal of Psychiatric and Mental health Nursing*, 1, pp. 115–23.

Wynne, B. (2003) 'Seasick on the Third Wave? Subverting the hegemony of propositionalism: response to Collins & Evans (2002)', *Social Studies of Science*, 33, pp. 401–17.

# 10

# Building Capacity for Evidence Based Management in Health Regions

*Judy Birdsell, Wilfred Zerbe, Petra O'Connell, Richard Thornley and Sarah Hayward*

## Background

The ability to create and use new knowledge is needed in all organizations to some degree. Organizational research capacity (ORC) refers to the creation of new knowledge and the use of extant research knowledge. For some organizations, including research centres and universities, the capacity to develop new knowledge is critical. For others, ORC represents a more subtle contribution to effectiveness. In this chapter we identify and examine the factors that contribute to ORC in organizations that primarily deliver health care services where the use of extant knowledge is important. ORC represents a framework for developing or introducing new ideas to increase efficiency or positive health outcomes. Because ORC is not a core requirement in most health service delivery organizations, understanding how to foster its development is a key question.

The purpose of this research was to develop a conceptual framework that could be used to understand the factors involved in the process of research utilization in health service delivery organizations and to use this framework to evaluate a provincial training program and make recommendations for future directions.

## The SEARCH program

This research took place in Canada, within Alberta's health system, and deals primarily with health regions. The Alberta Heritage Foundation for Medical Research (AHFMR), the provincial health research funding body, recognized the importance of organizational involvement in health research when it established the 'Swift Efficient Application of Research in Community Health' (SEARCH) program in 1996 as a 'partnership program to build capacity in the health system for producing and using research evidence to manage the health system'. SEARCH involves research funders, health authorities, universities and the health ministry, and provides an opportunity to develop local expertise for applied health research and evidence based decision making. Its purpose is to increase capacity to acquire, aggregate, interpret and apply health information for individual, regional and provincial health decisions and programs, and to facilitate more effective management of the health system. Despite the fact that most research knowledge must be used within organizational settings, there has been little emphasis on increasing our understanding of this process within the health system. To date, many of the approaches to knowledge transfer have focused on the individual behaviour of health providers in relation to health system problems.

## Research approach and findings

A focused literature review identified theoretical perspectives relating to organizational capacity for research including: (1) organizational learning/ learning organizations (Crossan et al., 1999; Hong, 1999; Marquardt, 1996; Senge, 1990); (2) innovation capacity (O'Connor and Rice, 2001); (3) absorptive capacity (Zahra and George, 2002); and, (4) knowledge management and transfer (Dougherty, 1999; Han, 2001; Hyde and Mitchell, 2000; Lee, 2000; Torjman et al., 2001). The literature also identified organizational culture and design enablers and barriers that influence organizational learning and knowledge management (Ahmed et al., 1999; Bate et al., 2000; Beeby and Booth, 2000; DeLong and Fahey, 2000; Elliot and O'Dell, 1999; Hong, 1999; Lee, 2000; Makri, 1999; Neufeld et al., 2001; Reigle, 2001; Tasi, 2001). However, none of these sources were in health care, nor did they provide a comprehensive framework or validated indicators and measures for the assessment of ORC in health service organizations. Since there was not an existing conceptual framework to use as a foundation to develop an assessment model, the literature was used as a guide to choose the areas of expertise that would contribute to an appropriate conceptual framework. This input from recognized experts in relevant areas was used to develop a model that would guide subsequent program evaluation design and data collection. A series of case studies was conducted to explore and refine the model. Finally, the resulting framework was used to help shape a telephone questionnaire to evaluate the SEARCH program. In the following sections each phase of the study and the results are described.

### Phase one: expert workshop: the development of a conceptual framework

Researchers with organizational disciplinary perspectives working in differing traditions and areas, plus expert practitioners, participated in a two-day workshop to begin developing the conceptual framework. They reached consensus that ORC could be provisionally defined as an organization's potential to acquire, assimilate, transform and exploit knowledge. They were influenced by work in 'absorptive capacity' (Zahra and George, 2002; Cohen and Levinthal, 1990).

Participants identified the levers, mechanisms and structures that management could use to influence ORC. They were divided into two similarly composed subgroups and asked to organize these elements into a coherent model, with liberty to add and subtract elements. It was decided that the two draft models would be used in developing a framework. These models were presented to the full group and then each subgroup refined the other group's model. The two models and brief explanatory comments are below.

The 'Box' model attempts to identify factors which can be tested for their contribution to the use of research:

- Factors both external and internal to the organization are deemed to contribute to research use.
- External factors include accreditation processes that look for evidence based decision making.
- Internal factors include expectations plus tangible features (highly educated staff, access to good library resources and so on).
- Moderating factors include the attitudes of senior management about research (that is, culture) and the clarity of the research knowledge.

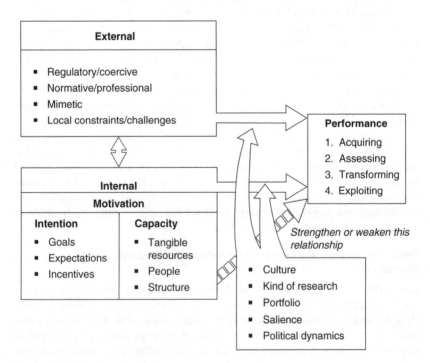

**Figure 10.1**  The 'box' model

An organization needs to focus on structure, culture, and
people to increase research capacity – in light of, and
perhaps shaping, the external context

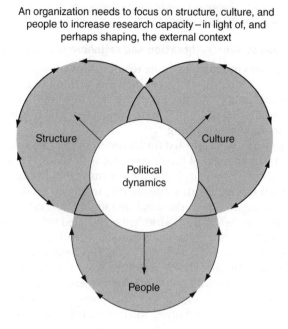

External environment

**Figure 10.2**   The 'circle' model

In the 'Circle' model, a similar set of factors contributing to research capacity were categorized into one of five interdependent groups:

(1) **Structure**, for example, official documentation, job descriptions with research in their mandate, incentives and logistics for sharing information.
(2) **Culture**, for example, valuing research and innovation, strong identity with a university.
(3) **People**, that is, aspects of individuals in the organization including leadership, skill sets and numbers with advanced education. Organizations can affect these three variables. Through these they may be able to shape the external environment, rather than adapt to it.
(4) **Political dynamics** overlay the above variables. This is where one acquires, assimilates, transforms and exploits new knowledge. Success results from good navigation in this area.
(5) The **external environment** is the backdrop within which the organization operates.

Although the two final models contain similar dynamics and comparable elements, participants indicated that it would be useful to retain both to inform subsequent research. Complete proceedings from the workshop are available elsewhere (Birdsell et al., 2002).

## Phase two: case studies: elaboration and refinement of the model

The next phase was intended to refine relationships among the categories in the models and to identify which components within categories were most salient to incorporating evidence based decision making. To do this, instrumental case studies (Stake, 1995) were conducted which were chosen for their ability to maximize learning.

Health authorities were selected for inclusion in the case studies based on two factors: (1) the strength of their experience with SEARCH (strong vs weak) and (2) their degree of research orientation (strong vs weak). Initially, one case in each cell was explored. Subsequently, to ensure good representation of regions of varying size, two additional case studies were carried out bringing the total to six. The health authorities were allocated into cells on the basis of expert input from five individuals familiar with health authorities and from five individuals familiar with the SEARCH program.

A key informant in each health region selected was asked to identify an area of recent action in which considering evidence had been part of the process. Subsequently, focus groups or interviews were conducted with key individuals who had been involved in the identified activity. The aims of the interviews were:

1. to learn about the organization's experience with the four major processes of knowledge acquisition, assimilation, transformation and exploitation; and
2. to learn how the organization's research related experience was shaped by the conceptual framework that incorporated people, structure, culture, political dynamics and the external environment.

The information gathering strategy included questions on: (1) the organization's motives for addressing the issue; (2) factors which influenced the approach taken; (3) experiences with gathering and using information; (4) decision making processes; and, (5) implementation of the planned course of action. Respondents were asked to think about an important process or decision that they had made recently where consideration of evidence had been part of the process.

Other questions were designed to assess aspects of the framework's key components:

- **Culture:** Did the values of the organization support or conflict with the approach? Did you have to justify your approach or was it assumed?
- **Politics:** What motivated you to use that approach? Was any special influence required?
- **Structure:** How was the approach supported? Was this formal or informal?

- **People**: To what extent was the skill and expertise available to support the approach used?
- **External environment**: What were the factors in the external environment that influenced your approach?

Notes were typed from all interviews and shared. Interviews were coded independently by two team members and a list of emerging categories was discussed and developed. Subsequently, all interviews were coded by one team member. Next, data elements from all six case studies were grouped together according to theme. Two team members independently extracted major themes then jointly developed a summary statement. Six themes were identified in the review of case studies: individual characteristics; resources; links and relationships; process; decision influences; and norms, beliefs and values. The following section is a summary of the highlights of each of these themes.

## (1) Individual characteristics

Certain personal attributes and activities were relevant in supporting action. They can be divided into two types: those that seemed to be solely the individual's attributes (for example, innovative, visionary manager, someone with initiative), and those influenced by the work situation (for example, underlying sense of implicit trust and faith by others in the individual, credibility of proponents of change). Individual characteristics, however, are only meaningful when considered in the context of other individuals or the situation; for example, leadership skills include understanding decision pathways in the organization and the ability to frame an issue so it becomes salient for senior management.

## (2) Resources

Resources were critical in two different ways:

(a) *as drivers*: financial incentives influenced the choice of areas for attention. If they were provided by an organization external to the health region this could be described as a 'resource pull'. In other cases, a lack of resources internally (for example, people, beds) were the drivers ('resource push').

(b) *as enablers*: in several cases, external organizations provided resources (for example, librarians at professional associations, travel funds) which enabled the use of evidence. Universities were not mentioned as enabling resources. Within larger regions, enhanced research capacity, such as staff with dedicated positions, specific research skills and content expertise, enabled concerted efforts toward incorporating evidence into decisions. In smaller regions, access to computers and the internet were important resources.

## (3)   Links and relationships

Links and relationships within the organization and with outsiders were important in all areas. Interestingly, the same organizations were often perceived as providing both helpful and unhelpful links, depending on the situation. When there was a personal relationship with a contact, the link was usually described as helpful. Other helpful external relationships involved formal or semi-formal groups or committees meeting to discuss issues of shared interest.

The most commonly mentioned organizations with whom relationships existed were other health authorities and individuals holding similar positions in other health authorities. Regions seemed most likely to seek information from regions with similar characteristics. Relationships with other community-based organizations were also frequently mentioned. Relationships with universities and AHFMR were mentioned less frequently and any positive implications were less evident unless they involved long-standing relationships between individuals.

In Alberta, although they are inextricably involved with decisions about patient care and health care delivery systems, most physicians are paid by a funding mechanism separate from the regional health authorities. Although they are generally formally 'outside' the health region, their actions influence many health care decisions. The relationships and links with physicians (both as individuals and often as practice groups in the community) were very important.

Links and relationships can be described as mediated and personal relationships. Mediated relationships involve networks which could be used for asking questions or professionals whose 'business' was information, such as librarians and booksellers. The reasons for these linkages included helping implement a change in some concrete way (instrumental) and assistance of a more conceptual nature. Instrumental linkages produced such things as policy manuals from other regions and reduction in duplication of efforts. Personal linkages were for reasons less directly linked to action, but potentially important nevertheless. For example, working with a profession to incorporate knowledge of certain tests into their training is expected to eventually produce action. In summary, linkages among individuals known to each other seem to be more helpful than more formal and impersonal relationships.

## (4)   Process

Processes which contribute to action are focusing on the issue, information gathering and implementation. Although they may occur progressively, there is not always a clear demarcation between them.

### (a)   Focusing on the issue

An issue must be on the agenda of key decision makers for action to occur. Several factors contributed to issues getting 'on the agenda'. These included:

- data (often collected internally, but sometimes from research done elsewhere)
- the action area addressed a strategic imperative
- broad ownership of the issue leading to higher salience for that issue
- appropriate framing so that the issue resonated with key decision makers
- good timing

### (b) Information gathering

The sources of information which were most highly valued by the smaller regions were from peer organizations, individuals with whom the person making the request had a personal relationship and on-line sources. Individuals had created their own methods of identifying legitimate sources of on-line information, such as using websites with .org or .edu extensions. Explicit use of organizational change knowledge had also been employed including the use of a change management model by one executive.

### (c) Implementation

This involved three subcomponents: *organizational structure, organizational routines* and *context*.

- In formal *organizational structures*, three dimensions seemed to contribute to action. First, clear roles and responsibilities enabled a change process to unfold in complex situations. Appropriate board or executive level committees provided a legitimate venue for raising issues and seeking support for action. In three of the larger regions, departments or individuals who focused on research and evaluation were instrumental in facilitating action.
- *Organizational routines* included interpersonal relationships, understanding the usual way of doing things in a specific setting and framing the action area so that it made sense to relevant decision makers. However, the most predominant routine discussed was that of participation. Region-wide initiatives involving large numbers of people assisted implementation. If the action involved few individuals, there were clear difficulties in widely implementing the action.
- Dimensions of the *context* within which action would occur either supported or created barriers to action. For example, senior management support and leadership actions were instrumental.

### (5) Decision influences

By studying situations where action had been taken, several themes emerged as indicated in Figure 10.3.

Some factors in the environment are distal to the decision and often impact all health regions or organizations in that community. For example, regulations regarding Alberta's mental health facilities influence care provided

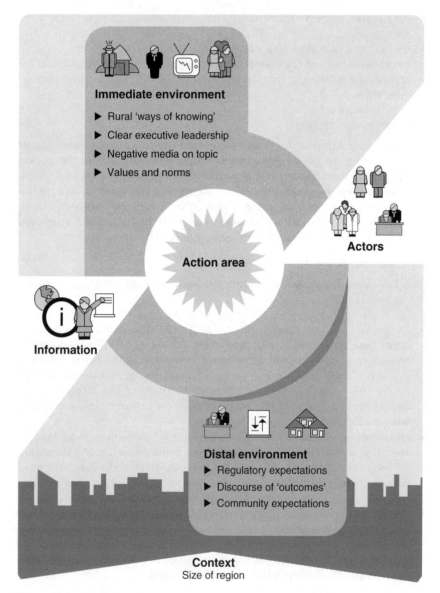

**Figure 10.3** Decision influences

for patients. Other factors are immediate to the decision zone. For example, a 'rural way of knowing' and clear executive leadership influence action.

Two elements, actors and information, seem to transcend 'distance' from the decision. Characteristics relating to the actors' individual attributes have already been discussed; personal attributes or those relating to a particular actor's group are also important. For example, rural physicians are a scarce resource so their involvement in any planned change is perhaps more salient than it may be in a large centre. Conversely, an action involving the large numbers of nurses in a region has the potential to influence an organization's culture.

In this analysis we are focusing on the potential impact of research evidence on decision making and service delivery. Thus it is important to examine the nature of information and how it is used to make decisions. Certain types and sources of information were valued highly, such as randomized control trials, specific websites and information from 'peer' organizations.

## (6)  Norms, beliefs and values

What individuals and organizations 'believe' about a situation powerfully influences action, although these beliefs are often difficult to clearly identify and articulate. Beliefs and values may operate on two intertwined, important levels: individual and organizational. Individual beliefs can be powerful adjuncts to change, but without the supportive environment of an organization which values and expects certain things, change may be difficult. It seems that when individual and organizational norms, values and interests are aligned, maximum progress can be achieved

The following beliefs and values were inherent in the cases examined:

- cost savings are important to regions (efficiency and cost benefit studies are important)
- operations (service delivery), education, and research and development need to be part of an integrated whole
- evaluation research is more important than knowledge development research
- the question of whether what is being done is good for the patient should be contemplated
- understanding and recognizing that effective service includes valuing the contributions and co-operation of others, including colleagues in the region and community agencies with overlapping or related mandates

An underlying theme emerges, indicating the importance of a region valuing research. When examining the presence and impact of research knowledge in the region, tension may be produced even in regions that deeply value research when they try to integrate research into operational settings. For example, even though potential significant cost savings realized from using research knowledge and support from the region was substantial, there were claims by some that operational funds were paying for research.

### Phase three: telephone survey: grounded program evaluation

The primary purpose of this survey was to evaluate the impact of the SEARCH program on participating organizations. In addition, the conceptual framework was further informed by this process. For example, participation in the SEARCH program produced an identifiable impact when projects were linked to areas of high importance to that organization.

Structured telephone interviews were conducted with individuals who were recommended as 'knowledgeable' about the region's involvement in SEARCH. Informants received the interview questions by electronic mail at least one week in advance of the telephone interview, which took approximately 50 minutes. On average, informants from the same health region agreed with respect to their overall assessments. The survey instrument comprised both open-ended questions and outcome measures. The questioning strategy was derived from evaluation questions identified in the Evaluation Framework (Blueprint) for the SEARCH program, input from the SEARCH Steering Committee and insights gained from the conceptual model work that preceded this survey. A more complete report of this program evaluation is available elsewhere (Birdsell and O'Connell, 2003).

## Key findings

There were three major components in the results: organizational impact, influence on organizational goals and factors predicting success of the SEARCH program in health regions.

### (1)  Organizational impact

The most immediate impact of the SEARCH program was to enhance resource development (human and research related funds) and improve access to information. SEARCH influenced the creation of positions with research/evaluation mandates and many of the regions were successful in acquiring new or additional funding based on proposals prepared or reviewed by SEARCH participants. Outcomes relating to priority health issue identification and influence on decision making depended on factors such as the participant's role in the organization, the salience of the SEARCH project to organizational priorities and an organizational culture that valued evidence based decision making. As anticipated, the greatest impact occurred in the community or public health sectors, which reflected where the SEARCH participants were employed and the types of projects undertaken.

### (2)  Organizational goals (related to participation in SEARCH)

Regions could not always clearly articulate their goals for participating in SEARCH or the nature of the benefit they hoped to realize through participation in the program. Despite this lack of clarity on what regions hoped to achieve through SEARCH participation, the majority of informants were satisfied with the contribution SEARCH made to their region. Those less satisfied tended to attribute this to a lack of purposeful engagement at the senior decision making level. Enhanced skills and knowledge gained by SEARCH participants and creation of unique networking opportunities were the two aspects most valued.

## (3) Success of SEARCH

From the program planning and delivery perspective, several factors seem to enhance success. For example:

- ensuring close involvement of executive staff in all aspects of the SEARCH program from recruitment to sharing results;
- targeting participants with roles in planning, information analysis and quality improvement;
- the alignment of the SEARCH projects with the priorities of the health region;
- the context within the health region including a culture of supporting evidence based decision making, organizations that have fewer competing opportunities for capacity building, the presence of a champion for the SEARCH program and infrastructure support for ongoing activities following completion of the SEARCH program;
- individual attributes of SEARCH participants including communication and educational skills and the ability to transform evidence into meaningful, relevant information.

## Building organizational research capacity: conceptual redux

The intent of this work was to develop a conceptual framework through which to consider organizational dimensions that may be important influences on the use of research evidence by those organizations. Figure 10.4 is the revised framework, which is based on the original two models developed, and modified using the case studies and the telephone survey. The components of this model can be summarized as follows:

- **Forces for action:** Those events or influences that cause the organization to 'attend to' a particular area.
- **Links and relationships with external individuals and organizations:** These were often the source of information. Personal relationships and mediated routes (for example, internet) are key.
- **Actors:** These can be individuals or 'groups' which influence action. Action is also more likely if senior managers, individuals with specific responsibilities for research or relevant areas, or individuals with excellent communication skills are involved.
- **Organizational structures and processes:** Those aspects of an organization that one can 'touch and feel'. Co-ordinating committees, research policies or expectations of senior executive are examples.
- **Information:** This is key to 'research transfer' as research results often materialize as information in some format. Information did not emerge as strongly as some other components, but given the particular focus of the model, it remains integral.

Forces for action                    Action area                    Links &
                                                                    relationships

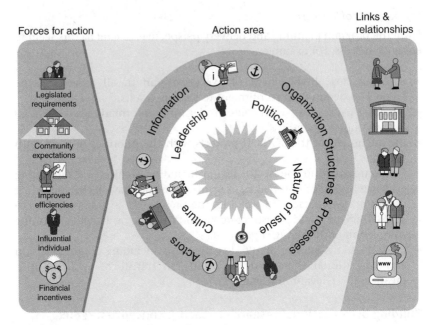

**Figure 10.4**   Organizational research capacity

- **Action area**: The focus of attention and where decisions are taken on a specific topic. It represents fluid and intangible dimensions; for example, organizational culture. Resources often come into play as 'enablers' in this area.
- **Leadership**: This is central to the action process. Leadership included clear executive leadership through business plans, putting the focal issue on the agendas of key committees and guiding participatory processes.
- **Politics**: Social relations involving authority are part of decision making processes in complex organizations. Politics are often intertwined with leadership dimensions and characteristics of various actors.
- **Nature of issue**: If the issue under scrutiny is tightly coupled with organizational priorities, effective action is more likely.

## Conclusion

Without a robust conceptual framework to apply to analyses of capacity for doing and using research in health organizations, efforts to build and evaluate such capacity are hampered. This study has developed, refined and applied such a framework in a province-wide context with diverse health care organizations.

The framework contributes to understanding how relevant research informs and aids operations and decisions to produce more positive outcomes. A generic model can be applied in varying settings to help assess, understand and plan both interventions and actions to increase the outcome of interest. It is anticipated that this model will be helpful in both general and specific ways.

## References

Ahmed, P., Loh, A. and Zairi, M. (1999) 'Cultures for continuous improvement and learning', *Total Quality Management*, 10(4/5), pp. S426–34.

Bate, P., Kahn, R. and Pyle, A. (2000) 'Culturally sensitive structuring: An action research-based approach to organization development and design', *Public Administration Quarterly*, 23(4), pp. 445–70.

Beeby, M. and Booth, C. (2000) 'Networks and inter-organizational learning: A critical review', *The Learning Organization*, 7(2), pp. 75–88.

Birdsell, J. and O'Connell, P. (2003) *The Impact of SEARCH on Participating Organizations: Evaluation Report* (Edmonton: Alberta Heritage Foundation for Medical Research. Technical Report).

Birdsell, J. M., Ginsburg, L., Golden-Biddle, K., Groeneveld, A., Langley, A., Underwood, J., Zahra, S. and Zerbe, W. (2002) *Assessing Organizational Research Capacity* (Edmonton, AB: Alberta Heritage Foundation for Medical Research).

Cohen, W. M. and Levinthal, D. A. (1990) 'Absorptive capacity: a new perspective on learning and innovation', *Administrative Science Quarterly*, 35, pp. 128–52.

Crossan, M., Lane, H. and White, R. (1999) 'An organizational learning framework: From intuition to institution', *Academy of Management Review*, 24(3), pp. 522–37.

DeLong, D. and Fahey, L. (2000) 'Diagnosing cultural barriers to knowledge management', *Academy of Management Executive*, 14(4), pp. 113–27.

Dougherty, V. (1999) 'Knowledge is about people, not databases', *Industrial and Commercial Training*, 31(7), pp. 262–6.

Elliot, S. and O'Dell, C. (1999) 'Sharing knowledge and best practices: the hows and whys of tapping your organization's hidden reservoirs of knowledge', *Health Forum Journal*, 42(3), pp. 34–7.

Han, F. (2001) 'Understanding knowledge management', *The Public Manager*, 30(2), pp. 34–5.

Hong, J. (1999) 'Structuring for organizational learning', *The Learning Organization*, 6(4), pp. 173–85.

Hyde, A. and Mitchell, K. (2000) 'Knowledge and management: the next big thing', *The Public Manager*, 29(2), pp. 57–60.

Lee, J. (2000) 'Knowledge management: the intellectual revolution', *IIE Solutions*, 32(10), pp. 34–7.

Makri, M. (1999) 'Exploring the dynamics of learning alliances', *Academy of Management Executive*, 13(3), pp. 113–14.

Marquardt, M. (1996) *Building the Learning Organization: A Systems Approach to Quantum Improvement and Global Success* (New York: McGraw-Hill).

Neufeld, G., Simeoni, A. and Taylor, M. (2001) 'High performance research organizations', *Research Technology Management*, 44(6), pp. 42–52.

O'Connor, G. and Rice, M. (2001) 'Opportunity recognition and breakthrough innovation in large established firms', *California Management Review*, 43(2), pp. 95–116.

Reigle, R. (2001) 'Measuring organic and mechanistic cultures', *Engineering Management Journal*, 13(4), pp. 3–8.

Senge, P. (1990) *The Fifth Discipline: The Art and Practice of the Learning Organization* (New York: Doubleday).

Stake, R. E. (1995) *The Art of Case Study Research* (Thousand Oaks, CA: SAGE).

Tasi, W. (2001) 'Knowledge transfer in intraorganizational networks: effects of network position and absorptive capacity on business unit innovation and performance', *Academy of Management Journal*, 44(5), pp. 996–1004.

Torjman, S., Leviten-Reid, E., Camp, C. and Makhoul, A. (2001) *From Information to Application: How Communities Learn* (Ottawa, ON: Caledon Institute of Social Policy).

Zahra, S. and George, G. (2002) 'Absorptive capacity: a review, reconceptualization, and extension', *Academy of Management Review*, 27(2), pp. 185–203.

# 11

# Pathways to Innovation in Health Care

*Sally Redfern, Fiona Ross, Susan McLaren and Sara Christian*

## Background

This chapter reports on a study commissioned by the UK National Health Service Executive to implement and evaluate an evidence based practice development program in the southeast of England (the STEP – South-Thames Evidence based Practice – projects). Each project related to a different clinical topic and was based in an NHS Trust and a university department operating in partnership. A project leader was appointed to each project. Each was evaluated locally and all were evaluated by an independent team.

In this chapter we present preliminary findings on the STEP projects' routes to innovation. The aim for this chapter is to investigate the process involved in implementing guidelines for change. The findings are discussed within a framework of organizational change and innovation based on Van de Ven et al.'s (1999) empirically-grounded theoretical model of 'the innovation journey'.

## An overview of contemporary literature

Achieving innovation in health care which can improve quality and outcomes for service users and health professionals is an integral component of clinical governance frameworks within the NHS (Department of Health, 1999). Despite advances made over the last decade, evidence based health care is in its early stages and is still practised in a health care system that is not evidence based (van Weel, 2003). Significant challenges therefore exist for management of change within the complex organizations of the NHS, added to which is the need to improve practice within the context of rapid organizational change and economic uncertainty (Iles and Sutherland, 2001).

Against this background of change and uncertainty, how can the pathway, or multiple pathways, to innovation in health care be managed? The early literature on organizational change presents the pathway to innovation as controllable, manageable, linear and predictable (King and Anderson, 2002). Stage models of change, which suggest a planned, rational sequence of steps to be followed within a linear process, represent this view. Examples include the 'unfreeze-change-freeze' stages based on force-field analysis (Lewin, 1951); the 'precede-proceed' model of Green and Kreuter (1980, 1991); and the six stages within the 'social marketing' model of Kotler (1984). Criticisms of stage models are that they oversimplify processes of organizational change, and are inflexible and complex (Ford and Walshe, 1994; Dunning et al., 1998; Perrin, 2002). Health care organizations with reasonably stable internal and external environments may be amenable to a relatively linear change process but unplanned, unanticipated events can disrupt this process (Ferlie and Shortell, 2001).

In contrast to the stage models are 'real world' iterative, dynamic, non-linear, contextual approaches, which emphasize cultural, macro- and micro-political factors within a context-process-content model of organizational change. The sum of previous decisions taken and policy outcomes, together with the need to consider complexity and contradiction created by individuals and groups as they encounter organizational change over time, are considered intrinsic to understanding change and formulating successful management strategies (Pettigrew et al., 1992). More recent conceptual analysis in the contextual area has differentiated receptive (favourable) from non-receptive (blocking) contexts for change which are dynamic. Receptive contexts are considered to be reversible if key individuals leading change are removed or if other events occur which exert a negative impact. Eight factors have been identified as influencing receptivity, including local policies, availability of key individuals leading change, intensity and scale of environmental pressures, organizational cultures, the nature of relationships between management and clinical staff, networks between organizations, clarity of priorities within the change agenda and its fit within the locale (Pettigrew et al., 2004). The empirically-grounded theoretical model of the 'innovation journey' proposed by Van de Ven et al. (1999) attempts to understand the process of organizational change in terms of a 'road map'. They refute the rational, linear, stage process of change. Instead, they suggest that, in complex, unstable organizations, the process of change is likely to follow a non-linear pattern of convergent and divergent activities with shocks, setbacks, loss of control and luck exerting an influence on the initiation, development and implementation processes.

Understanding the challenges and complexity inherent in changing practice of health professionals has been enhanced by findings of several empirical studies in the UK, notably Assisting Clinical Effectiveness (ACE, Miller et al., 1998), Promoting Action on Clinical Effectiveness (PACE, Dopson et al., 1999) and Framework for Appropriate Care Throughout Sheffield (FACTS, Eve et al., 1997). Findings from all three projects show that local ownership of the planned change is vital to success as is knowledge of the organizational culture and staff. Resources were also identified as intrinsic to supporting change in the PACE project. Rigorous adherence to a single model of change did not characterize the studies although the planning stages of PACE and FACTS drew on aspects of social marketing in meeting needs, perceptions and requirements of target groups, emphasizing that gaining agreement for change and meeting local priorities are vital for success.

In summary, more recent approaches to understanding and implementing change focus on analysis of pathways to innovation and the impact of setbacks and facilitators at different stages of the 'innovation journey'. This chapter explores the routes to innovation identified within the STEP projects by utilizing the Van de Ven model in an attempt to increase understanding of the process of change.

## Methods

Nine practice development projects each took a quasi-experimental approach, combining an element of action research (Meyer, 2001) to measure practice against evidence based standards before and after implementing change. The research included three components in the process of change that follow the framework of the Van de Ven model: initiation, development and implementation. The initiation phase was completed before, and the implementation and development phases after, receipt of funds awarded from 1997 to 2000.

## Initiation period: developing the partnership framework

This phase involved consultation with the commissioners and developing the strategy for recruiting NHS Trusts and designing a training program for the project leaders. All NHS Trusts in the region were invited to bid to take part. Of 31 applications, 24 Trusts were shortlisted, 21 attended for interview and nine were recruited.

At the time STEP started in the mid-1990s, the NHS was moving from an internal competitive market to an emphasis on quality, inclusivity and partnership. We applied Hudson et al.'s (1999) framework for collaboration to inform the development of our research and practice partnerships (Ross et al., 2001). The important themes for building partnerships were: assessing collaborative capacity across the organizations, articulating a clear purpose, ensuring wide organizational ownership, nurturing fragile relationships, and identifying collaborative, mutually beneficial outcomes for the NHS and university partners. A partnership agreement was established between each Trust and university centre. An academic leader/supervisor from the university and a clinical leader/manager in the Trust jointly managed each project.

Details of the projects in the nine centres are summarized in Table 11.1. The sample of practitioners consisted of nurses, midwives, therapists, doctors and

**Table 11.1** The nine projects

| Project | Centre | Clinical locality | Number of staff involved | Professional group |
|---|---|---|---|---|
| 1. Leg ulcer management | Community | Nursing services in one locality | 78 | Nurses |
| 2. Supporting breastfeeding women | Inpatient and community | Entire midwifery service | 119 | Midwives |
| 3. Management of pressure areas | Inpatient | A&E department | 36 | Nurses |
| 4. Nutritional support in acute stroke (nursing) | Inpatient | 12 wards | 81 | Nurses, therapists, doctors |
| 5. Nutritional management in acute stroke (dietetics) | Inpatient | 15 wards | 93 | Nurses, therapists, doctors |
| 6. Rehabilitation care options for stroke patients | Inpatient | 15 teams | 90 | Nurses, therapists, doctors |
| 7. Promotion of continence | Community | Entire nursing service | 71 | Nurses |
| 8. Multidisciplinary assessment of older people on discharge from hospital | Interface of inpatient and community | One ward | 7 | Nurses, therapists, doctors |
| 9. Family intervention for schizophrenia | Inpatient and community | Long-term intervention team | 14 | Health and social care workers |

social workers in the nine centres as indicated in the table. Each project was managed on a day-to-day basis by the project leader under the guidance of the clinical leader in the NHS Trust and the academic leader from the local participating university. Six of the nine project leaders were nurses and the others were a midwife, a dietician and a social worker. There were nine clinical leaders and six academic leaders (three had responsibility for two projects each).

## Developmental period

### Reviewing the evidence

Each project leader carried out a critical review of the available evidence on the selected clinical topic. In nursing, the lack of systematic reviews available to support evidence based practice is demonstrated by Thomas et al. (1999) who identified only 18 evaluations of clinical guideline implementation in nursing, midwifery and allied health professions that met Cochrane review criteria. In contrast, systematic reviews drawn largely from medical literature have identified good quality evidence to support practice (Grimshaw et al., 1995, 2001; University of York Centre for Reviews and Dissemination, 1999; Grol and Grimshaw, 2003). Use of clinical guidelines in conjunction with other methods of implementation, such as education of health professionals, opinion leadership, audit and feedback have been shown to maximize adherence by health professionals (University of York Centre for Reviews and Dissemination, 1999; Jamvedt et al., 2004). The importance of maximizing the potential impact of guideline adherence by health professionals through the incorporation of behavioural recommendations in their wording has been emphasized (Michie and Johnston, 2004).

### Contextual analysis

Contextual (also termed situational or diagnostic) analysis identifies organizational and external factors that can constrain or facilitate responsiveness to change (Pettigrew et al., 1992). Basing plans for change on analysis of barriers and facilitators has been identified as necessary for effective implementation of change (Grol and Grimshaw, 2003). Each project leader conducted a contextual analysis using a variety of methods including: documentary analysis, observation at meetings, group and individual interviews, staff questionnaires, and structured approaches (for example, force-field analysis, Lewin, 1951; assessment of work environment, Nolan et al., 1998; SWOT analysis: acronym for strengths, weaknesses, opportunities, threats).

### Implementation period

Projects used a multifaceted intervention approach combining three elements: evidence based guidelines; project leaders acting as change agents; and teaching staff to use the guidelines that were developed from the available evidence.

Each project leader was interviewed nine times by one of the evaluation team (SC), who interviewed them every three months to identify factors perceived as hindering (setbacks) or helping (facilitators) the change process and to follow up progress on previously identified factors. The academic and clinical leaders were each interviewed five times by SC for confirmatory evidence. The findings presented at this interim stage of the analysis are based on the first four interviews from the project leaders and the first three from the academic/clinical leaders and so address only the early periods in the process of change.

The procedure for analyzing the transcripts consisted of:

- coding setbacks and facilitators according to content and the categories of 'fluid participation of organizational personnel', 'top management', 'relationships with others' and 'infrastructure development' within the Van de Ven model;
- identifying evidence in clinical/academic leaders' transcripts that confirmed (or not) the project leaders' codes and calculating per cent agreement between them (rated arbitrarily as: <70%=low, 70–79%=medium, ≥80%=high agreement);
- ranking setbacks and facilitators according to number of agreements and deriving overall ranks across the nine projects, taking into account the number of projects ranked on each setback/facilitator, its median rank and range.

Combining the setbacks and facilitators, agreement on four projects (1, 4, 6, 7) by both academic and clinical leaders was high; for three projects (2, 5, 8) it was high by one leader and medium by the other; and for two projects (3, 9) it was medium for both. None scored low.

## Findings

### Initiation period

The initiation period was long and complex, and involved detailed negotiation. Funding was agreed at the end of the first year, which was followed by a further year of activity on negotiating access, finalizing design of the projects and conducting preliminary work (Box 11.1).

### Developmental period

Project leaders searched electronic databases, reports, consensus statements, standards and guidelines in publications of expert groups for evidence on their topics. For five projects, systematic reviews were available. For two, project leaders undertook a systematic review according to Cochrane criteria.

**Box 11.1**  Setting up the projects

| | |
|---|---|
| Dec 1995 | Meeting at NHS Regional Office. |
| Nov 1996 | Full proposal submitted following negotiations and development. |
| Jan–Mar 1997 | Recruitment of 9 NHS Trusts. |
| May 1997 | Workshop with Trusts, funders and researchers. |
| Mar–Dec 1997 | Academic leaders work with Trusts to define management arrangements, recruit project leaders, make site visits, establish steering groups, design studies, scope the interventions, establish Trust networks and facilities for project leaders. |
| May–July 1997 | Independent evaluation team negotiates ethical clearance. |
| May–Sep 1997 | Evaluation team conducts site visits. |
| Dec 1997 | Project leaders start with 2-week training on: orientation to Trusts and universities; aims, methods and timetable for projects; skills in critical appraisal of guidelines, research design, change management and presentation. |

The contextual analyses found predominant barriers to be: constraints in staff resources in seven centres (low numbers, high workloads, time pressures); organizational restructuring in three (local Trust mergers, national services integration); and problem teamwork in two. In contrast, facilitators identified in four centres included existence of established support services, systems and skilled personnel.

### Implementation period

#### Teaching frontline staff

All the projects used formal teaching sessions, such as interprofessional workshops. Most (7 of 9) also used informal methods such as clinical visits and discussion in guideline development groups. Dissemination approaches included newsletters, Trust briefings and steering groups.

#### Setbacks and facilitators described by project leaders

Table 11.2 lists the setbacks and facilitators identified in the early stages for the nine projects and overall rank. Each setback/facilitator belongs to one of four categories: colleague relations, leadership/management, organizational resources, project progress and workload. 'Frontline staff' is the first-ranked setback and also the first-ranked facilitator. As a setback, project leaders described some staff as resistant to the changes being introduced, confused

**Table 11.2** Setbacks and facilitators identified by project leaders

| Setbacks | Overall rank | No. of projects ranked | Median rank | Rank range | Facilitators | Overall rank | No. of projects ranked | Median rank | Rank range |
|---|---|---|---|---|---|---|---|---|---|
| **Problems with:** | | | | | **Helpful:** | | | | |
| **Colleague relations** | | | | | **Colleague relations** | | | | |
| Frontline staff | 1 | 9 | 1 | 1–3 | Frontline staff | 1 | 8 | 1.5 | 1–5 |
| Medical staff | 5 | 7 | 5 | 2–7 | Other project leaders | 6 | 8 | 7 | 6–10 |
| Other project leaders | 8 | 5 | 6 | 2–7 | Therapists/clinical specialists | 7 | 6 | 4.5 | 3–7 |
| Therapists/clinical specialists | 12 | 2 | – | 5, 7 | Medical staff | 10 | 4 | 5.5 | 1–7 |
| | | | | | Home partner | 12 | 2 | – | 7, 10 |
| **Leadership/management** | | | | | **Leadership/management** | | | | |
| Trust middle management | 4 | 7 | 4 | 2–6 | Trust middle management | 2 | 9 | 2 | 1–5 |
| Academic leader | 7 | 5 | 4 | 2–5 | Academic leader | 3 | 8 | 3 | 1–5 |
| | | | | | Top trust management | 4 | 7 | 2 | 1–4 |
| **Organizational resources** | | | | | **Organizational resources** | | | | |
| Resource availability | 3 | 8 | 3.5 | 2–7 | Resource availability | 5 | 9 | 6 | 1–9 |
| Organizational disruption | 9 | 4 | 4 | 1–7 | Trust environment | 11 | 3 | 6 | 4–8 |
| **Project workload** | | | | | **Project workload** | | | | |
| Work overload and project progress | 2 | 8 | 1 | 1–4 | Own personal qualities | 8 | 5 | 6 | 3–7 |
| Personal inadequacies | 6 | 7 | 6 | 5–10 | Project leader training program | 9 | 5 | 7 | 5–10 |
| Home-work imbalance | 10 | 3 | 8 | 7–9 | | | | | |
| Duplication of projects | 11 | 2 | – | 1, 7 | | | | | |

about the project or threatened by it. Project leaders found it difficult to get access because staff were too busy, low in morale or preoccupied with organizational upheaval. Other frontline staff, on the other hand, facilitated the project by being enthusiastic, helpful, resourceful and keen to be involved. Leadership and management issues featured as setbacks (rank 4 and 7) but were ranked higher as facilitators (rank 2, 3 and 4). As setbacks, some middle managers were described as being inaccessible or threatened by the potential of any negative findings. In two centres, the project leader described loss of a supportive clinical leader who was replaced by less committed managers. Other project leaders, on the other hand, reported middle managers to be accessible, welcoming, supportive, enthusiastic and influential in overcoming hurdles. The same was reported for top managers of the Trusts who gave the projects a high profile throughout the Trust.

The academic leader was ranked 3 as a facilitator and 7 as a setback. Setbacks referred to inaccessibility and busyness, or the academic leader having expectations about the project that the project leader thought unrealistic. Facilitative academic leaders were described as accessible, supportive, resourceful and stepping in to deal with crises.

Resources available for the projects featured high (rank 3) as a setback in eight projects, though all the project leaders also described certain resources as facilitators (rank 5). Prominent in the list of resource setbacks was lack of, or inadequate, office space, computer/email/internet facilities, secretarial support, library services or funds for essential running costs such as stationery, postage, travelling expenses, staff training and equipment.

Medical staff featured more prominently as a setback (rank 5) than as a facilitator (rank 10). Some doctors were described as being inaccessible or lacking in commitment to the project. Others showed their scepticism through resistance or obstructiveness. One project leader described her success in 'taming' a powerful 'old school' medical consultant who, she said, expected to take control of her project. She tamed him, she said, by treading carefully, using her charm and impressing him with her medical knowledge. She described the outcome as a complete reversal in the consultant's behaviour; he became so enthusiastic and involved in the project that junior doctors soon followed his lead.

Work overload and difficulty in keeping to deadlines emerged as the second-ranked setback. Perceived personal inadequacies identified were lack of confidence, feeling incompetent in comparison with other project leaders and having to cope with isolation and 'outsider' status. Personal qualities described as facilitative included personal drive, ability to cope under pressure, self-confidence and previous experience.

## Trend over time of setbacks

Table 11.3 summarizes the trend over time in the early phases for each project of the top five setbacks. By concentrating on trends in setbacks,

**Table 11.3**  Linearity of the top five setbacks

| Project | Frontline staff (1ˢᵗ) | Workload (2ⁿᵈ) | Resources (3ʳᵈ) | Middle management (4ᵗʰ) | Medical staff (5ᵗʰ) | L:NL |
|---|---|---|---|---|---|---|
| 9 | NL | n/a | NL | NL | NL | 0:4 |
| 2 | NL | NL | NL | L | NL | 1:4 |
| 4 | NL | NL | NL | NL | L | 1:4 |
| 5 | NL | NL | NL | L | NL | 1:4 |
| 8 | L | NL | NL | NL | NL | 1:4 |
| 7 | L | NL | NL | NL | n/a | 1:3 |
| 1 | L | NL | NL | L | NL | 2:3 |
| 6 | L | NL | L | NL | L | 3:2 |
| 3 | NL | L | L | L | L | 4:1 |

L = linear, NL = non-linear.
*Note*: Linearity was determined by analyzing setbacks and facilitators. A linear classification indicates that the change was unidirectional and progressive. A non-linear classification indicates the occurrence of divergent and convergent activities.
n/a = not applicable (that is, not mentioned in this centre).

rather than those of facilitators too, the analysis demonstrated the process of successful (or unsuccessful) innovation. A setback could, for example, become a facilitator after a period of problem-solving and resolution.

A linear classification indicates that the change was unidirectional and progressive. A non-linear classification indicates the occurrence of divergent and convergent activities. Interpretation of the trend as linear or non-linear was estimated from project leaders' comments about each setback over the four interviews together with any facilitators they identified that were relevant to the setback. The following excerpts from summaries of two project leaders' comments on medical staff support illustrate our interpretation of a trend as linear or non-linear:

*Indication of a linear trend*: Some medical consultants were threatened by the project. One refused to cooperate during the first six months of the project. By the third interview, at seven months, medical staff were consistently no longer viewed as a setback because a very supportive and involved medical consultant had replaced the obstructive predecessor and continued to give the project support for the remainder of its life.

*Indication of a non-linear trend*: Initially accessing junior doctors was difficult. The project leader reported obstruction from a medical consultant who argued that any introduction of change should be entirely a medical responsibility. The project leader reported success in changing his mind – within three months he had become involved and cooperative. By the third interview, at seven months, junior doctors were refusing to sign up for multiprofessional training sessions with nurses and therapists. By the fourth interview, the doctors were co-operating and had become positive and involved in the project.

Differences emerged in the classification of the nine projects as following a linear or non-linear trend for each setback. For frontline staff, four projects (1, 6, 7, 8) were classified as linear and five (2, 3, 4, 5, 9) as non-linear. For workload, the trend for seven projects was non-linear and linear for just one (3). Workload was not raised as a setback in project 9. For resources, two projects (3, 6) emerged as linear and the other seven as non-linear. For middle management in the Trusts, four projects (1, 2, 3, 5) were linear and five non-linear, and for medical staff, three (3, 4, 6) were linear and five non-linear (not raised as a setback by project 7).

The last column in Table 11.3 shows the linear:non-linear ratio of these five setbacks for each project. The first five projects (9, 2, 4, 5, 8) show the trend in their process of change to follow a predominantly non-linear path, whereas two projects (6, 3) take a more linear path. Projects 7 and 1 fall in between these two groups with a tendency towards non-linearity.

In the next section, project 8 is presented as a brief case study of the process of change in the early phases of the project. The case study illustrates the detailed level of information that was gained about complex change processes.

## Case study: project 8

The aim of this project was to develop and implement evidence based guidelines on multidisciplinary health and social needs assessment for older people. Unusually, this project was managed by the community NHS Trust, but the project leader was based in a hospital ward for older people, resulting in a complex partnership that also included the university. Figure 11.1 summarizes impacts on the process of change in its early phases according to the Van de Ven model.

The unfunded initiation period leading to appointment of the project leader focused on building partnership relationships and conducting feasibility work. The 'shock' that contributed to receptivity of the organizations to participate was a critical report of discharge arrangements for older people carried out by the local community health council.

The contextual analysis carried out in the developmental period (staff interviews and a SWOT analysis) identified anxieties about workload and challenges to existing professional roles and practice, while perceived benefits were seen to be time saving, reducing duplication and improving the quality of information and teamwork. Interviews with the project leader in the early implementation phase revealed that, in contrast to the majority of projects where frontline staff was the first-ranked setback, perceptions of work overload and inadequate resources emerged as the most dominant

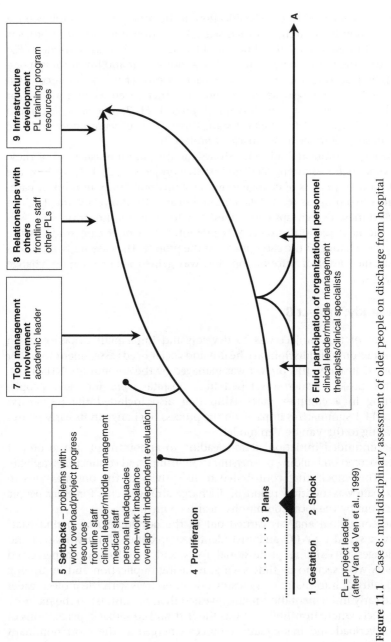

**Figure 11.1** Case 8: multidisciplinary assessment of older people on discharge from hospital

**5 Setbacks** – problems with:
work overload/project progress
resources
frontline staff
clinical leader/middle management
medical staff
personal inadequacies
home–work imbalance
overlap with independent evaluation

**7 Top management involvement**
academic leader

**8 Relationships with others**
frontline staff
other PLs

**9 Infrastructure development**
PL training program
resources

**6 Fluid participation of organizational personnel**
clinical leader/middle management
therapists/clinical specialists

**4 Proliferation**

1 Gestation    2 Shock    · · · · · · 3 Plans

PL = project leader
(after Van de Ven et al., 1999)

A

setback for this project leader. This may have reflected the pressure of working with hospital and community staff as well as the need to juggle competing priorities of leading change and meeting the milestones expected in the project. This setback did not have a corresponding facilitator.

Developing multidisciplinary guidelines requires clinical staff to abandon individual systems which, in the context of a busy ward for older people with nursing shortages, was challenging for the project leader. Perhaps not surprisingly, frontline staff were identified as a major setback because they were busy and working under pressure. However, this setback was balanced in the project leader's view by the role of the ward sister and geriatrician who were resourceful, helpful and keen to enhance the ward profile through its role in the project. Management support was perceived as variable in that the community manager was supportive and accessible, unlike the hospital manager who was more remote. Other issues seen to be setbacks were anxieties about personal capacity and managing demands of work with those of home.

Although this case study draws only on interview data from the development and early implementation phases, the pathway of change shows a non-linear pattern. Conclusions reached so far suggest that the leadership skills of the project leader were crucial to overcoming setbacks and managing the emotional, interpersonal and organizational challenges of unpredictable change.

## Discussion and conclusions

The STEP program described here investigated the process of change in nine practice development projects introduced by change agents (project leaders). In contrast to other empirical studies in the UK (ACE, Miller et al., 1998; PACE, Dopson et al., 1999; FACTS, Eve et al., 1997), unique features of STEP were standardization in a quasi-experimental study design across projects together with contextual analysis, process measurement and independent evaluation (and outcome evaluation not reported here). The focus on the process of change provides some understanding of the initial journey of innovation from initiation of the projects, through development of guidelines for change, to implementation of the guidelines.

The time it takes to set up practice development projects and forge productive partnerships in complex NHS organizations is amply illustrated by the protracted initiation period which required two years of negotiation for securing funding and establishing university-NHS Trust partnerships, followed by an intensive two-week training course to prepare project leaders for the work ahead. This time investment in initiation is justified in Hudson's model of collaboration, which recognizes the time needed to establish a legitimate basis for partnership (Hudson et al., 1999). During the developmental period, project leaders had to review available research literature on their clinical topic, a task that took much longer for those whose topic had no published systematic review to draw on in support of evidence based practice. Also, the contextual analysis gave project leaders an understanding of the culture of their organization and its readiness for change; an approach recognized as necessary for effective implementation of change (Grol and Grimshaw, 2003).

The implementation period was extremely intensive for the project leaders. They developed evidence based guidelines with colleagues, ran teaching sessions for staff on how to use the guidelines, and facilitated the changes in practice by supervising and guiding staff. The emergence for most projects of frontline staff as the most important setback and facilitator is understandable, given the variability among overworked NHS staff in their willingness to be committed, helpful and open to the need for change. Four of the top five setbacks (frontline staff, resource availability, clinical leader/middle management and medical staff) identified in the early phases featured also as facilitators, three of which were in the top five.

The weight of evidence supporting the process of change as following a non-linear rather than a linear route in complex organizations is supported by the preliminary findings in most of these projects. Non-linearity features to the greatest extent in five projects and to a lesser extent in two. Two projects demonstrated more of a linear trend.

The facilitators that emerged as important support previous research that identifies essential levers for successful change in health care practice to be organizational commitment, active support from key stakeholders, recognition of the importance of change, a credible change agent who has direct contact with practitioners, and ownership of the innovation vested in the target workers (Bircumshaw, 1990; Dunning et al., 1998; Kitson et al., 1996; Miller et al., 1998; Wood et al., 1998; Dopson et al., 1999). The important facilitators in the STEP program related to colleague relations, leadership and management, and organizational resources. The project leaders were credible and committed change agents who worked tirelessly with frontline staff to ensure their involvement and co-operation. Other key stakeholders were medical and therapy colleagues, and managers/leaders who provided resources, promoted collaborations and took action to overcome obstacles. Ownership of the innovation by frontline staff was more likely to occur when staff were immersed in what was happening right from the start.

The STEP program involved development as well as research activity in real-world organizations which left us sometimes having to compromise on methodological rigour. The information collected on setbacks and facilitators during the process of change relied on interviews from project leaders who may have been selective in what they recalled or revealed. The interviews with academic and clinical leaders validated the project leaders' accounts but they too could have been selective. Also, the interviews with project leaders reported here all occurred during the development phase and very early stages of implementation. Later interviews, not reported here, may provide a different perspective. Therefore, the conclusions we have drawn on linearity of trend need confirmation.

Implications of this research for policy and health care practice are:

- Implementing change requires financial resource and management support at all levels (that is, frontline, managerial and strategic) in the organization.
- Change agents need credibility and status to work effectively with frontline workers and all key stakeholders to initiate change.
- Change agents need support structures such as academic and clinical leadership, access to organizational information and resources, opportunity for educational and personal development, and peer support to overcome feelings of isolation.
- Change in clinical practice is constrained by organizational instability due to events such as staff changes and new policy targets.

Five years in the life of complex, dynamic, unstable NHS organizations provide an important glimpse of the processes involved in initiating, changing and evaluating practice. It is for this reason that contextual approaches to the study of change suggest that investigation should be longitudinal over substantial time and address the temporal interconnection of events which make an impact on the organization (Pettigrew et al., 1992). The Van de Ven 'road map' of the typical innovation journey is emerging as an appropriate model for the STEP projects. The findings support the journey outlined in the model showing the process of change in these complex, unstable organizations as following, in most cases, a dynamic, non-linear pattern of divergent and convergent activities.

## References

Bircumshaw, D. (1990) 'The utilization of research findings in clinical nursing practice', *Journal of Advanced Nursing*, 15(11), pp. 1272–80.

Department of Health – *see* UK Department of Health.

Dopson, S., Gabbay, J., Locock, L. and Chambers, D. (1999) *Evaluation of PACE Programme*. Final Report (Oxford: Oxford Healthcare Management Institute, Oxford and Wessex Institute for Health Research and Development, University of Southampton, Southampton).

Dunning, M., Abi-Aad, G. and Gilbert, D. (1998) *Turning Evidence into Everyday Practice* (London: Kings Fund).

Eve, R., Golton, I. and Hodgkin, P. (1997) *Learning from FACTS: Lessons from the Framework for Appropriate Care throughout Sheffield* (Sheffield: University of Sheffield Publications).

Ferlie, E. B. and Shortell, S. M. (2001) 'Improving the quality of healthcare in the United Kingdom and the United States: a framework for change', *Milbank Quarterly*, 79(2), pp. 281–315.

Ford, P. and Walshe, M. (1994) *New Rituals for Old: Nursing through the Looking Glass* (Oxford: Butterworth–Heinemann).

Green, L. W. and Kreuter, M. W. (1991) *Health Promotion Planning: An Educational and Environmental Approach* (London: Mayfield).

Green, L. W., Kreuter, M. W. and Deeds, S. G. (1980) *Health Education Planning: A Diagnostic Approach* (California: Mayfield).

Grimshaw, J., Freemantle, N. and Wallace, S. (1995) 'Developing and implementing clinical guidelines', *Quality in Healthcare*, 4, pp. 55–64.

Grimshaw, J. M., Shirran, R., Thomas, R. et al. (2001) 'Changing provider behaviour: an overview of systematic reviews of interventions', *Medical Care*, 39(Supplement 2), pp. 2–45.

Grol, R. and Grimshaw, J. (2003) 'From best evidence to best practice: effective implementation of change in patients' care', *Lancet* 362(9391), pp. 1225–30.

Hudson, B., Hardy, B., Henwood, M. et al. (1999) 'In pursuit of inter-agency collaboration in the public sector', *Public Management*, 1(2), pp. 235–60.

Iles, V. and Sutherland, K. (2001) *Organisational Change: A Review for Healthcare Managers, Professionals and Researchers* (London: National Co-ordinating Centre for NHS Service Delivery and Organisation R&D, London School of Hygiene and Tropical Medicine).

Jamvedt, G., Young, G. M., Kristoffersen, D. T., Thomson-O'Brien, M. A. and Oxman, A. D. (2004) 'Audit and Feedback: effects on professional practice and healthcare outcomes', *The Cochrane Library*, 4.

King, N. and Anderson, N. (2002) *Managing Innovation and Change: A Critical Guide for Organisations* (London: Thomson).

Kitson, A., Ahmed, L., Harvey, G. and Seers, K. (1996) 'From research to practice: one organisational model for promoting research-based practice', *Journal of Advanced Nursing*, 23, pp. 430–40.

Kotler, P. (1984) 'Social marketing of health behaviour', in L. W. Fredericksen, I. J. Solomon and K. A. Brehoney (eds), *Marketing Health Behavior: Principles, Techniques and Applications* (New York: Plenum Press).

Lewin, K. (1951) *Field Theory in the Social Sciences* (New York: Harper).

Meyer, J. (2001) 'Action research', in N. Fulop, P. Allen, A. Clarke and N. Black (eds), *Studying the Organisation and Delivery of Health Services: Research Methods* (London: Routledge).

Michie, S. and Johnston, M. (2004) 'Changing clinical behaviour by making guidelines more specific', *British Medical Journal*, 328, pp. 343–5.

Miller, C., Scholes, J. and Freeman, P. (1998) *Evaluation of the 'Assisting Clinical Effectiveness' Programme* (Brighton: Centre for Nursing and Midwifery Research, University of Brighton).

Nolan, M., Grant, G., Bown, J. and Nolan, J. (1998) 'Assessing nurses' work environment: old dilemmas, new solutions', *Clinical Effectiveness in Nursing*, 2, pp. 145–56.

Perrin, B. (2002) 'How to and how not to evaluate innovation', *Evaluation*, 8(1), pp. 13–28.

Pettigrew, A., Ferlie, E. and McKee, L. (1992) *Shaping Strategic Change* (London: Sage).

Pettigrew, A., Ferlie, E. and McKee, L. (2004) 'Receptive and non-receptive contexts for change', in A. Clarke, P. Allen, S. Anderson, N. Black and N. Fulop (eds), *Studying the Organisation and Delivery of Health Services* (London: Routledge).

Ross, F., McLaren, S., Redfern, S. and Warwick, C. (2001) 'Partnerships for changing practice: lessons from the South Thames Evidence based Practice project (STEP)', *NT research*, 6(5), pp. 817–28.

Thomas, L. H., McColl, E., Cullum, N., Rousseau, N. and Soutter, J. (1999) 'Clinical guidelines in nursing, midwifery and the therapies: a systematic review', *Journal of Advanced Nursing*, 30(1), pp. 40–50.

UK Department of Health (1999) *A First Class Service: Quality in the New NHS* (London: HMSO).

University of York Centre for Reviews and Dissemination (1999) 'Getting evidence into practice', *Effective Healthcare Bulletin*, 5(1), pp. 1–16.

Van de Ven, A., Polley, D., Garud, R. and Venkataraman, S. (1999) *The Innovation Journey* (New York: Oxford University Press).

van Weel, C. (2003) 'Translating research into practice: commentary', *Lancet*, 362(9391), p. 1224.

Wood, M., Ferlie, E. and Fitzgerald, L. (1998) *Achieving Change in Clinical Practice: Scientific, Organisational and Behavioural Processes* (Warwick, England: Centre for Corporate Strategy and Change, Warwick Business School, University of Warwick).

# 12
# Is Evidence Based Organizational Innovation a Delusion?

*Rod Sheaff, Susan Pickard and Bernard Dowling*

## Introduction

'Evidence basing' the choice of organizational innovations is becoming a new public management orthodoxy (Landry et al., 2001; Schwartz and Rosen, 2004) under such rubrics as 'evidence based policy', 'evidence based management', 'evidence based purchasing' (of services) and 'evidence based healthcare' (Muir-Gray,1997; Lohr et al., 1998). It is common to hear doctors argue that managers can hardly advocate evidence based medicine when managers and policy makers are not doing likewise (Muir-Gray, 1997, p. 57). Evidence basing health policy and management directly rebuts such complaints. However, health sector evidence from England gives reasons to wonder whether this goal of evidence basing decisions about organizational innovation may at times be a delusion. This chapter identifies some of the challenges to evidence based organizational innovations. It then explores the evidence related to organizational innovation in nine English NHS primary care trusts and uses a 'realist' concept of ideology to understand what kinds of organizational innovation are occurring.

## Background

One reason for evidence basing is to identify which policies are likely, as UK government rhetoric puts it, 'to work'. In particular, evidence basing can identify innovations which are bound to fail because they rest on a false 'program theory'; that is, the theory implicit in every policy about what actions are necessary and sufficient to achieve the policy's ends. For example, the UK recently attempted to apply a policy for managed care of frail elderly patients believing that as in America (Kane and Huck, 2000) this would reduce unplanned hospital admissions by up to a half. However, the program theory for that policy was soon shown to rest on two dubious assumptions: first, that the alternatives to hospital care which the US study presupposed also existed in England; and, second, that the criterion of two unplanned admissions in the past year was a good predictor of future unplanned admissions (Roland et al., 2005). Since the 1970s many governments have promoted evidence based medicine (EBM) partly as a means of cost containment, partly as a means of de-politicizing awkward 'rationing' decisions (Hunter, 1995), and partly as a means of integrating medical decision makers more closely into general (lay) health management (Harrison, 2002).

In health services, organizational innovations can be defined as the implementation of new ways of organizing health care; that is, new divisions of labour, governance regimes, organizational structures, incentive systems, property rights and managerial techniques. So defined, organizational innovations include new clinical technologies insofar as the latter are used for organizational rather than purely therapeutic purposes (for example, when outcome indicators such as severity indicators are used for rationing purposes besides clinical management purposes). Attempts to base organizational innovations on evidence rely upon two explicit analogies with EBM:

1. Evidence basing assists public sector managers in legitimizing and therefore implementing innovations (Ferlie et al., 2002), including organizational innovations.
2. Suitably adapted, methods of evidence basing can validly be transposed from the clinical into the organizational sphere.

However, the second assumption has been challenged on technical, methodological and theoretical grounds.

The technical challenge is that the methodological problems of evidence basing are more complex and acute for organizational than for clinical innovations (Lohr et al., 1998; Lilford et al., 2003) especially in regard to research design. Quantitative organizational research tends to consist of cross-sectional analyses. Experimental studies are rare and randomized control trials almost unheard of (Sheaff et al., 2004). Surrogates for these methods are hard to design and execute well. A more radical methodological challenge is that social sciences research investigates conscious human actions not natural processes. Since social research records the beliefs, motivations and actions through which organizational innovations occur and produce their effects, it is hardly surprising that the published evidence about the effectiveness of organizational innovations is mostly case study or other qualitative reports. Although methods for combining evidence from multiple qualitative studies (Boulton and Fitzpatrick, 1997; Tranfield et al., 2003) remain underdeveloped, there is no reason to think these deficiencies are insurmountable in principle. Nevertheless, both these challenges allow that, although it is difficult to do and good examples are scarce, the evidence basing of organizational innovations is possible in principle.

The third challenge is more fundamental. Many organizational innovations; the choice of descriptions and explanation of them; and the social theory and definitions of 'evidence' which underlie these descriptions are often contested. This is most visible in such controversial innovations as the 'marketization' of health services, but also in more modest innovations especially when the innovation reduces the income or power of an individual worker, organization or occupational group. Then managers or policy makers face a substantial problem in persuading others to comply with the innovation. In doing so, they often deploy not only technical knowledge but ideology in the sense of an integrated, comprehensive belief system. This belief system encompasses a substantial normative component with functions that include the justification of particular social relationships, governance structures and/or policy decisions.

Concepts and theories of ideology are no less contested than organizational innovations and health policy themselves, and these debates have generated a large literature. One way to differentiate theories of ideology is by how sharp a conflict they perceive between the normative task of legitimizing organizational innovations and the scientific task of evidence basing technical evaluations of (the same) innovations. At one pole, sociological concepts of ideology from de Tracy to Mannheim (1936) to Durkheim, and via Weber's (1946) accounts of 'legitimacy', to more recent writers such as Chiapello and Fairclough (2002) essentially define ideology as a belief system whose contents essentially reflect or express the social circumstances and hence normative standpoints of the authors who originated it. Since all belief systems have a particular social origin, all are therefore normatively coloured and so it follows that a purely objective discourse is unattainable, including a purely objective description and evaluation of organizational innovations. Thus Durkheim (1982), for instance, defines ideology as the use of 'a priori' concepts to order and select evidence. However, this view is less challenging to the idea of organizational evidence basing than might first appear. For what applies to organizational ideologies also applies to the 'paradigms' of natural science, each of which also has its own particular social origin and normative character (Kuhn, 1970). Accordingly, the social origins of ideology pose in principle no greater (or smaller) a problem for the evidence basing of organizational innovations than they do for evidence basing in, say, biology. Evaluators of organizational innovations can minimize the risks to objectivity by deliberately making their evaluations as value free as they can, seeking a 'perspective which gives evidence of the greatest comprehensiveness and the greatest fruitfulness in dealing with empirical materials' (Mannheim, 1936, p. 271).

The more trenchant challenge comes from the opposite pole. Realist concepts of ideology (for example, Connelly, 2000) disagree that purely evidence based social science is unattainable just because theories and researchers are bound to have some particular social origin. Objectivity is attainable in the sciences and indeed it is what empirical research establishes (or refutes). The realists, however, are more pessimistic about what damage normative beliefs can do to evidence basing. The realists agree with the viewpoint outlined above that ideology and science alike have a normative component. However, the realists differ by arguing that, in a science, the normative component is limited to methodological rules specifying how to produce empirically valid knowledge of causal relationships. In ideologies, the normative component is utterly different. It is a prior requirement to justify particular social structures, policies or (in the present case) organizational innovations, on the basis of evidence if possible but, if not, irrespective of evidence. Consequently,

ideology, as a system of representations, is distinguished from science in that in it the practico-social function is more important than the theoretical function (function as knowledge). (Althusser, 1969, p. 231)

Given this view, the main barrier to evidence basing organizational innovations is not the truism that knowledge is a human and a social product. The barrier arises when the dominant motive for evaluating an organizational innovation is to legitimize a particular policy or the interests of, say, a particular occupational group or political faction; and when the only way to do this is to ignore or elide parts of the evidence about the innovation's actual or intended effects on other people (Schwartz and Rosen, 2004). In health systems, this is more likely to occur in organizational than technical evaluations (Lavis et al., 2002; Schwartz and Rosen, 2004).

A realist concept of ideology implies that, when organizational innovations arouse conflicts of interests, evidence based evaluation becomes a positive obstacle to implementation. Under what might be called the 'circumstances of ideology', policy makers and managers cannot explicitly state all the foreseen effects of an organization innovation for one or more of the following reasons:

1. Its ends appear inconsistent (for example, both to reduce car use and win the political support of oil companies).
2. To avoid giving hostages to fortune, so that the innovators can claim success whatever happens.
3. To avoid arousing opposition, criticism or unpopularity.
4. It rests on untested or invalid assumptions or predictions ('program theory').
5. Its ends are formulated ambiguously in order to appeal to opposing constituencies (Hjern and Porter, 1981).
6. To gain implementers' compliance by obfuscating any adverse outcomes for them.

If these reasons prevent policy makers or managers from formulating what outcomes an organizational innovation is intended to achieve, evidence based evaluations in terms of those outcomes become logically impossible (Lohr et al., 1998). A realist theory of ideology implies that, when the circumstances of ideology exist, the evidence basing of organizational innovations is not just difficult but impossible.

The remainder of this chapter compares the second, critical realist account of ideology and its implications for evidence based organizational innovation with recent evidence from English NHS primary care about what kinds of organizational innovation are occurring in English primary care; how far they are evidence based; and, when they are not evidence based, why that is.

## Methods

As evidence about what innovations are occurring at the local level in English Primary Care Trusts (PCTs), we undertook case studies in nine PCTs, purposely selecting a maximum variation sample in terms of governance structures. Using data from key informants, documents, database evidence and official websites, we made triangulated case studies of each, including a list of reported attempts at organizational innovations during the period autumn 2001 to early 2003. We defined organizational innovation as the adoption of new working practices for organizing, managing, resourcing and monitoring primary care provision for the purpose of achieving NHS policy objectives. We counted either an explicit decision to implement the innovation, or attempts to plan, finance and practically implement the innovation as evidence of adoption. 'New' we defined as 'first introduced to the study site within the preceding two years', even if examples of the same innovation already existed elsewhere.

A claim that a given innovation was evidence based was reduced to four assertions:

1. Evidence about the organizational outcomes it would produce existed when the innovation was adopted.
2. On balance the evidence supported adopting the innovation (which presupposes assertion 1).
3. This evidence was available to the adopters (which also presupposes assertion 1).
4. The adopters made the existence of supporting evidence a necessary condition for adopting the innovation (which presupposes the three previous assertions).

To test whether evidence existed (assertion 1) we searched databases available to NHS managers and staff for evidence relevant to each reported innovation.

If such evidence was absent, we assumed that they could not have adopted the innovation on that basis. Determining whether the balance of evidence favoured adopting each innovation for which evidence did exist (assertion 2) would have required making numerous systematic reviews. That was beyond our resources and beyond most PCTs' resources too (Wilkin et al., 2000). So this stage was limited to consulting any relevant systematic reviews among the studies found. PCT decision making bodies are dominated by GPs and (non-medical) NHS managers. To determine whether any extant evidence had been available to them (assertion 3), we checked whether the relevant evidence had been published in sources that they would generally seek evidence about health care innovations in. For GPs this meant Bandolier, Effective Health Care Bulletins and the *British Medical Journal's* database, which McColl et al. (1998) say account for 65 per cent of GPs' mentions of databases used. Only anecdotal evidence exists about where NHS managers seek such material, but it suggests that the HMIC database (a superset of Department of Health, King's Fund) and HELMIS (Health Management Information Service) databases and Department of Health guidance are their preferred sources. On these databases we first limited the search to primary care (or near-cognate terms such as 'general practice', 'community care' and so on) and publication before December 2002 because later evidence could not have influenced the adoption decisions reported. Then, we searched under keywords relevant to organization (for example, 'manage*', 'model*', 'skill-mix', 'cost*' and so on).

To test the fourth assertion it was necessary to establish whether each innovation was adopted for evidential or 'practico-social' reasons. Cases where evidence basing was not attempted at all, or only as an afterthought (for example, as a 'post-facto' legitimization), would be instances of the latter. We therefore examined the reasons which our informants stated or implied had motivated the innovations they mentioned and the sources from which they became aware of the innovation. Insofar as organizational innovation was not evidence based, it became necessary to assess how far the aforementioned circumstances of ideology existed.

These methods err on the side of overestimating the degree to which organizational innovations in PCTs are evidence based. If any evidence existed at all in the sources we checked, we assumed that someone in the PCT might have examined it. A single empirical study, however limited its data, counted as availability of evidence. We counted not only experiments or trials, but also case studies as evidence. (We arbitrarily defined the existence of ten or more studies as an 'extensive' evidence base.) We have assumed that where evidence existed, PCTs acted in conformity with it. Against this, checking only specific (though extensive) sources of evidence leaves open the possibility that relevant evidence supporting a given innovation might have existed elsewhere even when it was absent where we looked. Insofar as they make it relatively easy to demonstrate at least minimal evidence basing, these methods place a greater burden of proof on the critical-realist account of ideology.

## Results

From the case studies, we tabulated the numbers of innovations found, their origins and extent of evidence base. Although informants at every site were directly asked what service changes had occurred, even some nationally-promoted innovations (for example, cancer guidelines) were not mentioned in all sites. Widespread innovation is evident. We found 61 types of organizational innovation projects, 21 of them in more than one site. Every PCT could report at least nine such projects. Site D had 21. These projects had three main immediate sources (beyond which further sources may lie; for example, many national guidelines are based on earlier research). National government and professional bodies were the immediate source of 14 projects. Six had sources directly in health research literature; 36 originated from local enthusiasts or inventors. The other four had mixed origins. Most (38/61, that is 62 per cent) were at least minimally evidence based (Table 12.1).

The first line of data in Table 12.1 shows that only three innovations – the 'advanced access' system for GP booking systems and nurse triage; National Service Frameworks giving standards for the organization and clinical content of certain services; and, general practice development plans – were found in all nine sites. Of these innovations, more than ten studies providing evidence about the effects of implementing National Service Frameworks were found; fewer than ten studies were found giving evidence about advanced access; and none provided evidence about the effects of practice development plans on patient care. The next line shows that one innovation was found in six of the sites and there was only a small evidence base for it, and so on until, in the last line, we find that 40 (3 + 18 + 19) innovations were found in only one site and of these innovations there was

Table 12.1   Adoption and evidence bases (numbers of projects)

| Number of | | Level of evidence | | |
|---|---|---|---|---|
| Sites | Innovations | Extensive | Small | None |
| All (9) | 3 | 1 | 1 | |
| 6 | 1 | 0 | 1 | 0 |
| 5 | 1 | 1 | 0 | 0 |
| 4 | 5 | 2 | 1 | 2 |
| 3 | 2 | 0 | 2 | 0 |
| 2 | 9 | 1 | 7 | 1 |
| 1 | 40 | 3 | 18 | 19 |

extensive evidence for three, small evidence for 18 and no evidence for the remaining 19. Although a small proportion of the total, the more widely adopted innovations tended to be those with the stronger evidence bases. Many informants saw the evidence base as the proper criterion for deciding whether to adopt an organizational innovation. For instance:

> when we put a community mental health worker into one of the deprived rural practices, it was done on the basis of a proper evaluation project. And then once that pilot period was over, and the evaluation indicated it was a success and it was rolled out. (PCT Chair, site E)

Another PCT that had evidence of 'five practices who were over-prescribing dramatically' (PCT Chair, site G), adopted a 28-day limit on prescriptions and made substantial savings. Evidence basing generally appeared easiest for innovations in the aspects of clinical work especially prescribing, about which PCTs have sufficient and timely data by which to evaluate organizational innovations. More sporadically, we found attempts to include evidence about user preferences in service reviews. In site A for example:

> we've now got a PALS [Patients Advisory and Liaison] service which again might highlight issues that we would need to look at, so I think that there's information out there and we're trying to pull it all together into work, kind of, [a] meaningful format...but I mean we are still very much dependent upon, in some cases, [what] people are actually telling you about near misses for example. (Chief executive, site A)

The evidence about service quality collected from user groups or complainants tended to be qualitative, even anecdotal.

The evidence basing that first legitimized an organizational innovation was also used to help implement it through tacit appeals to 'clinical effectiveness', 'patients' needs' or 'professional self-respect':

> Q: 'What kind of data do you [PCT] use to impose peer pressure...?'
> A: 'Comparative...analysis. So we've done comparative analysis by GP on radiology referrals, pathology referrals, outpatient referrals, so that there is a league table if you like where, well you can see where you are. It's non-an...it's not anonymized, we have open meetings for all GPs to attend, we discuss the results.' (PEC Chair site G)

Other studies have also found that NHS staff are more likely to adopt innovations which they believed would benefit their patients (Modell et al., 1998; Ferlie et al., 2002).

Some PCTs made a 'lucky hit' by adopting an innovation for which supporting evidence appeared after they had adopted it; for example, for nurse triage in general practice (Richards et al., 2002). In certain cases, where evidence supported an organizational innovation, it did so only under specific conditions or caveats (Griffin, 1998; Grol et al., 1998). In a few cases the published evidence was conflicting or equivocal; for example, feedback to GPs on their prescribing practice (O'Connell et al., 1999); or unfavourable to the innovation (Salisbury, 1997). It was not uncommon for PCTs to make post-adoption 'evaluations' although, in some cases, the decision to replicate an innovation was apparently made before evaluation results or other evidence were available. The same can occur at national level; for example, with the Evercare project (Boaden et al., 2005). 'Symbolic' evidence basing is apparently intended to legitimize post-facto an innovation made for other reasons (Lavis et al., 2002).

Other attempts to evidence base innovation have floundered on practical obstacles which our case studies suggested remain widespread in the NHS. Data collection is patchy; whilst NHS prescribing data are exemplary, they are also exceptional. Financial and referrals' data are quite widely collected, but our study PCTs only had erratic access to data collected from NHS Trusts. Even when evidence was available and warranted an organizational innovation, financial constraints pre-empted the innovation in two sites:

> it's very difficult, we spend all our time trying to save small amounts of money that can be channelled into local projects... one has to say that in reality for 90 percent, it's about financial balance... and trying to get money out of the secondary and acute sector back so that we can invest more in primary and community care. (PCT Chair, site E)

The same problem stymied site G's attempts to train its staff in evidence based practice. Generally, if evidence evaluating the need for or likely effects of an organizational innovation was already available, PCTs used it. Yet, even by our generous definition, a good third of PCT organizational innovations were not evidence based but adopted for other reasons, as Allery et al. (1997) also found. There were two main reasons why. Whilst the introducing of an invention made elsewhere can be evidence based, an original invention (that is, first use of a technique) cannot be. However, only a minority of innovations reported into our study sites were claimed as new, locally originated inventions. The other reason was that the innovation either was already a national policy (for example, National Service Frameworks, which include technical and organizational innovations), or PCTs saw it as a way to implement national policy (for example, NHS targets for 24 hour access to a health professional). PCT management, including organizational innovation, has become increasingly subject to central control and the corresponding incentives and penalties. The incentives to meet the targets and adopt the recommended innovations were both normative;

We are a National Health Service, we are not a Local Health Service, we cannot therefore ignore the aims that are set by the Secretary of State through parliament. (Chief Executive, site D)

and material;

if those standards are breached then...the effect is the removal of the chief executive. It's quite clearly understood. (Strategic Health Authority lead, site H)

Consequently:

it becomes much easier to deliver local changes, there is a real imperative, a real driver, it focuses people's minds and it's much easier to get things, to get the changes through...because we're being driven to, you know, and we've got to make sure that these are delivered. (Chief Executive, site B)

Provided that 'effective' is defined as 'effective in realizing national policy', these pressures make the evidence basing of such innovations valuable to managers. However the purposes of organizational innovations were not always so clear:

there's very little transparency in the NHS and it's, I always feel as though somehow patient confidentiality has been transferred to management. And trying to get to the bottom of issues is very, very difficult, particularly as a lay person. (Primary Care Trust Chair, site G)

This informant was an academic with an interest in health services, who might be expected to find NHS management less opaque than most other PCT chairs would. In general, NHS guidance often stated requirements for specific organizational innovations, and, in some cases, what 'problem' this requirement related to, but less often defined what ends were served by solving it. This applied to some potentially far-reaching innovations; for example, user involvement in PCTs (Pickard and Smith, 2001).

We also found evidence of targets (defining the objectives of organizational innovations) becoming hostages to fortune. Such targets have either remained unpublicized (for example, performance management uptake targets) or been tacitly relaxed (for example, the target for all hospital accident and emergency patients to wait less than four hours has tacitly been relaxed to a 98 per cent target). Subsequent research has also exposed the doubtful assumptions or 'program theory' of certain recent organization innovations; for example, whether nurse practitioners really do provide primary care more cheaply than doctors (Venning et al., 2000). However, we found little evidence of overt conflict about organizational innovations. One PCT chair told us that some general practices are frankly I would say suspicious, as they were suspicious of the Health Authority. They tend to think that the Primary Care Trust is a replacement for the Health Authority. (PCT Chair, site D)

Certain GPs were sceptical of the value or longevity of organizational innovations such as PMS contracts:

a lot of the reasons fund holding fell down, I think were predictable right from the start. And I would say the same about PMS frankly. I think PMS doesn't have a future. The role it has doesn't make any sense to me. (GP, site A)

Although we heard reports of passive GP non-compliance with organizational innovations, overt GP resistance was exceptional. The most concerted resistance that we found involved several practices in site A but that concerned GP workloads not innovation.

## Difficult or delusion?

Attempts to base decisions about possible organizational innovations upon evidence are becoming normal in English primary care (Allery et al., 1997; Coleman and Nicholl, 2001) although, when it occurs, the evidence relevant to organizational innovations is often of a qualitative, even informal nature. Thus, the evidence basing of organizational innovations is a matter of degree in terms both of the volume of evidence and its formality. PCTs have obvious scope for improving the data collection and analytic techniques required for evidence based decision making. Evidence basing organizational innovations is often difficult in NHS primary care, but is still nevertheless widespread enough to gainsay claims that the very idea is a delusion.

Even with the most generous interpretation, though, a substantial minority of organizational innovations in NHS primary care are not evidence based. The present study found five of the seven circumstances of ideology: ambiguous and inconsistent ends; avoiding hostages to fortune; innovations based on untested or invalid assumptions; and opaque policy imperatives reinforced with strong incentives to adopt particular innovations irrespective of evidence.

A critical realist concept of ideology thus yields testable predictions about which types of organizational innovation are least likely to become evidence based and why. To that extent, it corrects over-ambitious expectations for evidence based management and policy making. Yet the circumstances of ideology are quite specific. Where they do not apply, the attempt at evidence basing is difficult, but not a delusion.

Defining the intended outcomes of an organizational innovation is a precondition for evidence basing. Even when the circumstances of ideology apply, they do not necessarily prevent an 'outside' researcher from discovering the nature of the 'problem' and whose problem the proposed innovation is intended to solve; who is likely to oppose this solution; and why. It would be naïve to expect policy makers or managers always to welcome this type of research. Nevertheless, this type of analysis can extend the scope for evidence based scrutiny of organizational innovations in healthcare and more generally.

## References

Allery, L. A., Owen, P. A. and Robling, M. R. (1997) 'Why general practitioners and consultants change their clinical practice: a critical incident study', *British Medical Journal*, 314(7084), pp. 870–4.

Althusser, L. (1969) *For Marx* (London: Penguin).

Boaden, R. et al. (2005) *Evercare Evaluation Interim Report: Implications for Supporting People with Long-term Conditions* (Manchester: National Primary Care Research and Development Centre), accessed 2005-08-02, http://www.npcrdc.man.ac.uk/ Publications/ evercare%20report1.pdf.

Boulton, M. and Fitzpatrick, R. (1997) 'Evaluating qualitative research', *Evidence Based Health Policy and Management*, 1(4), pp. 83–5.

Chiapello, E. and Fairclough, N. (2002) 'Understanding the new management ideology: a transdisciplinary contribution from critical discourse analysis and new sociology of capitalism', *Discourse and Society*, 13(2), pp. 185–208.

Coleman, R. and Nicholl, J. (2001) 'Influence of evidence based guidance on health policy and clinical practice in England', *Quality in Health Care*, 10, pp. 229–37.

Connelly, J. (2000) 'A realistic theory of health sector management', *Journal of Management in Medicine*, 14, pp. 262–71.

Durkheim, E. (1982) *The Rules of Sociological Method* (New York: Free Press).

Ferlie, E., Fitzgerald, L. and Wood, M. (2002) 'Getting evidence into practice: an organisational behaviour perspective', *Journal of Health Services Research and Policy*, 5, pp. 96–102.

Griffin, S. (1998) 'Diabetes care in general practice: meta-analysis of randomized control trials', *British Medical Journal*, 317(7155), pp. 390–6.

Grol, R., Dalhuijsen, J., Thomas, S., Veld, C., Rutten, G. and Mokkink, H. (1998) 'Attributes of clinical guidelines that influence use of guidelines in general practice: observational study', *British Medical Journal*, 317(7162), pp. 858–61.

Harrison, S. (2002) 'New Labour, modernisation and the medical labour process', *Journal of Social Policy*, 31, pp. 465–85.

Hjern, B. and Porter, D. O. (1981) 'Implementation structures. a new unit of administrative analysis', *Organization Studies*, 3, pp. 211–27.

Hunter, D. (1995) 'Rationing: the case for muddling through elegantly', *British Medical Journal*, 311(7008), p. 811.

Kane, R. L. and Huck, S. (2000) 'The implementation of the Evercare demonstration project', *Journal of the American Geriatrics Society*, 48(2), pp. 218–23.

Kuhn, T. S. (1970) *The Structure of Scientific Revolutions* (Chicago: Chicago University Press).

Landry, R., Amara, N. and Lamari, M. (2001) 'Utilization of social science research in Canada', *Research Policy*, 30, pp. 333–49.

Lavis, J. N., Ross, S. E., Hurley, S. E. et al. (2002) 'Examining the role of health services research in public policy-making', *Milbank Quarterly*, 80(1), pp. 125–54.

Lilford, R. J., Dobbie, F., Warren, R., Braunholtz, D. and Boaden, R. (2003) 'Top-rated British business research: has the emperor got any clothes?', *Health Services Management Research*, 16, pp. 147–54.

Lohr, K. N., Eleazer, K. and Mauskopf, J. (1998) 'Health policy issues and applications for evidence based medicine and clinical practice guidelines', *Health Policy*, 46, pp. 1–19.

Mannheim, K. (1936) *Ideology and Utopia* (London: Routledge Kegan Paul).

McColl, A., Smith, H., White, R. and Field, J. (1998) 'General practitioners' perceptions of the route to evidence based medicine: a questionnaire survey', *British Medical Journal*, 316(7128), pp. 361–5.

Modell, M., Wonke, B., Anionwu, E., Khan, M., See-Tai, S., Lloyd, M. and Modell, B. (1998) 'A multidisciplinary approach for improving services in primary care: randomized controlled trial of screening for haemoglobin disorders', *British Medical Journal*, 317(7161), pp. 788–91.

Muir-Gray, J. A. (1997) Evidence based Healthcare (Edinburgh: Churchill Livingstone).

O'Connell, D. L., Henry, D. and Tomlins, R. (1999) 'Randomized controlled trial of effect of feedback on general practitioners' prescribing in Australia', *British Medical Journal*, 318(7182), pp. 507–11.

Pickard, S. and Smith, K. A. (2001) 'A third way for lay involvement: what evidence so far?', *Health Expectations*, 4, pp. 170–9.

Richards, D. A., Meakins, J., Tawfik, J., Godfrey, L., Dutton, E., Richardson, G. and Russell, D. (2002) 'Nurse telephone triage for same day appointments in general practice: multiple interrupted time series trial of effect on workload and costs', *British Medical Journal*, 325(7374), p. 1214.

Roland, M., Dusheiko, M., Gravelle, H. and Parker, S. (2005) 'Follow up of people aged 65 and over with a history of emergency admissions: analysis of routine admission data', *British Medical Journal*, 330(7486), pp. 289–92.

Salisbury, C. (1997) 'Postal survey of patients' satisfaction with a general practice out of hours cooperative', *British Medical Journal*, 314(7094), pp. 1594–8.

Schwartz, R. and Rosen, B. (2004) 'The politics of evidence based health policy-making', *Public Money and Management*, 24, pp. 121–7.

Sheaff, R., Sibbald, B., Campbell, S., Roland, M., Marshall, M., Pickard, S., Gask, L., Rogers, A. and Halliwell, S. (2004) 'Soft governance and attitudes to clinical quality in English general practice', *Journal of Health Services Research and Policy*, 9, pp. 131–8.

Tranfield, D., Denyer, D. and Smart, P. (2003) 'Towards a methodology for developing evidence-informed management knowledge by means of systematic review', *British Journal of Management*, 14, pp. 207–22.

Venning, P., Durie, A., Roland, M., Roberts, C. and Leese, B. (2000) 'Randomized controlled trial comparing cost effectiveness of general practitioners and nurse practitioners in primary care', *British Medical Journal*, 320(7241), pp. 1048–53.

Weber, M. (1946) *The Methodology of the Social Sciences* (Glencoe Ill: Free Press).

Wilkin, D., Gillam, S. and Leese, B. (eds) (2000) *The National Tracker Survey of Primary Care Groups and Trusts* (Manchester: National Primary Care Research and Development Centre).

# Part IV

# How Do Organizations Manage Across Boundaries?

# 13
## Systemic Transformational Change in Tobacco Control: An Overview of the Initiative for the Study and Implementation of Systems (ISIS)

*Allan Best, Ramkrishnan Tenkasi, William Trochim, Francis Lau, Bev Holmes, Timothy Huerta, Gregg Moor, Scott Leischow and Pamela Clark*

## Introduction

Tobacco control efforts in North America are at a crossroads. Although considerable progress has been made over the past few decades towards understanding which tobacco control strategies are effective, translating such scientific knowledge into practice remains a challenge (Ellis et al., 2003). Tobacco control advocates and public health workers are active in almost every community; however, much good science that would enhance their efforts sits unused in journals and reports. Unfortunately, there exists very little research to explain why the 'discovery–development–delivery' path has not been navigated successfully (Ellis et al., 2003; Estabrooks, 2003; National Cancer Institute, 2003).

The US National Cancer Institute-funded Initiative on the Study and Implementation of Systems (ISIS), whose work is detailed in this chapter, is aimed at moving tobacco control to the next level. Our belief is that the failure of the 'discovery–development–delivery' process stems primarily from the complexities of the system – multiple private and public organizations, from local to international in scope, offering a patchwork of uncoordinated programs – in which tobacco control is embedded. The complexities of that system must be addressed in order to move to the next level of tobacco control and, in fact, to avoid backsliding on gains that have been made.

ISIS's goal, therefore, is to develop a comprehensive research-to-practice initiative by approaching the tobacco control community as a trans-organizational system (multiple organizations linked together) working collaboratively towards common ends. In order optimally to design and implement such a system, we need to map out and refine three key

189

elements/architectures (Tenkasi et al., 1998) related to the effective functioning of organizations and trans-organizational systems: the strategic/market architecture, which refers to an organization's practices for relating to its business environment; the social architecture, which refers to organizational design; and the technical architecture, which refers to the technical know how and tools involved in task accomplishment.

ISIS has chosen three approaches to systems thinking to further our understanding of these architectures and enable us to create a 'combined toolbox' that will aid in the development of outcome-oriented implementation strategies. System dynamics modeling will allow us to develop a model of a trans-organizational strategic/marketing architecture; network analysis will enable us to identify the optimal social interaction patterns required for a successful trans-organizational system; and knowledge management can further our understanding of technical architectures, identifying the current state of knowledge and its use in practice, as well as identifying gaps. Together, these processes will drive what we are calling the 'systemic transformational change' (STC) that is needed to enable significant breakthroughs in the next generation of tobacco control. Although ISIS focuses on tobacco control, ultimately our work is intended to serve as a prototype or proof-of-concept for applying the approach to other key public health challenges.

We describe the current tobacco control environment and the ISIS initiative and its three components. We also discuss the underpinning concept of systemic transformational change, which expands to the macro-level the concepts of large-scale organizational change (LSOC) originally articulated by Mohrman and colleagues, and which we describe as 'a system-level change, made through collaborative action, that transforms the character of the system in ways that significantly alter its performance'.

## Tobacco control: an overview

Since the 1964 release of the United States Surgeon General report, North America has made tremendous strides in tobacco control. Smoking, a habit that had captured one in two Americans in 1964, now has a prevalence rate of one in four (CDC, 1999). Laws in many states prohibit smoking in public places. In Canada, smoking prevalence has decreased from an estimated high of 50 per cent in 1965 to 21 per cent in 2002 (Health Canada, 2003). The US Occupational Safety and Health Administration and Canadian Centre for Occupational Health and Safety have both acknowledged second-hand smoke as a health hazard for the workplace (Canadian Centre for Occupational Health and Safety, 2004; US Department of Labor, 1994). In many ways, tobacco has become the 'poster child' for the successful implementation of population-level health strategies.

Unfortunately, perhaps because of such successes, there is a growing movement to treat the 'tobacco problem' as solved; much of the public believes that tobacco control is no longer a pressing problem (Jadad, 2004). Nothing could be further from the truth. In the recent economic downturn, funding has been dramatically cut, and infrastructure for much of the existing tobacco control network is being dismantled, adding economic pressure to current inefficiencies in tobacco control efforts. An ever-vigilant tobacco industry is becoming more sophisticated in its marketing approach, taking advantage of the lack of cohesion in the field of tobacco control. Outside North America, the use of tobacco is an ever-increasing concern (WHO, 2002). Add to the environment a widely diverse group of organizations and stakeholders who often operate independently rather than collaboratively, and it is apparent that tobacco control is at a critical juncture.

Attempts are being made to address such concerns. The US Department of Health and Human Service's (DHSS) initiative to reduce mortality and morbidity associated with tobacco use via a 50 per cent reduction in the number of Americans who smoke, and the emergence of a clear set of evidence based best practice recommendations in tobacco control, indicate the ongoing commitment to tobacco control. Efforts supporting the development and dissemination of evidence based recommendations in tobacco control include the *Clinical Practice Guideline Treating Tobacco Use and Dependence* of the Public Health Service (Fiore et al., 2000) and the Community Guide project (Truman et al., 2000), a multi-agency effort convened by the US Department of Health and Human Services, both of which are based on scientific meta-analysis and synthesis efforts such as the Cochrane Collaboration for developing evidence based clinical practice (2003). Yet another effort towards the dissemination of evidence based practices is a multi-agency (government, advocacy groups and charitable foundations) initiative resulting in a report entitled 'A National Blueprint for Disseminating and Implementing Evidence based Clinical and Community Strategies to Promote Tobacco-Use Cessation' (the Adult Blueprint) (US DHHS, 2002). Similar efforts have been undertaken for cessation among youth and pregnant women. Dissemination efforts such as Plan, Link and Act with Evidence based Tools (PLANET), a portal site for the development of cancer control programs led by the National Cancer Institute, represent important steps towards tobacco control goals.

Ultimately, however, these initiatives address only part of the landscape (Kerner et al., 2003). Realizing the efforts of tobacco control requires a new approach to dissemination – in effect, a broader and scientifically credible assault on the complexities of the system and the barriers to change. There exists a broad, growing consensus in tobacco control that new dissemination methodologies are needed, both to bring the potential of these evidence based tobacco control practices to fruition, and to harness the collaborative effort of stakeholders in the process (Jadad, 2004).

## Initiative on the study and implementation of systems (ISIS): moving research to practice

Effectively translating tobacco control discoveries into practice means addressing the complexities and dynamics of the system in which tobacco control is embedded. Such is the approach of the two-year, US National Cancer Institute-funded Initiative on the Study and Implementation of Systems (ISIS), both in response to critical current needs in tobacco control, and as a proof-of-concept for applying such a linking approach to similar challenges in other key public health areas. The following sections provide an overview of the initiative.

### ISIS project teams

Four teams play essential roles in ISIS' work: a core team, an innovation team, an advisory group, and tobacco control experts. Our core team – Scott Leischow, PhD, Acting Associate Director of the US National Cancer Institute's Behavioral Research Program; Pamela Clark, PhD, Senior Research Scientist at Battelle Centers for Public Health Research & Evaluation; and Project Leader Allan Best, PhD, Senior Scientist at Vancouver Coastal Health Research Institute – is responsible for ISIS overall. Our innovation team involves leading systems thinkers representing a diverse range of disciplines, including management sciences, population and public health, public policy and administration, mathematics, and the emerging discipline of integration and implementation sciences. This group of world-class scientists met in May 2003 to develop a framework for ISIS and in December 2003 to refine strategy. Our advisory group consists of international experts who offer their expertise on an ad hoc basis. Tobacco control experts have been consulted through a variety of methods, the most important of which have been two ISIS Systems Thinking Summits. The purposes of the summits, held in June 2003 and January 2004, were to introduce key members of the tobacco control community to central concepts of system and network approaches; to get feedback on the project's scope and approach; and to encourage dialogue and strengthen a sense of cohesion in the field. A third event was a workshop in November 2003 to gather data about the dynamic forces at play in tobacco control, for the purpose of system dynamics modelling. Work teams focusing on system dynamics modeling, network analysis, knowledge management and systemic transformational change produced a 'source document' released in September 2004 that includes recommendations on immediate interventions as well as long-term strategies for co-ordinated tobacco control at the national, state and community levels.

### The ISIS approach

Integrated systems thinking encompasses a set of methodologies that help explain the behaviour of a system, both in terms of the totality of the components and their dynamic interaction. ISIS proposes that an approach based on integrated systems thinking will fill the gap between research and practice that drives public health outcomes. The current tobacco control environment can be understood in terms of 'three Ds' (Discovery, Development and Delivery), which in turn can drive outcomes such as reduced prevalence and consumption, morbidity and mortality. The Delivery phase still suffers from a gap in linking current research to clinical and public health practice, which we feel can be effectively addressed by integrated systems thinking methodologies.

ISIS is integrating three key approaches to systems thinking – system dynamics modeling, network analysis and knowledge management – to enable understanding and development of three key elements/architectures related to the effective functioning of organizations and trans-organizational systems: strategic/marketing architecture, social architecture and technical architecture, respectively. The result will be a set of tools that can drive efficient dissemination and implementation of evidence based tobacco control practice and ultimately system change. ISIS builds upon the framework in the Clinical and Community Guides, the Adult Blueprint and existing dissemination efforts to prototype a new, integrated systems approach to evidence based public health practice. Within the scope of this project, some promising research efforts are already underway, which will be discussed under each heading.

System dynamics modeling is a computer-aided approach to policy analysis and design which addresses dynamic problems arising in complex social, managerial, economic or ecological systems (Richardson, 1996). This approach will help us understand and model an ideal strategic/market architecture and arrive at a combined market strategy for the tobacco control system. In this area, an ISIS team led by Professor George Richardson of the State University of New York at Albany (SUNY) has created an ambitious system dynamics model of the factors in tobacco usage (see Figure 13.1), as well as a mathematical model to project the effects of tobacco adoption and cessation variables in specific groups of smokers over a 40-year period.

Network analysis – Tobacco control efforts are currently in the hands of a wide range of participants, including government agencies, advocacy groups, local coalitions, charitable foundations and public health authorities. The science of network analysis – broadly speaking, understanding paths of knowledge and influence among networks of people, and using these relationships to drive more efficient communication and collaboration – will help us develop the system's social architecture by revealing and quantifying effective collaborative relationships among individuals and groups, driving dissemination strategies and helping reduce duplication of effort. In this area, Professor Noshir Contractor of the University of Illinois at Urbana-Champaign, Professor Keith Provan of the University of Arizona and Dr Timothy Huerta of Vancouver Coastal Health Research Institute have prototyped a simulation of network relationships among a sample group of tobacco control stakeholders (see Figure 13.2).

194

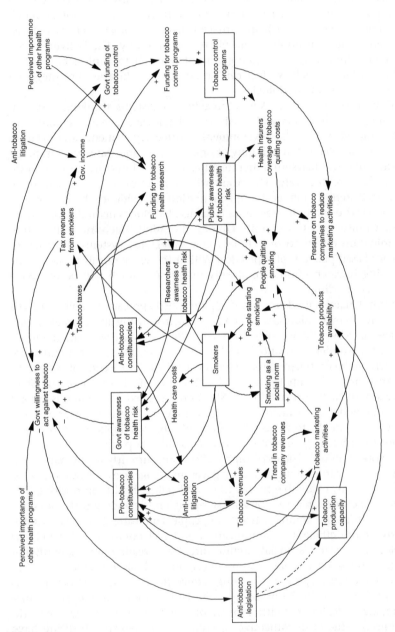

**Figure 13.1** A conceptual map of the tobacco control system

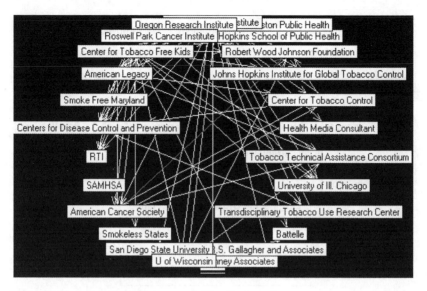

**Figure 13.2**   A mapping of interorganizational networks

Knowledge management – The science of knowledge management – which includes strategies, processes and technologies for identifying, capturing and leveraging knowledge to benefit an organization or network of organizations – is essential to an understanding of the technical architecture, which refers to the technical know-how, tools, methods, processes, routines, problem-solving strategies and steps involved in task accomplishment, needed for a tobacco control system. Associate Professor Francis Lau of the University of Victoria is researching the development of a knowledge management infrastructure for public health (see 13.3).

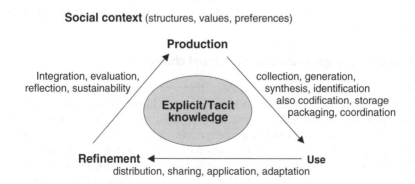

**Figure 13.3**   A conceptual knowledge management framework in health

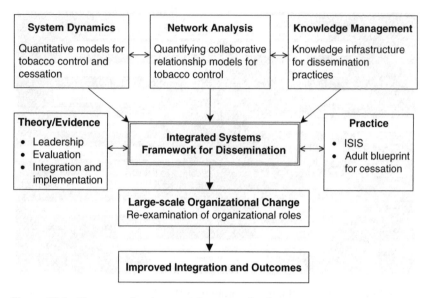

**Figure 13.4**   The nexus for change at the system level

The approach we are proposing involves integrating these three existing sets of tools and applying them to the development of strategies that drive system change. Figure 13.4 provides an overview of how we might integrate these tools around the problem of dissemination strategies for tobacco control.

The system change referred to in the diagram is critical to the initiative's success. Organizations involved in tobacco control have been slow to evolve from their current roles in the process and foster efficient collaborative strategies for action. The science of large-scale organizational change (LSOC) – understanding how organizations change their processes, procedures and behaviours – will help us understand how to drive evolution among players in this field.

## Reframing large-scale organizational change

A family of related concepts has been frequently and interchangeably used in the organizational theory and development literature to indicate a deep and all-encompassing transformation in the 'state of an organizational system' that can realize positive consequences for the system (Camden-Anders, 1999). These concepts – transformational (Adams, 1984; Ackerman, 1996; Davidson, 1996; Owen, 1991; Blumenthal and Haspeslagh; 1994, Harmann and Hormann; 1990, Fletcher, 1990; Nutt and Backoff, 1997; Elmes and Wynkoop, 1990), fundamental (Mohrman et al., 2003), large-scale (Nadler, 1988; Mohrman et al., 1989), second-order (Nutt and Backoff, 1997), discontinuous (Tushman et al., 1998), radical (Skibbins, 1974; Brown and Eisenhardt, 1997; Newman and Nollen, 1998), revolutionary (Gersick, 1991; Romanelli and Tushman, 1994; Tushman and O'Reilly, 1996; Sastry, 1997), configurational (Meyer et al., 1993), and/or quantum change (Miller and Freisen, 1980; Miller and Freisen, 1984) – are often associated with fundamental shifts in mindsets and behaviours of system actors, and with the incorporation of new skills, resources, strategies, structures, practices and goals (Tenkasi et al., 1998).

Mohrman and colleagues articulated the concept of large-scale organizational change as a 'planned' approach to create '[such] lasting fundamental change in the character of an organization that can significantly alter its performance' (Mohrman et al., 1989). Mohrman, Senge, Stacey and other organizational change theorists such as Axelrod and Cohen point out that such fundamental change can be the result of a planned effort even in a chaotic environment, where organizations are subject to the unforeseen and unknowable (MacIntosh and MacLean, 1999; Axelrod and Cohen, 1999; Stacey, 1992; Mohrman et al., 1989; Robertson, 1990, Simon, 1978).

The implementation of such designed LSOC has become increasingly important in recent years, as organizations continually attempt to reconfigure themselves to meet the challenges of an ever-shifting competitive landscape (Tenkasi et al., 1998; Mohrman et al., 1997; Mohrman and Tenkasi, 1996). In contrast to serendipitous or emergent organizational change, planned LSOC is a fundamental or transformational change that is deliberate, purposive, systemic and complex, and typically encompasses the whole organization within a finite time window (Tenkasi et al., 1998; Mohrman et al., 2003; Mohrman and Tenkasi, 1996). It is based on deliberate or wilful action (that may or may not involve representation and participation from employees), typically from the leadership, and is purposive in that the change is initiated based on some defined end such as becoming more organizationally effective, profitable, cost-efficient and/or competitive. These changes are systemic in nature by focusing on interdependent changes to multiple sub-systems of the organization. Typically they also involve the whole organization such as divisions and business units that may be further composed of sites, departments and teams, all requiring a change to a new modus operandi within a fixed time boundary.

Although its effectiveness has been explored at the inter-organizational level (Cummings, 1984), planned LSOC has mainly focused on transformations at the organizational level. However, given that several of these organizational systems are complex and elaborate systems comprised of multiple divisions, regions, locations and sites (Mohrman and Tenkasi, 1996; Mohrman et al., 2003), lessons learned from experiences at the organizational level can be very relevant to understanding transformation at the system level (Boje and Wolfe, 1989; Cummings, 1984). By expanding the concepts of LSOC to focus on macro-level dynamics, systemic transformational change can be defined as 'a system-level change, made through collaborative action that transforms the character of the system in ways that significantly alter its performance'.

## Critical success factors for large-scale organizational change

A starting point for translating findings from the organizational level to the systems level is a consideration of the critical success factors associated with planned LSOC. Mohrman and Tenkasi (1994, 1996) conducted a four-year longitudinal study of 12 *Fortune* 100 organizations from diverse industrial sectors (for example, electronics, insurance, oil and natural gas, aircraft design and manufacture) that underwent fundamental planned changes in their strategic/market, technical and social architectures to realize more effective performance. The intent of this longitudinal, prospective study was not only to understand factors at the total organization level that contributed to success or failure in realizing the intended aims of the change, but also systematically to compare matched business units (divisions, regions, sites, and so on) within each organization (68 in total across the 12 organizations) to understand their differential success in implementing the intended aims of the change.

Based on the results of the study, it was clear that the implementation of such fundamental planned change had two interrelated components – organization-wide change implementation and local-level learning. While there were organization-wide aspects to the planned change, effective operation within an organization-wide architecture that is changing also depended on the ability of the many units and sub-units of the organization to take up these new directions, and implement them locally, and further learn to establish local practices in response to each unit's unique task environment and contingencies, while still keeping the broader change mandate in context.

The elements of organization-wide change implementation that contributed to success were:

1. A clear and easily understandable communication strategy that emphasized the need, rationale and purposes of the change.
2. Framing the change in a way that captured the energies of people and offered them a clear vision of where the organization was heading.
3. Crafting the change in an integrated and systemic manner, and communicating clearly how all the changes fit together.
4. Viewing and presenting the change as evolutionary, subject to continuing learning and adjustment.
5. Ensuring that the behaviours of key/central opinion leaders are seen as consistent with the new directions.
6. Ensuring that input is sought from a broad constituency in the design and direction of the change, as well as the continuing decisions in implementation.

The dynamics at the local level (sites, units, teams, and so on) that were associated with successful implementation of the change were:

1. Creating locally-shared meanings of the new way of doing business.
2. Functioning in an integrated fashion, ensuring any particular unit could understand its own contribution, as well as how it fit with other units' contributions to create 'the big picture'.
3. The creation of internal feedback systems that help units monitor how they are doing in terms of outcomes (performance) and adherence to operating values (for example, self-managing teams).
4. Learning from experience by systematically documenting successes and failures (lessons learned) and disseminating these lessons to all the members of the unit.
5. Creating 'personal meaning', often facilitated by the local leadership, so that individuals in a unit can identify with change and their place in it.
6. Developing 'change capability' at the unit-level, through formal and informal training systems.

## Systemic transformational change: applying the critical success factors at a systems level

Lessons learned at the organizational level can be applied to the system level; however, some critical distinctions must be given due consideration to facilitate the translation. These distinctions stem primarily from the differences in the basic natures of organizations and systems. Organizations, regardless of their size and complexity, are still tightly-coupled (Weick, 1979), hierarchically-regulated systems with defined lines of command and control. Trans-organizational systems, on the other hand, are loosely-coupled (Weick, 1979) peer institutions; there is no 'common leader' with defined lines of authority across the constituent entities who can mandate such a change. The tobacco control system, for example, consists of independent institutions with their own leaders, funding sources, unique agendas, and beliefs and opinions on how best to effect tobacco control. Enlisting these disparate entities to become part of a common change framework will require focused attention to the following four key elements:

1. Creating buy-in for the need for change and the model of change: Constituents must agree that a common, concerted effort that optimizes the efficiencies of the member entities and reduces duplication of efforts will be more effective than unco-ordinated, independent initiatives focused on similar ends. Constituents should also be convinced that the proposed approach for understanding and redesigning the system (an assessment of the three key elements/architectures of the system through system dynamic modelling, knowledge management and network analysis) will

be effective in realizing efforts. ISIS' plan to 'pilot' its approach using the North American Quitline Consortium may help substantially in creating buy-in for further work.

2. Creating a common vision: A key principle of systemic transformational change is the need for participants collectively to define and negotiate the desired 'end-state' (Boje and Wolfe, 1989). Demonstration of proof-of-concept, for instance, through a pilot study or a pre-diagnosis (Tichy, 1983), can help crystallize issues and facilitate the formation of a focused and mutually agreeable vision based on the input of key stakeholders.

3. Involving constituents in analysis and design of change implementation and in establishing local-level learning processes: There are three primary approaches to analysis and design of change: 1) member-dominated; 2) researcher-dominated; 3) collaborative (Tichy, 1983). The member-dominated approach is preferred where the assessment is not complex, where there is minimal need to contribute to scientific knowledge, and where there is greater need for member commitment to use the results. The researcher-dominated approach is preferred where the assessment can be studied without heavy reliance on organizational members' local knowledge and understanding, where theoretically-derived propositions are being tested, and/or where there is minimal concern with members using the results, or learning from the assessment. The collaborative approach – which will be used for ISIS – is preferred where there is a complex assessment requiring scientific knowledge and tools along with local, in-depth knowledge of the organization, where time is available for interactive collaborative learning and problem-solving, and where it is necessary that members are committed to the results themselves, as well as to becoming a 'learning organization' through continuing to use concepts and techniques for continuing self-assessment and design (Senge, 1990).

4. Creating a participative structure and process to enable the systemic transformational change: The changing of systems requires the development of an overall participative framework for the analysis and design process. Following completion of the current two-year ISIS theory integration phase, we will propose a participative design phase to create a comprehensive implementation plan. We believe the following steps that are typically associated with LSOC processes can be applied to systemic transformational change:

(a) Boundaries of the system being redesigned must be clarified, and the desired outcomes spelled out. Until such a step is taken there may not be sufficient support to continue with the process. In some cases, the scope of the system to be redesigned is clear, but the place to begin is not. In such cases, defining a target organization(s) becomes a critical sub-step. A unit that is functioning well, but could improve further, represents the best starting point for successful redesign since it will facilitate rapid diffusion if the outcomes are successful (Pasmore, 1988).

(b) Key stakeholders – those who can influence the success of the redesign effort – must be identified, and a trans-organizational steering committee formed to sanction the overall redesign effort, and review results against internal and external expectations. Questions to be considered ongoing by the steering committee include: Will there be broad or narrow participation in the redesign? How long should the redesign take? How much will it cost? In the long run, it pays for all key stakeholders to agree about the nature and scope of the redesign even if it means some delay in order to obtain consensus (Pasmore, 1988). The final outcome of this stage is a preliminary vision statement – an expression of the values underlying the effort and a statement of its intended outcomes and 'end state'.

(c) Another important step is to create a trans-organizational design team whose functions include analyzing the system and suggesting how it should be redesigned. The design team should act as the representative body for all parts and levels of the system and assist in educating others about the redesign process, communicating information about the process and redesign, planning for implementation of changes and participating in evaluating the changes and revising them as necessary. The design team should overlap with the steering committee by one or two members to facilitate communication, and reflect demographics as well as the 'politics' of each organization.

(d) The next step is conducting the analysis and formulating proposals for redesign, which is usually carried out by the design team with the assistance of a researcher/consultant. In the case of ISIS, the parallel will be a multidisciplinary research team combined with a technical assistance strategy. The steering committee, design committee and research resource people should jointly decide on the most viable proposal before communicating them publicly.

(e) The next step is to create an implementation plan, including training required for individuals to perform under the 'changed conditions', and evaluation of the change ongoing. Two reasons for evaluating changes that have been implemented are 1) that the redesign may have fallen short of desired outcomes, or 2) internal or external changes may force a rethinking of design decisions. In the first case, simple one-time adjustments may be all that are needed; the latter may require that the system possess an ongoing mechanism to assist with change and the required learning.

In sum, the LSOC literature applies quite directly to the challenge of systemic transformational change. The overall system – as opposed to a single organizational system – is more complex and will require more substantial co-ordination and resource support, but the principles provide a strong starting point for systemic transformational change.

## Conclusion

The application of systems thinking to dissemination practices in tobacco control holds the promise of an integrated, dynamic process with several key benefits, including the development of clear collaborative relationships within the tobacco control community, and alignment of resources and networks towards (a) effective, evidence base practices, (b) more efficient, non-overlapping use of resources, and (c) a quantitative and qualitative understanding of the impact of tobacco control activities on public health outcomes.

The initial efforts described above are part of a process designed to lead to such an application for tobacco control, as well as other public heath efforts in time. Table 13.1 outlines key short and long-term objectives of this program.

To work efficiently and effectively in today's environment, public health must adapt the same kind of systems methodologies that now drive the

**Table 13.1**   Short and long-term objectives of ISIS

| Methodology | Short-term (12 months) | Long-term (two–five years) |
| --- | --- | --- |
| System dynamics modelling | Quantitative simulation of change in specific population of smokers over time. Model for cessation based on data in Clinical and Community Guides. | An integrated system dynamics model for tobacco control factors with clear policy recommendations. |
| Network analysis | Network analysis of tobacco control organizations based on existing network data. | Network based structure and tools for future collaborative tobacco control efforts. |
| Knowledge management | Expert review of current dissemination efforts (such as PLANET) and analysis of knowledge management needs. | Knowledge management and translation infrastructure, systems, and tools for tobacco control efforts. |
| System change | Understand organizational change factors in effective tobacco control dissemination practices. | Integration with systems, network and knowledge management models for tobacco control, towards implementation and co-ordination of an effective national tobacco control strategy. |

competitiveness of the private sector and that are essential if we are to successfully translate our science into practice. This effort represents a first step in creating a clear deliverable – effective dissemination of evidence based tobacco control practices – while serving as a framework for a new, rigorous approach for other public health issues.

## References

Ackerman, A. L. (1996) 'Development, transition or transformation?', *OD Practitioner*, 28, pp. 5–25.

Adams, J. (1984) *Transforming Work: A Collection of Organizational Transformation Readings* (Alexandria VA: Miles River Press).

Axelrod, R. and Cohen, M. D. (1999) *Harnessing Complexity: Organizational Implication of a Scientific Frontier* (New York, NY: The Free Press).

Blumenthal, B. and Haspeslagh, P. (1994) 'Toward a definition of corporate transformation', *Sloan Management Review*, 35, pp. 101–6.

Boje, D. M. and Wolfe, T. (1989) 'Transorganizational development: contributions to theory and practice', in D. M. Boje (ed.), *Readings in Managerial Psychology* (Chicago: Chicago Press).

Brown, S. L. and Eisenhardt, K. M. (1997) 'The art of continuous change: linking complexity theory and time-paced evolution in relentlessly shifting organizations', *Administrative Science Quarterly*, 42, pp. 1–34.

Camden-Anders, S. (1999) *Transformation Change: Illusion or Reality?*, PhD thesis, Benedictine University, Lisle, IL.

Canadian Center for Occupational Health and Safety (2004) *Environmental Tobacco Smoke (ETS): General Information and Health Effects* (Ottawa: Canadian Center for Occupational Health and Safety).

CDC – *see* US Centers for Disease Control and Prevention

Cummings, T. G. (1984) 'Transorganizational development', *Research in Organizational Behavior*, 6, p. 367.

Davidson, M. (1996) *The Transformation of Management* (Boston, MA: Butterworth Heinemann).

Ellis, P., Robinson, P., Ciliska, D., Armour, T., Raina, P., Brouwers, M., O'Brian, M. A., Gauld, M. and Baldassarre, F. (2003) *Diffusion and Dissemination of Evidence-based Cancer Control Interventions* (Rockville, MD: US Agency for Healthcare Research and Quality).

Elmes, M. B. and Wynkoop, C. (1990) 'Enlightened upheaval and large-scale transformation', *Journal of Applied Behavioral Science*, 26, p. 245.

Estabrooks, C. A. (2003) 'Translating Research into Practice: Implications for Organizations and Administrators', *Canadian Journal of Nursing Research*, 35, pp. 53–68.

Fiore, M. C., Bailey, W. C. and Cohen, S. J. (2000) *Treating Tobacco Use and Dependence* (Rockville, MD: US Department of Health and Human Services).

Fletcher, B. (1990) *Organizational Transformation* (New York, NY: Praeger).

Gersick, C. (1991) 'Revolutionary change theories: a multilevel exploration of the punctuated equilibrium paradigm', *Academy of Management Review*, 16, pp. 10–36.

Harmann, W. and Hormann, J. (1990) *Creative Work: The Constructive Role of Business in a Transforming Society* (Indianapolis, IN: Knowledge System).

Health Canada (2003) *The National Strategy: Moving Forward – The 2003 Progress Report on Tobacco Control* (Ottawa, ON: The Tobacco Control Liaison Committee of the Federal Provincial Territorial Advisory Committee on Population Health and Health Security).

Jadad, A. (2004) 'Keynote Address', in *Web Assisted Tobacco Interventions* (Toronto ON: Centre for Addiction and Mental Health).

Kerner, J., Vinson, C. and Cynkin, L. (2003) 'Cancer Control PLANET – Plan, Link and Act with Evidence-based Tools', Paper presented at the Priester Conference, Phoenix, Arizona.

MacIntosh, R. and MacLean, D. (1999) 'Conditioned emergence: a dissipative structures approach to transformation', *Strategic Management Journal*, 20, pp. 297–318.

Meyer, A., Tsui, A. and Hinings, C. R. (1993) 'Configurational approaches to organizational analysis', *Academy of Management Journal*, 36, pp. 1175–95.

Miller, D. and Freisen, P. (1980) 'Archetypes of organizational transition', *Administrative Science Quarterly*, 25, pp. 268–99.

Miller, D. and Freisen, P. (1984) *Organizations: A Quantum View* (Upper Saddle River, NJ: Prentice-Hall).

Mohrman, A. M. Jr, Mohrman, S. A., Ledford, G. E. Jr, Cummings, T. G. and Lawler, E. E. III (1989) *Large-scale Organizational Change* (San Francisco, CA: Jossey-Bass).

Mohrman, S. A. and Tenkasi, R. V. (1994) 'Learning during transition: phase one findings of a 12 company longitudinal study', Paper presented at the Learning During Transition Seminar, Center for Effective Organizations, University of Southern California.

Mohrman, S. A. and Tenkasi, R. V. (1996) 'Learning during transition: phase two findings of a 12 company longitudinal study', Paper presented at the Learning During Transition Seminar, Center for Effective Organizations, University of Southern California.

Mohrman, S. A., Mohrman, A. M. Jr and Tenkasi, R. V. (1997) 'The discipline of organizational design', in S. Jackson and C. Cooper (eds), *Creating Tomorrow's Organization: A Handbook for Future Research in Organizational Behavior* (New York: Wiley).

Mohrman, S. A., Tenkasi, R. V. and Mohrman, A. M., Jr (2003) 'The role of networks in fundamental organizational change: a grounded analysis', *Journal of Applied Behavioral Science*, 39, pp. 301–23.

Nadler, D. A. (1988) 'Organizational frame-bending: types of change in the complex organization', in R. Killmann and T. Covin (eds), *Corporate Transformation* (San Francisco, CA: Jossey-Bass).

National Cancer Institute (2003) *The Nation's Investment in Cancer Research: A Plan and Budget Proposal for Fiscal Year 2005* (Bethesda, MD: US Department of Health and Human Services).

Newman, K. and Nollen, S. (1998) *Managing Radical Organizational Change* (Thousand Oaks, CA: Sage).

Nutt, P. and Backoff, R. (1997) 'Transforming organizations with second-order change', in R. W. Woodman (ed.), *Research in Organization Change and Development*, Vol. 10 (Greenwich, CT: JAI Press).

Owen, H. (1991) *Riding the Tiger: Doing Business in a Transforming World* (Potomac, MD: Abbott).

Pasmore, W. A. (1988) *Designing Effective Organizations: The Sociotechnical Systems Perspective* (New York: Wiley).

Richardson, G. P. (1996) 'System Dynamics', in S. Gass and C. Harris (eds), *Encyclopedia of Operations Research and Management Science* (Boston: Kluwer Academic).

Robertson, J. D. (1990) 'Transaction-cost economics and cross-national patterns of industrial conflict: a comparative institutional analysis', *American Journal of Political Science*, 34, pp. 153–89.

Romanelli, E. and Tushman, M. (1994) 'Organizational transformation as punctuated equilibrium: an empirical test', *Academy of Management Journal*, 37, pp. 1141–66.

Sastry, M. A. (1997) 'Problems and paradoxes in a model of punctuated organizational change', *Administrative Science Quarterly*, 42, pp. 237–75.

Senge, P. (1990) *The Fifth Discipline: The Art and Practice of the Learning Organization* (New York: Currency Doubleday).

Simon, H. A. (1978) 'On how to decide what to do', *The Bell Journal of Economics*, 9, pp. 494–507.

Skibbins, G. (1974) 'Organizational evolution', in B. Fletcher (ed.), *Organizational Transformation* (New York: Praeger).

Stacey, R. (1992) *Managing the Unknowable: Strategic Boundaries Between Order and Chaos in Organizations* (San Francisco, CA: Jossey-Bass).

Tenkasi, R. V., Mohrman, A. M. Jr. and Mohrman, S. A. (1998) 'Accelerated learning during organizational transition', in S. A. Mohrman, J. R. Galbraith and E. E. Lawler III (eds), *Tomorrow's Organization: Crafting Winning Capabilities in a Dynamic World* (San Francisco, CA: Jossey-Bass).

Tichy, N. (1983) *Managing Strategic Change: Technical, Cultural and Political Dynamics* (New York: Wiley).

Truman, B. I., Smith-Akin, C. K. and Hinman, A. R. (2000) 'Developing the guide to community preventive services: overview and rationale', *American Journal of Preventive Medicine*, 18, pp. 18–26.

Tushman, M., Anderson, P. and O'Reilly, C. (1998) 'Levers of organizational renewal: innovative streams, ambidextrous organizations, and strategic change' in, D. Hambrick, D. A. Nadler and M. Tushman (eds), *Navigating Change: How CEOs, Top Teams, and Boards Steer Transformation* (Boston, MA: Harvard Business Press).

Tushman, M. and O'Reilly, C. (1996) 'Ambidextrous organizations: managing evolutionary and revolutionary change', *California Management Review*, 38, pp. 8–30.

US Centers for Disease Control and Prevention (1999) *Cigarette Smoking Among Adults – United States 1997* (Atlanta, GA: Centers for Disease Control and Prevention).

US DHHS – *see* US Department of Health and Human Services.

US Department of Health and Human Services (2002) *A National Blueprint for Disseminating and Implementing Evidence-Based Clinical and Community Strategies to Promote Tobacco-Use Cessation* (Bethesda, MD: National Cancer Institute).

US Department of Labor (1994) 'Indoor air quality', in *Federal Register*, 59, pp. 15968–16039.

Weick, K. E. (1979) *The Social Psychology of Organizing* (New York: McGraw-Hill).

World Health Organization (2002) *The World Health Report* (Geneva: World Health Organization).

# 14

## Organizational Boundaries and Inter-Group Relationships

*Paula Hyde*

### Introduction

Little has been written about the effects of organizational restructuring and redesign on organizational boundaries although boundaries between working groups are readily identified by organizational members (Schneider, 1991) and modernization of working practices within large organizations has led to increased boundary complexity (Gabriel, 1999). Reactions to this complexity are neither standard nor entirely predictable, but may be illuminated through exploration of psychodynamic understandings of 'boundary'.

This chapter explores boundaries and cross-boundary working in UK health services. Health care policy in the UK in the 1980s and 1990s focused on structural rearrangements aimed at improving health care such as the introduction of general management, mergers and delayering. More recently, beginning around 1998, policy effort has increasingly been directed at bringing about cultural changes such as the introduction of clinical governance and lifelong learning strategies (UK Dept of Health 2000, 2003). At the same time much front line effort is being expended on service redesign – the rearrangement of facilities, staff and patient pathways in search of more streamlined services, greater throughput and improved patient experiences (Locock, 2001; McNulty and Ferlie, 2002). These frequent changes threaten organizational boundaries for health care workers. In contrast, boundaries between professional groups have remained more constant as professional bodies support health professionals in delineation of their roles and professional training follows specified programs. Recent moves in UK health policy, through the introduction of the Modernisation Agency, have introduced a focus on changing working lives with the emphasis on redesigning workers' roles. These attempts to change traditional roles threaten professional boundaries and are likely to increase defensive activity amongst professional groups.

This chapter presents a series of four case studies from different mental health services within one larger organization and uses psychodynamic conceptions of boundary from several perspectives to explore service functioning. Finally, the effects of restructuring on organizational boundaries generally are explored.

## The concept of boundary

Boundaries separate a system from its environment and within the system they separate parts and processes. They determine relationships between systems and affect the degree of integration and differentiation within and between systems (Schneider, 1991). They also provide for the establishment of identity at individual, group and organizational levels (Hirschhorn and Gilmore, 1992; Miller, 1990; Hirschhorn, 1988).

The concept of boundary has been explained by using the example of an infinite line where one side of the line was safe and familiar; the other side dangerous, unknown and exciting. Moreover, this line may be strong and resilient or fragile and thin (Gabriel, 1999). The line analogy can be applied to the individual, groups and organizations. Alternatively, it has been suggested that a boundary is better considered as a region representing the discontinuity between the tasks of one system and the systems with which it transacts. The region is not stable or static but locates activities that 'mediate relations between inside and outside' (Miller, 1990, p. 172). Indeed, it has been noted that the more one examines the boundary itself the less clear it becomes (Gabriel, 1999).

Boundary has been considered at the individual, family, group and organizational level (Roberts, 1994; Kanter, 1983). At the individual, intrapsychic level Freud described boundaries evolving to delineate the id by the ego (Freud, 1932). These intrapsychic boundaries act to strengthen boundaries between reality and fantasy (fantasy arising from the id to satisfy desires). The ego must, however, negotiate between the id and superego to achieve individual integration of the personality. Boundary has been described as 'coextensive with the ego' (Gabriel, 1999, p. 98). These intrapsychic boundaries enable transactions between the individual and the outside world (Schneider, 1991). Such transactions continue between the individual and his/her working environment.

Most workers do not operate in isolation. In health services in particular, staff are clustered around professional groupings, in their 'professional family'. Each professional group has clear responsibilities and identities within the hospital. Family therapy often focuses on role and generational boundaries in order that individual identity and family relatedness may be sustained whilst maintaining the family boundary. Roles are important within families as the blurring of boundaries can lead to role confusion; that is, a child acting as parent (Schneider, 1991). Indeed, family therapy concepts have been applied to organizations specifically for their focus on clarifying boundaries (Hirschhorn and Gilmore, 1980). Professional groupings share some similarities with this analysis of family therapy, as they have a hierarchical career system and roles can be very clear cut with certain tasks being conducted by specific professional groupings. These roles and hierarchies can be compared to those within the family group.

Health service workers are also clustered around service areas such as accident and emergency or maternity departments. These clusters may involve many types of workers in a team or group working to achieve common goals. Bion explored group functioning and suggested that, in addition to sharing common tasks, groups can support fantasies that do not relate to task performance (Bion, 1961). He suggested that groups are understandable only in terms of psychotic processes where the negotiation of boundaries between fantasy and reality may lead to fantasies such as dependency, salvation and persecution. Furthermore, it has been suggested that defence against psychotic anxiety is one of the main forces binding individuals into institutionalized activity (Jaques, 1953). Group dynamics during the evolution of a group demonstrate how boundaries are established and negotiated. Being a member of a group involves seeing oneself as part of the group and accepting group norms. Where group cohesiveness evolves, boundaries between members are reduced and boundaries between the group and other groups become more clearly defined. Leadership also affects group boundaries; for example, powerful leaders whom everyone will follow strengthen group boundaries. Group boundaries can be strengthened by identification of internal scapegoats or external enemies (Janis, 1972). Conflicts between groups can be understood as efforts to reassert group boundaries while enhancing internal integration (Schneider, 1991). Health service teams demonstrate many aspects of group functioning as they come together to complete their work task.

Boundary issues present at the group level exist not only within groups in organizations but also exist between the organization and the external world (Miller and Rice, 1967). Organizational boundaries are far more complex than those of the family (Hirschhorn and Gilmore, 1980) and are increasingly complex as organizations import agency staff, contract out services and form partnerships with other organizations (Gabriel, 1999). Boundaries between the organization and the outside world can be strengthened by isolating operations, creating niches and by controlling the flow of inputs and outputs, effectively withdrawing from the boundary (Schneider, 1991). Schneider argued that public sector organizations such as hospitals are unable to define and negotiate external boundaries because of considerable external control of task performance and organizational structures. However, despite many attempts at organizational restructuring, professional families and team groups retain the ability to carve out niches, control the flow of inputs and outputs or isolate business operations.

Much psychological work is needed to maintain boundaries as they offer a defence against anxiety (Hirschhorn, 1988; Roberts, 1994); however, in spite of this, defending boundaries can generate anxiety and the defence itself may provoke further threats (Gabriel, 1999). It has been argued that workers operating at the organization's boundaries experience anxiety from both external threats and internal defensive activity (Hirschhorn, 1988). They tend to retreat from the boundary to a safe quarter. Indeed, frenzied searches for safe havens or niches are common in fragmented organizations (Kanter, 1983). Health workers operate on the boundary of organization that forms between the patient and the service.

Whilst these pairings (family; professional, group; team) may be analogous they are not directly transferable terms. Indeed, Freud (Freud, 1932) warned against going too far in drawing comparisons between individual psychology and the functioning of society. These boundaries are often unconscious, dynamic systems affected by changes in staffing, clients, organizational systems and many other factors. They may, however, illuminate some aspects of organizational functioning which are not easily explained by other means. This exploration of cross-boundary working within the health service sheds light on organizational processes generally, and on the effects of organizational restructuring specifically.

## The case examples: mental health services

Between 2001 and 2002 four case studies were conducted as part of a wider study (Hyde, 2002). Each case study involved extended observations and interviews as well as informal conversations with mental health managers, staff, patients and carers as they went about their business. The purpose of the study was to gain some understanding of organizational dynamics of mental health teams by exploring how staff understood the work that they did and the operation and organization of their teams (Gabriel, 1999; Miller, 1990; Roberts, 1994). Formulations and interpretations were discussed and explored with participants as each case study progressed. The study considered organizational dynamics broadly with specific consideration of organizational defences. The interconnectedness of and interplay between various boundary systems emerged as an important feature. This outcome should not be surprising as defensive activity, whilst not always successful, is aimed at strengthening boundaries and thereby reducing anxiety.

The case studies took place within a larger mental health and social care trust, which had been recently formed by merging the mental health sections of several previously distinct organizations. The studies took place at a psychiatric ward, an occupational therapy department, a psychiatric hostel and within a community mental health team. The cases were differentiated by facilities for care, staff groupings and levels of illness of patients. They were also differentiated by degree of patient contact; residential or appointment, and by their location on the hospital site or in the community. All services were offered to people experiencing severe mental illness according to their degree of illness.

Managers allowed the study to take place expressing hope that it would reduce anxiety about organizational change, particularly at the hostel, and increase staff efficiency on the ward. The participants agreed to take part in the study to help outsiders understand their experiences.

A brief description of each setting is given before exploring boundaries in relation to these cases. In each case, only those findings that relate to boundary issues are presented.

## The psychiatric ward

The ward was situated on the second floor of a mental health unit toward the rear of a large general hospital site. There were four psychiatric wards and other specialist psychiatric departments in the same building. The primary task on the ward involved containment and control of the patients (Hyde, 2002). Patients were locked in and were allowed short visits off the ward although, in reality, they rarely got time away from the ward. They had to wait for staff to unlock doors for them; for example, the door to the washing machine and laundry room or the door to the bathroom. The environment was dilapidated with little functional equipment. The ward lacked basic essentials such as enough food to eat and opportunities for activity other than watching television.

The ward had more patients than beds and staff were concerned that a patient may return early from hospital leave and have no bed available. The staff were under constant pressure to admit new patients and discharge existing ones. Staff were often busy in the office as patients waited outside the office door to ask for their money, cigarettes or domestic items such as towels or milk. One member of staff was posted by the locked door and was required to record observations on a chart of each patient at required time intervals. Staff roles on the ward were allocated each shift, so that junior members of the team were often given responsible roles such as ward co-ordinator (manager) even though they lacked the authority with other staff to get simple tasks done. One ward co-ordinator could not persuade any of the other nurses to collect a prescription from the pharmacy department. The staff carried personal alarms, which could be sounded if a member of staff was in danger. False alarms frequently sounded usually because staff accidentally triggered their alarm system or were stationary for long enough for the alarm to activate automatically.

Occasionally a patient would be restrained or forced to have treatment. This involved several staff manhandling the patient to a secure area and giving an injection or series of injections in a process known as 'acuphase'. Although the acute phase was rare, there was a 'cycle of frustration' on the ward whereby patients had to ask then wait for staff to meet many of their daily needs. On one occasion a patient asked to wash some clothes in the washing machine. He had to wait until a nurse met his eye, which took some time. The nurse went to find the key and subsequently the patient was sent to get his clothes. While he was away the keys were given to another nurse who had some washing to do. When the patient returned he was told that he had to put his name on a list because the machine was being used. The patient then had to go through a similar process to get a pen. He did not become angry but it was easy to see how patients could become frustrated and angry. Equally, the staff felt under considerable pressure from both external demands to take new admissions and from constant requests from patients for milk, keys, money and information about their care.

The psychiatric ward illuminated some of the threats to intrapsychic boundaries faced by mental health workers. Mental health services were provided to offer care to patients and/or to offer a place where they might be contained and controlled (Bott, 1976). The work itself involved close contact with patients whose intrapsychic boundaries were understood to be disrupted to some extent, causing excessive anxiety in neurosis or distorted perceptions of reality in psychosis (Klein, 1952). However, psychotic processes have been identified as a normal part of personality development and mental health workers could identify with the distress of their patients. This distress threatened to overwhelm staff at times and therefore threaten their own sanity. The staff were detailed with the task of helping patients to strengthen intrapsychic boundaries so that the patient might recover. Attempts were made to achieve this through the use of medication or psychological therapies. The staff tried to protect their own intrapsychic boundaries whilst negotiating the disturbances of those in their care.

Dangers to staff were signalled by the physical presence of alarm systems in case of attack and the locked doors to prevent patient escape. The locking away of equipment, food and personal belongings of the patients led to increased demands upon the staff that threatened to run out of control and overwhelm the staff. The allocation of managerial roles to junior members of ward staff meant that simple jobs did not get done and led to a reduction of control over the ward environment. For example, junior staff were ineffectual when insisting on immediate repairs to ward equipment such as the cooker, which was broken for the duration of the study. The lack of available activity for patients increased their boredom and frustration and led to an increase in the demands they made upon the staff. Outbursts of frustration, in rare cases, led to forced treatment which enabled staff to exert physical control over the patients and demonstrate their effectiveness. Staff attempted to protect their intrapsychic boundaries by retreating from patients to the ward office and employed means of reducing exchanges between them, such as avoiding eye contact, whilst still being in close proximity.

## The occupational therapy department

In contrast, the occupational therapy department, which was on the ground floor of the same psychiatric unit, was a quiet place staffed by occupational therapists and occupational therapy assistants. Their primary task was to care for patients once they were well enough to leave the ward and to provide occupational therapy activities aimed at supporting the patients' discharge from hospital. The staff came from one professional group and took tasks according to seniority. Roles and responsibilities were clearly defined as qualified staff took referrals for patients from the ward and assessed the patient on the ward to decide whether they were suitable. This process allowed them to limit the number of patients they saw and to limit the level of anxiety generated by the work. Planning meetings often focused on what could be done in the future when the department was fully staffed and when a better service could be offered.

The qualified staff took part in case reviews and discharge planning meetings that involved repetition of information, often to similar staff groups. The occupational therapy assistants offered a small range of activities to patients, such as cooking or craft activities. Patients were normally brought down one at a time but occasionally assistant staff led group activities. Patients had to be 'well enough' to go to the department and by that time they had often been discharged from the hospital. Their readiness to attend the department was specified by the senior staff. Staff were also able to visit patients at home for a period of weeks after their discharge although they rarely did this.

In the occupational therapy department the staff were able physically to distance themselves from the patients almost totally. They considered various patients during most of their meetings, thereby remaining in contact with the imagined patient. The occupational therapists had been trained in their roles and had a hierarchical career system. Training involved being taught how to be objective and not to become overly involved with patients. The idea being that, if one were too preoccupied with the patient's suffering, effective work would become impossible. This allowed for professional boundaries that were protective of the individual. Professional boundaries can be very clear cut with certain tasks conducted by specific professional groups. Professional roles and hierarchies may be compared to those within the family group. Within families role and generational boundaries exist to allow individual identity and family relatedness whilst reinforcing the family boundary. In the occupational therapy department professional boundaries were very clearly defined and the occupational therapists could be described as having protected intrapsychic boundaries by strengthening their professional boundaries and limiting their personal contact with patients. Here one professional grouping operated together, expending considerable energy in policing their professional and departmental boundaries. There were clearly defined roles and responsibilities yet there was also homogeneity in the team as they had developed a clear hierarchy and family identity.

## The hostel

The hostel was a large building that offered 16 patients their own room and some communal areas in which to live. The hostel staff were able to accept or reject patients for admission, following assessment, and the hostel was under-occupied. As a result, staff used spare patient bedrooms as offices and places to meet for patient reviews.

Residents at the hostel had been previously treated on the psychiatric ward but they were unable, as yet, to return home. They were expected to stay at the hostel for one to two years whilst they became more able to live independently. The hostel staff were wary of increasing dependency in the residents and as a consequence the residents were left to their own devices for much of the time. The staff occupied the dining room and office and one of the kitchens and enacted routines such as having breakfast and reading the paper. Residents were often excluded from decision making about their care with review meetings starting without the resident, who was invited in later for a discussion and to hear what decisions had been made. The residents' conditions were slow to change and the role of the staff was to demonstrate skills and encourage independence. Life at the hostel was monotonous for the staff but residents were allowed out alone and were often out for most of the day. Living conditions for residents at the hostel were far better than those they could expect on leaving.

At the hostel, residents posed little threat to intrapsychic boundaries of the staff as their condition was stabilized and the staff were able to maintain some considerable distance between themselves and the residents. The staff group were from mixed professional backgrounds, although the majority of staff were nurses and support workers. The staff group functioned in similar ways to those described by Bion (Bion, 1961) who suggested that the group can sustain fantasies that do not relate to task performance. In the absence of a team leader, the hostel staff had adopted patient routines and were sometimes unaware of the needs of the residents. For example, some residents were unable to prepare meals for themselves but did not receive help as the staff were fearful of promoting dependence. As the hostel was away from the hospital site, the physical boundary provided by the building enabled staff to operate in ways that would have been unacceptable within the hospital. They were able to withdraw from the boundary between themselves and the patient and sustain a fantasy of active rehabilitation as residents who needed supporting in community activities were referred to the community team.

## The community team

The staff of the community team were said to be dynamic and effective as they supported people with severe mental illnesses living in the community. The staff were encouraged to take more patients than they were supposed to and much of their role involved persuading clients to take their medicines under threat of returning to hospital. Staff took responsibility for individual patients and undertook the majority of tasks regardless of professional background.

The team was housed in a community centre and had a locked door to their section. They had been amalgamated with a team of social workers who divided the office with a row of cupboards to separate themselves. Most of their work took place in the clients' own homes and staff were held individually responsible for the well-being of their client group.

The clients were often acutely ill and so posed some threat to the intrapsychic boundaries of the staff who had to reason with them and attempt to ensure that they took their medicines. The staff were concerned to build good relationships with their clients so that they might understand the need for medication and be able to make contact in a crisis. In effect, the organization was 'boundaryless' for the community team as their work could take place anywhere in the community (Hirschhorn, 1988). This posed some problems for the workers as they did not have the usual safety nets a health service organization may offer such as other staff for back up in an emergency. This led to an emphasis on professional boundaries and intra-professional pairings in the office. Exclusions were set on the tasks that could be performed by occupational therapists (injections) and nurses (longer-term rehabilitation). The social workers who were being amalgamated into the team began by separating themselves in the office using physical boundaries to exert some boundary control.

## Managing across boundaries

The excerpts of case examples presented here demonstrate that responses to threats to intrapsychic boundaries varied according to the degree of exposure of staff to distressed patients. On the ward, staff were locked in with acutely ill patients at the height of their mental disturbance or distress. The staff retreated from patients and employed means of reducing exchanges between them whilst remaining in close proximity. They shared responsibility for patients so that they dealt with patient tasks rather than individual people. In the occupational therapy department the staff were able physically to distance themselves from patients almost totally and the hostel staff occupied resident spaces and enacted life on their behalf. Consideration of these personal boundaries in mental health services demonstrates the unique difficulties faced by mental health workers by the nature of their work.

Modern mental health services commonly use medication and cognitive behavioural therapies to treat patients. These interventions have been shown to be effective, yet they also promote the fantasy of the 'magic pill', which when taken reduces all distress and restores normality. Whilst there are many factors in play, psychodynamic insights into the staff experience can demonstrate how staff become able to relate to patients' experiences whilst containing difficult emotions. Staff can then recognize their own emotional reactions and maintain their individuality and intrapsychic integrity.

The occupational therapy department offered one example of clearly defined professional boundaries. Here, the occupational therapists had retreated from the boundary with the patients through the use of restrictive referral and appointment systems, thereby strengthening their professional boundaries and limiting their personal contact with patients. Here the professional boundary resembled a family with emphasis on clearly defined roles and responsibilities according to grade. These hierarchies are also present in other mixed services where professionals also retain some connection with their speciality that may allow the leader of the mixed team to be overruled on their behalf. This happened in the community team where the occupational therapists did not do injections and nurses did not do longer-term rehabilitation. Family therapy concepts may be informative in understanding professional boundaries and the boundaries of other role specific staff groupings. Attempts to alter such boundaries threaten role confusion as a result of blurred boundaries.

Furthermore, explorations of group functioning that draw on understandings of group dynamics may go some way towards explaining some aspects of team functioning. Mental health teams normally include psychiatrists, nurses, nursing assistants, occupational therapists, psychologists and social workers. These workers may be located together to perform their work tasks and therefore function with similarities to those groups described by Bion (Bion, 1961), where group cohesiveness derives from clear group boundaries. These ideas are not mutually exclusive and either approach may offer useful insights into cross-boundary working within the larger organization.

Boundary issues present at the group level also exist between the organization and the outside world (Miller and Rice, 1967) and these boundaries can be strengthened by creating niches for work or controlling the flow of patients (Schneider, 1991). The mental health services in this study were all part of one larger, recently formed mental health and social care trust. There were clear access points to the overall service described above which put the ward and community mental health team at the boundary of the organization, whereas the hostel and occupational therapy department were able to control patient flow and protect themselves from boundary violations (see Figure 14.1). Patients entered the service via referral from a general practitioner or accident and emergency department directly onto a ward or

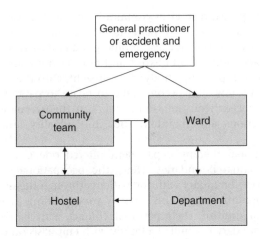

**Figure 14.1**   Routes of patients through psychiatric services*
*Patients enter mental health services by referral from a general practitioner or accident and emergency department. They may be admitted to a psychiatric ward or be under the care of the community mental health team. Only subsequently may they access hostel or department services.

to a community mental health team. Whilst they may be referred on, for hostel or department services, these services were better able to limit their intake of new patients.

The ward and community team formed a buffer for the hostel and the department. This may explain why the hostel and the department were operating under capacity with fewer patients than they were capable of treating. In contrast, the ward and community team were operating over capacity having more patients than they should. Defensive activity varied across teams, but all teams attempted to retreat from the boundary of care by some means. Managers operated at some distance from the service, holding meetings away from centres of care and judging the operations of the service on the content of the meetings. Some managers were unaware of the realities of service provision to the extent that they thought the ward staff were inefficient or hostel staff were highly anxious about organizational change. This distancing of health service managers from the services for which they are responsible has been noted elsewhere (Heginbotham, 1999; Peck and Norman, 1999).

The boundaries described here are often unconscious, dynamic systems affected by changes in staff, patients, organizational systems and many other factors. Indeed, their dynamism is essential as exchanges across boundaries allow for the development of identity and individuality for the individual, the group or the organization. Exchanges that enable adventures into the unknown offer excitement and the opportunity to be effective. Where boundaries are tightly policed, much energy is expended and anxiety is not successfully avoided. Boundaries operating in the health service can shed some light on organizational processes in other settings. As organizations are reformed and restructured, boundaries between departments can become more rigid leaving those at the boundary of the organization under considerable pressure as flow of inputs (patients in this case) into the system slows down. In this study, the restructuring of mental health service organizations, which had amalgamated a number of services, did not improve cooperation and understanding between services. Indeed, the reorganization itself generated anxiety relating to threatened boundary violations.

The introduction of the Modernisation Agency as part of *The NHS Plan* (UK Department of Health, 2000) has generated a different approach to modernizing the health service, one that is concerned with redesigning work roles and draws on principles of business process redesign. When these changes are considered in the light of this paper, it is likely that attempts to redraw professional boundaries will result in unforeseen effects in other areas of service function that may be understood by examining boundaries and cross-boundary working. Changes that affect boundary threaten individuality and identity, and generate defensiveness and anxiety that is not conducive to effective organizational learning. Consideration of 'boundary' may allow staff reactions and resultant organizational functioning to be better understood.

Rather than seeing boundaries as obstacles, they may be viewed as essential to effective organizational functioning as boundary is the area where relations are mediated between the inside and outside. Challenges to intrapsychic boundaries threaten individual integrity and sanity, whereas restructuring at the professional and group level threaten role confusion through blurred boundaries or loss of clarity of task respectively. Increasing complexity of organizational boundaries (including those above) leads to the creation of niches and restricted flows of inputs and outputs in an attempt to retreat from the organizational boundary. Each of these effects will have a negative resultant effect upon organizational capacity for learning and may go some way to explain aspects of organizational functioning that are not easily explained by other means.

## Conclusion

Boundaries are elusive and the closer one looks at them the less clear they become (Gabriel, 1999). This chapter has demonstrated how psychodynamic insights around boundaries can illuminate processes at the level of the individual worker, the work group and the organization. Drawing analogies between families and professional functioning, and groups and team functioning, offers a means of understanding issues relating to borders.

Mental health services are perhaps particularly illuminating because the work itself requires attention to be paid to psychological functioning. For staff working in contact with patients, personal boundaries are under continuous threat. Staff must find some way to protect themselves whilst being effective in their work. They have a professional identity to draw upon that can offer protection and individuality as well as other benefits of family life. The staff team evolve together in a group addressing their work task and sharing fantasies about their purpose that do not always relate to the task. Boundaries at the organizational level are extremely complex. This chapter has considered the boundary between the organization and the external world and boundaries between services, including the routes that patients take through the system. This examination reveals how some services managed to distance themselves from the organizational boundary by creating a niche for themselves or by restricting the flow of patients into the service.

There is no ideal boundary state for any organization; however, recognition of the threat to identity and individuality posed by restructuring offers insights into consequent reactions of staff groups. In addition, understanding of the function of organizational boundaries may go some way to explain the resistance to organizational change associated with organizational restructuring.

## References

Bion, W. R. (1961) *Experiences in Groups and other Papers* (London: Tavistock).
Bott, E. (1976) 'Hospital and society', *British Journal of Medical Psychology*, 49, pp. 97–140.
Freud, S. (1932) 'The ego and the id', in J. Strachey (ed.), (1961) *The Standard Edition of the Complete Psychological Works of Sigmund Freud*, vol. 19, (London: Hogarth Press).
Gabriel, Y. (1999) *Organizations in Depth* (London: Sage).
Heginbotham, C. (1999) 'The psychodynamics of mental health care', *Journal of Mental Health*, 8(3), pp. 253–60.
Hirschhorn, L. (1988) *The Workplace Within* (Cambridge, MA: MIT Press).
Hirschhorn, L. and Gilmore, T. (1980) 'The application of family therapy concepts to influencing organizational behavior', *Administrative Science Quarterly*, 25, pp. 18–37.
Hirschhorn, L. and Gilmore, T. (1992) 'The new boundaries of the 'boundaryless' company', *Harvard Business Review*, May–June, pp. 104–15.
Hyde, P. (2002) *Organizational Dynamics of Mental Health Teams*, PhD Thesis, University of Manchester, England.
Janis, I. L. (1972) *Victims of Groupthink* (Boston: Houghton Mifflin).
Jaques, E. (1953) 'On the dynamics of social structure', *Human Relations*, 6, pp. 10–23.
Kanter, R. M. (1983) *The Changemasters* (New York: Simon & Shuster).
Klein, M. (1952) *Developments in Psychoanalysis* (London: Hogarth Press).
Locock, L. (2001) *Maps and Journeys: Redesign in the NHS* (Birmingham: HSMC, University of Birmingham).
McNulty, T. and Ferlie, E. (2002) *Re-engineering Healthcare: The Complexities of Organizational Transformation* (Oxford: Oxford University Press).
Miller, A. J. and Rice, A. K. (1967) *Systems of Organizations: The Control of Task and Sentient Boundaries* (London: Tavistock).
Miller, E. J. (1990) 'Experiential learning in groups, 1: the development of the Leicester Model', in E. Trist and H. Murray (eds), *The Social Engagement of Social Science*, Vol. 1: *The psychological perspective* (London: Free Association Books).

Peck, E. and Norman, I. J. (1999) 'Working together in adult community mental health services', *Journal of Mental Health*, 8(3), pp. 231–42.

Roberts, V. Z. (1994) 'The organization of work', in A. Obholzer and V. Z. Roberts (eds), *The Unconscious at Work: Individual and Organizational Stress in the Human Services* (London: Routledge).

Schneider, S. C. (1991) 'Managing across boundaries in organizations', in. M. F. R. Kets De Vries (ed.), *Organizations on the Couch: Clinical Perspectives on Organizational Behaviour and Change* (Oxford: Jossey Bass).

UK Department of Health (2003) *Delivering HR in the NHS Plan* (London: Department of Health).

UK Department of Health (2000) *The NHS Plan* (London: Department of Health).

# 15

# Effective Health Care CHAIN (Contacts, Help, Advice and Information Network): Breaking Down Barriers between Professions, Organizations, Researchers and Practitioners in the UK and Canada

*David Evans, Laura McAuley, Nancy Santesso, Jessie McGowan and Jeremy Grimshaw*

Research findings cannot improve population outcomes unless health care systems, organizations and professionals use them in practice and in policy making. Clinical and health services research produces new knowledge that has the potential to contribute to more effective patient care (Mulrow, 1994). However, this has no impact if health care systems, organizations and individual professionals fail to be aware of or utilize new knowledge generated by research (Grimshaw et al., 2001). Unfortunately, one of the most consistent findings in health services research is that the transfer of research findings into changes in practice is unpredictable and can be a slow and haphazard process (Agency for Healthcare Research and Quality, 2001). This results in policy makers and service managers being unaware of research that could improve their decision making and, consequently, patients are denied treatments of proven benefit. Many decisions at the organizational or health care system level do not explicitly consider the available evidence, which leads to the avoidable implementation of ineffective or even potentially harmful policies. There is considerable evidence of a knowledge translation (KT) gap in health care practice and policy. Studies in the United States and The Netherlands suggest that about 30 to 40 per cent of patients do not routinely receive care according to current scientific evidence and about 20 to 25 per cent of care provided is not needed or potentially harmful (Schuster et al., 1998; Grol, 2001). Similar research in Canada has identified knowledge gaps. For example, suboptimal performance has been observed in retinal screening rates and cardiovascular risk factor management in diabetic patients (Buhrmann et al., 2003; Shah et al., 2003), in the use of ACE inhibitors in heart failure patients (Tu et al., 1999) and in the continued use of benzodiazepines in the elderly (Pimlott et al., 2003). The different conception of research and KT held by researchers and decision makers creates a mismatch in expectations often leading to frustrations for both parties and a failure of knowledge translation (Lomas, 1997). It has been argued that a new relationship is needed between researcher and decision maker to increase mutual respect and communication in both directions. This relationship would benefit decision makers' communication of research needs in addition to researchers' ability to convey results in an appropriate and timely form (Evans and Haines, 2000). Experience from the United Kingdom's (UK) National Health Service supports this notion. Despite substantial investment in health services research of direct relevance to the service, (through the National Health Service's Research and Development Programme), the translation of research evidence into changes in policy and practice has been patchy and problematic (Muir-Gray, 1997). It follows that greater engagement between the various stakeholders across health and health-related research would be beneficial. For researchers, greater engagement would at the very least enable better alignment of their work to the needs of health care professionals and service managers. For health care systems and the managers and professionals who deliver services, greater engagement with researchers would facilitate more effective and timely dissemination of knowledge generated through research. Moreover, improved communication and the sharing of ideas and needs across research and service offer the possibility of creating a dynamic process to replace the failing, passive, linear model of 'getting research into practice'. The new relationship between research and service would thus be fluid, responsive and underpinned by mutual awareness of needs and evidence.

There has been ongoing interest in the value of networks to facilitate knowledge exchange and use. There is a strong emphasis on both the benefits of a network for individuals and the importance of supporting the communication. Networks can work to 'socialize' members into each other's fields, create an acceptance of each other's norms, and develop trusting relationships and an openness to sharing knowledge. It has been shown that people who identify with a group, exchanging experiences and practice, can create a shared language and vocabulary which enable the 'discovery and development of improved practice' (Fenton et al., 2001). However, in order to support the network, it is important to use appropriate active communications technology because it is not enough to simply provide repositories of information or activities of passive dissemination of information (Creech and Willard, 2001). People need to be linked to each other to provide opportunities to converse, as relationships require conversations to strengthen them.

## Origins of CHAIN in the UK

The idea for establishing CHAIN (Contacts, Help, Advice and Information Network) arose in the London region of the UK's NHS in the late 1990s. Despite considerable activity in health services research and evidence based practice in the UK, individuals who wanted to start making use of research evidence in their practice, to link up with health care professionals elsewhere to undertake research, to implement changes based on research evidence, or to get involved in influencing the research agendas, found it a considerable challenge making the necessary connections. (This need was demonstrated by the volume of enquiries from health care professionals and managers to the R&D administrative office.) It seemed that if connections were made at all, they were haphazard and reliant on serendipity. A major reason for this disconnect was the fact that no map existed to show who was involved in research, evidence based practice (EBP) and related education and training. There was no way to know if colleagues were willing and able to offer advice or help, or of colleagues to link up with to undertake a project, even when they might have been found within the same organization. People with new interests in research and evidence based practice were inhibited and this reduced the potential for inter-organizational and multi-professional collaborations.

## Features of CHAIN

CHAIN was established as a means of addressing the identified informational and communications insufficiency by providing a map and a channel of communication with and between interested people, including researchers, clinicians, managers and teachers. An environmental scan was undertaken before the development of CHAIN to ensure that existing resources would not be duplicated. The scan was completed several years ago and at that time many relevant virtual and traditional networks were identified for health care professionals interested in research and evidence based practice. An interesting feature of these existing networks was that they appeared to reinforce rather than break down boundaries between professions, specialties and stakeholders. Typically, the networks would either focus exclusively on one group (that is, doctors, nurses, physiotherapists, and so on) or alternately would focus on a single disease or part of the body (with single or multi-disciplinary groups involved). Thus a network existed for nurses with an interest in research and development (at the time administered by the King's Fund), and an online network, 'Drs.net', provided virtual space for networking between physicians. There were separate networking opportunities for health care professionals with an interest in diabetes and those with an interest in coronary heart disease, but neither offered a forum for exchanging experience across these fields. In short, aside from e-mail discussion lists, no network welcomed a broad cross-section of interested parties and consequently no network was facilitating linkage between the various stakeholders.

This chapter describes the development and evolution of the CHAIN network, which aims to facilitate knowledge sharing, creation and dissemination. It also allows the building of relationships linking users and researchers and providing training opportunities in research use and knowledge translation skills. Members have access to CHAIN resources, including contact details and self reported interests of other members, and agree to try to respond to queries from other CHAIN members. In addition, CHAIN can be used for a targeted 'push' of information to members based upon their self reported interests. By being broad and inclusive, CHAIN addresses this need, providing a mutual support network and an informal virtual space where these critical interfaces are propagated, setting it apart from other networks. The overall objectives are to enable people to support each other in producing and using research evidence, and to breakdown boundaries between research and practice, the health care professions, and the organizations involved in the heath care system (Russell et al., 2004). Figures 15.1 and 15.2 give an indication of the breadth of experience within CHAIN.

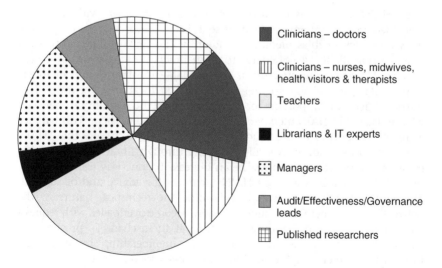

**Figure 15.1** CHAIN members' professions

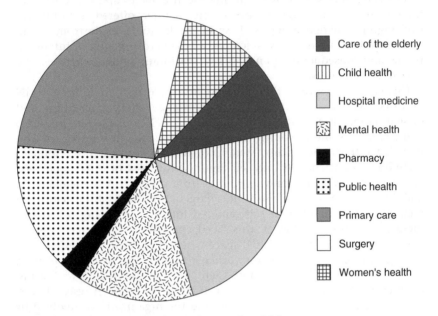

**Figure 15.2**   CHAIN members' main interests/specialties

## The CHAIN directory

The CHAIN directory is the listing of all CHAIN members with their self-identified areas of interest and expertise. It is the resource at the core of the network which enables members to identify and make contact with each other. It is available free of charge to all members via a password-protected website. However, the directory is not available in libraries and members cannot make it available to their colleagues on local area networks. This restricted access is important for maintenance of the equilibrium between what is asked of CHAIN members, and what is offered to them. This balance is absolutely critical to the functioning of the network. Were the CHAIN directory to be made universally available through libraries and hospital intranets, there would doubtless be an increase in 'one-way traffic'; that is, non-CHAIN members asking CHAIN members for advice and/or support. The resultant imbalance would undermine the reciprocal nature of the network, as some members would inevitably become overloaded with requests and queries despite demanding little from it themselves. To prevent this CHAIN has offered free and unrestricted membership, simultaneously imposing 'members only' restrictions to the network directory.

Being free of charge and welcoming all who have an interest in research/EBP, CHAIN has enlisted a wide cross-section of people from the health care 'family of organizations', who have agreed to the principles of membership. These principles include signing up to a reciprocal relationship whereby each member submits information about their own interests, skills and activities, with their contact details, for inclusion in the network directory. By joining CHAIN, each member signals his or her willingness to be contacted by other members and agrees to provide help on request, if possible. In return, each member is granted access to the network directory and all members. This 'transaction' is fundamental to the way CHAIN functions on a number of levels. In purely practical terms, it serves to keep the flow of messages within manageable limits, eliminating the drain of 'one-way traffic'. What is less obvious, but of equal importance, is the way that the self-selecting nature of membership influences the character of the network. Since the network is voluntary and founded on the principle of mutual support, the CHAIN membership is inherently biased towards more enthusiastic individuals who are keen to offer help when they can. Not surprisingly, this is a major advantage in the context of eliciting replies to a query or a call for help.

Unlike an e-mail discussion group, CHAIN does not operate on the basis of circular messaging. Rather, CHAIN networking is founded on 1:1 e-mails, either generated by members themselves, or tightly targeted and sent by CHAIN facilitators to appropriate groups on behalf of members (see below). Because CHAIN is not dominated by information technology experts or academics, but is a cross-section of stakeholders, this works well as the tight targeting ensures that members only receive messages relating to their own self-identified fields of interest. Members can update their interest profiles at any time, and routine updating is undertaken on a six-month rolling schedule.

## Targeted messages

Targeted messages are sent out to groups of members by CHAIN facilitators. Targeting is as precise as possible so as to avoid sending unwanted messages, which would serve to devalue the 'currency' of a CHAIN e-mail. In order to maintain the rigour of targeting, individual members are not enabled to send out multiple messages themselves. Members can communicate independently 1:1; however, if CHAIN members wish to broadcast a message to a group of members, this must be done through a CHAIN facilitator in the central CHAIN office. This filtering ensures that targeting is consistent, appropriate and precise. Targeted messages originate either from members' requests or suggestions or as a result of intelligence gathered by CHAIN from other sources. The following are examples of various types of targeted messages:

- Calls for help finding evidence – when individuals are seeking help in locating the latest evidence on a subject.
- Calls for help in implementing evidence – when people are seeking advice or examples of strategies or policies for the application of evidence.

- Calls for collaborators – for many possible reasons such as putting together a research bid, writing an evidence based guideline, working on a local policy. This would include researchers seeking to engage potential users of research evidence in the design and conduct of their research.
- Educational and training opportunities such as offers of bursaries, studentships, and so on.
- Invitations to participate in relevant events such as conferences or seminars. (These include calls for papers and posters as well as invitations to attend. This would include both events involving researchers keen to disseminate the results of their research and those highlighting issues which might benefit from research.)
- Targeted dissemination of summaries of robust research evidence (such as in the journal *Effective Health Care*).
- Research calls/funding opportunities.

Since CHAIN began in 1997, the balance of targeted messages has shifted. The most noticeable change has happened in relation to the nature of messages calling for help from other members. In the early days, the messages from members seeking help in finding evidence dominated. Recently, however, many more messages have been concerned with the translation of evidence into local policy. This change may reflect greater awareness of and ease of access to sources of evidence among health care professionals and managers. It also suggests that more CHAIN members now value each other's experience and support in the context of implementing changes in policy and practice, more than in finding the evidence.

## Evaluation

In 2002/3 researchers from University College London undertook a comprehensive independent evaluation of CHAIN (Russell et al., 2004). The key findings showed that CHAIN 'provides an example of how knowledge can be targeted, personalized, and made meaningful through informal social processes. It offers a mechanism for people to span the divisions between organizations and professional groups, to capture obscure items of codified knowledge, to share and shape the know-how and know-what of implementing evidence, and to link novices with experienced practitioners who are motivated to help them solve problems.'

The researchers identified a number of factors critical to the success of CHAIN:

- Firstly, the skilled staffs at the centre of CHAIN help establish, maintain and develop the networking processes. They perform four key functions: ensuring that the database of members is up to date; targeting messages to appropriate subgroups based on members' interests; reminding members of the opportunities for networking; and affirming the principle of reciprocity.

- Secondly, the nature of CHAIN's communication by simple e-mail enables its members to draw on what one author has called 'the strength of weak ties'.
- Thirdly, CHAIN provides both the medium and the impetus for small groups of people to come together and set about making sense of a common problem.
- A final critical success factor for CHAIN is silent or passive participation, known as 'lurking' – reading the e-mail postings to a group without posting a reply.

## The future of CHAIN in the UK

Recently, CHAIN became a component part of a major new initiative for health and social care in the UK, National Health Service University (NHSU). NHSU is a multi-faceted corporate university which was established to offer educational opportunities to more than a million people who work in health and social care in England (Iles and Sutherland, 2000). Developing and supporting learning communities was one of NHSU's early objectives, and CHAIN is a tried and tested way of doing that, having evolved in the health care sector over a number of years. NHSU has continued to support the existing Effective Health Care CHAIN, which has research and evidence based practice as its common theme. It has also replicated the CHAIN model of facilitated networking to grow an additional learning community which has another interest as its theme. This second UK CHAIN, launched in spring 2004, focuses on workplace-based learning. Plans are in place to replicate the model with at least four further themes. The principles of mutual support and reciprocity which have successfully underpinned the original CHAIN would be central to all, and members of each CHAIN would be able to make contact with members of the wider community of members from all CHAINs when appropriate. The announcement in November 2004 that NHSU is to be absorbed into a new entity in 2005, the National Institute for Learning, Skills and Innovation, (NILSI), casts some doubt over these plans; however, the objectives of the NILSI are consistent with the work of CHAIN and it is hoped that the network(s) will continue to flourish.

## CHAIN in Canada

To date, CHAIN has been a UK resource, with less than 2 per cent of members being based outside of Great Britain. The launch of CHAIN Canada in 2004 was an exciting new development. The Canadian network initiative is led by The Cochrane Effective Practice and Organisation of Care (EPOC) Review group in collaboration with the Centre for Best Practice, Institute of Population Health, University of Ottawa. Those wishing to join CHAIN can do so online from the EPOC website at: http://www.epoc. uottawa.ca/CHAINCanada/.

CHAIN Canada is an independent network with provincial and national levels of operation and its own identity. However, when networking with a wider community is desirable, members are able to link with CHAIN in the UK and vice versa. It is anticipated that the ability to draw from knowledge and experience on both sides of the Atlantic will further broaden the perspectives of CHAIN. Current members of CHAIN in the UK were asked about their interest in collaborating with a Canadian CHAIN. Responses included potential suggestions on areas where collaboration would be valued. One of the most frequent suggestions concerned funding application. Here, suggestions included preparing joint applications, preparing parallel applications to allow greater generalizability of findings, and being kept abreast of funding opportunities. Other suggestions included opportunities for 'exchanges' with Canadian peers to allow learning and broadening of experience, and facilitation from Canadians in the interpretation and understanding of Canadian research literature.

## Feedback

The following is a small selection of the many messages in support of CHAIN which have been provided by members:

- 'with all those members with real practical experience it (CHAIN) is a fund of knowledge', Dr Christina Maslen, Researcher and National Guidance Developer, Bath, England.
- 'having access to such wide knowledge and experience is invaluable', Ms Catherine Breen, Clinical Effectiveness Manager, Berkshire, England.
- 'inexpensive and environmentally friendly...an excellent resource', Susan Watt, Royal College of Nursing, Edinburgh, Scotland.
- 'a significant contribution to advancing quality and governance in the UK', Dr Ian Davidson, Consultant Psychiatrist and Clinical Director, Cheshire and Wirral Partnership NHS Trust, England.
- '...if it (CHAIN) did not exist, it would have to be invented', Prof. Frank Sullivan, Professor of Research & Development in Primary Care, Dundee University, Scotland.
- '...a highly valued and unique service...providing enhanced collaboration and communication', Prof. Sheila Hollins, Professor of Psychiatry of Learning Disability, St George's Hospital Medical School, London, England.
- '...an all-important brokerage, marrying research capacity to clinical, real-world needs', Prof. George Kernohan, Professor of Health Research, University of Ulster, Northern Ireland.
- 'I've found the network particularly valuable', Prof. Angela Coulter, Chief Executive, Picker Institute Europe, Oxford, England.
- '..the "filtering" approach works well and means that messages are neither intrusive nor too many', Prof. Philip Burnard, Vice Dean, University of Wales, Cardiff, Wales.

## Discussion

CHAIN offers a model for supporting improvements in the generation and uptake of research evidence in health care by facilitating communication between willing, motivated individuals from a wide range of backgrounds. The focus therefore is on connections between individuals rather than the organizations. This may seem odd given that it originated in the UK, which on the surface has a centralized 'national health service'. The reality today, however, is that the service comprises at least 650 employing organizations in health care alone, with many more social care organizations becoming part of the combined health and social care sector. Many researchers and teachers, though connected, are not employees of the NHS, but of universities and colleges. Even those organizations within the NHS do not have a common structure, so effective communication across and within organizations through formal channels is notoriously unreliable. We also know that changing organizational behaviour is far from being a rapid process (Iles and Sutherland, 2000). In this context, although the ambitious, evidence based national policies of recent years have promised widespread improvements in care and the reduction of inequalities, in reality, organizational culture has frequently hindered rather than facilitated research-led improvements. The CHAIN approach recognizes that motivated individuals, and the 'soft networks' of which they are informal members, can provide intelligence, networking opportunities and ultimately far more effective communication, enabling rapid improvements in the relevance of research and quality of health care. This is often despite rather than because of the behaviour of their organizations, which in many cases seems biased against developments 'not invented here'.

The prospect of motivated individuals from research and health care being able to identify and communicate with each other across the Atlantic as well as within their own health economies is particularly exciting. We look forward to some interesting connections, comparisons and collaborations in the near future. Internet links to the UK and Canada CHAIN networks are:

CHAIN UK homepage: http://www.nhsu.nhs.uk/chain (accessed March 2, 2004)
CHAIN Canada homepage: http://www.epoc.uottawa.ca/CHAINCanada (accessed March 2, 2004)

## References

Agency for Health Research and Quality (2001) *Translating Research Into Practice (TRIP)-II* (Washington, DC: Agency for Health Research and Quality).

Buhrmann, R., Assaad, D., Hux, J., Tang, M. and Sykora, K. (2003) 'Diabetes and the eye', in J. E. Hux, G. L. Booth, P. M. Slaughter and A. L. Laupacis (eds), *Diabetes in Ontario: An ICES Practice Atlas*. (Toronto: Institute for Clinical Evaluative Sciences).

Creech, H and Willard, T. (2001) *Strategic Intentions: Managing Knowledge Networks for Sustainable Development* (Manitoba: International Institute for Sustainable Development).

Evans, D. and Haines, A. (eds) (2000) *Implementing Evidence Based Changes in Health Care* (Abingdon: Radcliffe Medical Press).

Fenton, E., Harvey, J., Griffiths, F., Wild, A. and Sturt J. (2001) 'Reflections from organization science on the development of primary health care research networks', *Family Practice*, 18(5), pp. 540–4.

Grimshaw, J. M., Ward, J. and Eccles, M. P. (2001) 'Getting research into practice', in D. Pencheon, J. A. Muir-Gray, C. Guest and D. Melzer (eds), *Oxford Handbook of Public Health* (Oxford: Oxford University Press).

Grol, R. (2001) 'Successes and failures in the implementation of evidence based guidelines for clinical practice', *Medical Care*, 39(8 Suppl. 2), pp. 46–54.

Iles, V. and Sutherland, K. (2000) *The Management of Change in the NHS* (London: SDO).

Lomas, J. (1997) *Improving Research Dissemination and Uptake in the Health Sector: Beyond the Sound of One Hand Clapping* (Hamilton: McMaster University, Centre for Health Economics and Policy Analysis).

Muir-Gray, J. A. (1997) *Evidence-based Healthcare: How to Make Health Policy and Management Decisions* (Edinburgh: Churchill Livingstone).

Mulrow, C. D. (1994) 'Systematic reviews: rationale for systematic reviews', *British Medical Journal*, 309, pp. 597–99.

Pimlott, N. J., Hux, J. E., Wilson, L. M., Kahan, M., Li, C. and Rosser, W. W. (2003) 'Educating physicians to reduce benzodiazepine use by elderly patients: a randomized controlled trial', *Canadian Medical Association Journal*, 168(7), pp. 835–9.

Russell, J., Greenhalgh, T., Boynton, P. and Rigby, M. (2004) 'Soft networks for bridging the gap between research and practice: illuminative evaluation of CHAIN', *British Medical Journal*, 328(7449), p. 1174.

Schuster, M., McGlynn, E. and Brook, R. (1998) 'How good is the quality of health care in the United States?', *Milbank Quarterly*, 76, pp. 517–56.

Shah, B., Mamdani, M. and Kopp, A. (2003) 'Drug use in older people with diabetes', in J. E. Hux, G. L. Booth and A. L. Laupacis (eds), *Diabetes in Ontario: An ICES Practice Atlas* (Toronto: Institute for Clinical Evaluative Sciences).

Tu, J. V., Austin, P., Rochon, P. and Zhang, H. (1999) 'Secondary prevention after acute myocardial infarction, congestive heart failure and coronary artery bypass graft surgery in Ontario', in C. D. Naylor and P. M. Slaughter (eds), *Cardiovascular Heath and Services in Ontario: An ICES Atlas.* (Toronto: Institute for Clinical Evaluative Sciences).

# 16

# Do Organizational Interventions in Health Care Reform Enhance Health Systems Performance?

*Orvill Adams and Gülin Gedik*

## Introduction

Health systems have undergone overlapping generations of reforms in the last century, including the founding of national health care systems and the extension of social insurance schemes. In the 1970s, primary health care was promoted as a route to achieving affordable universal coverage – the goal of health for all. The 1980s and 1990s witnessed the introduction of market forces into health care and there is now a move towards primary health care-led health systems that will do the following (WHO, 2003):

- Build on Alma-Ata principles of equity, universal access, community participation and intersectoral approaches.
- Take account of broader population health issues, reflecting and reinforcing public health functions.
- Create the conditions for effective provision of services to poor and excluded groups.
- Organize integrated and seamless care, linking prevention, acute care and chronic care across all components of the health system.
- Continuously evaluate and strive to improve performance.

Although significant policy changes and developments have been achieved, dissatisfaction with health system performance has become an issue of increasing concern. In industrialized countries, this has centred on cost issues, quality assurance and access. In developing/transition countries, discontent has focused on these same issues, plus availability and equitable distribution of basic services, abuses of power, financial mismanagement and corruption, and lack of responsiveness.

Health sector reform has, therefore, been on the agenda of most countries. The reform agenda was triggered by factors arising from both outside and within the health sector. The external factors include the external environment and the pressures originating from political, social and economic conditions. The internal factors include epidemiological trends, resource constraints in the health sector, inefficiencies and people's changing expectations. Furthermore, the international and bilateral agencies have influenced the agenda and in some countries have even driven the reform efforts (Saltman and Figueras, 1997; Savas and Gedik, 1999).

Throughout the world, governments are now assessing their health services provision in response to common problems such as inefficiency, user dissatisfaction, low quality of care and failure to reach the poor. These problems are attributed primarily to lack of incentives and mechanisms for good performance and lack of instruments to assist health care providers to change their behaviour.

Interventions in service provision and their impact still remain one of the least well-understood of all health care reforms. The provision of services is defined as 'the combination of inputs in a production process that takes place in a particular organizational setting and that leads to the delivery of a series of interventions' (WHO, 2000). Nowadays, health services provision is organized in many different ways. Health services can be implemented in more dispersed or more concentrated configurations, or in hybrid arrangements. Health care delivery involves a complex network of settings. Some service providers act as individual independent providers (hospitals, practices) whereas some are part of a system or network. Since health systems are organized differently, various policy reforms have been introduced in different contexts. This leads to a new perspective for looking at organizational models that explores the interventions that affect performance whatever the institutional arrangements.

Such interventions require actions at all levels of the system, including some at government level, some at provider level and some at user level. Decentralization and autonomy are some of the common organizational interventions in the health sector; these aim to improve performance by shifting decision making control to the lower levels and providers. Accountability accompanies them as an important characteristic. Increased accountability is often called for as an element in a wide variety of interventions in reforming health systems. Integration of services, both functionally and managerially, and type of ownership are some other aspects considered to have an impact on the performance of systems. The users are also increasingly playing an important role in health services, as they can hold the provider accountable. Effective mechanisms to provide adequate information and opportunities to allow user involvement are needed. However, the evidence on the impact of these interventions on health system performance is still limited. There is an immense need for further research.

## Health systems' performance

Health systems' performance considers what is achieved with respect to the objectives of good health, responsiveness and fair financial contribution through optimal use of resources. Thus, assessing how health systems perform means looking at what they do and how they carry out functions, as well as what they achieve.

Differences in the design, content and management of health systems translate into differences in a range of socially valued outcomes, such as health, responsiveness or fairness. Decision makers at all levels need to quantify the variation in health system performance, identify factors that influence it and articulate policies that will achieve better results in a variety of settings.

The World Health Report 2000 suggests a framework for the assessment of health systems. Figure 16.1 illustrates the framework which highlights four basic functions (financing, provision, stewardship and resource generation) and three objectives (health, responsiveness and fair financial contribution) (WHO, 2000; Murray and Frenk, 2000).

For system objectives of 'health' and 'responsiveness' both the average level and the distribution are important. However, for the third objective, concerning financial contribution, the interest is more in the distribution and not the average level. For example, the distinction between the overall level of responsiveness and how it is distributed in the population is important and it is always desirable to achieve more health and more responsiveness. The level of health financing is a key policy choice in any society, but it is not an intrinsic goal. Rather, what matters is that the financial burden should be fairly distributed across groups. Societies will inevitably differ on the weighting distribution and the average level (see Figure 16.2).

Any systematic attempt to understand the performance of health systems should include both process/functions and objectives. This chapter uses the WHO framework in Figure 16.1 to frame the review; however, not all functions

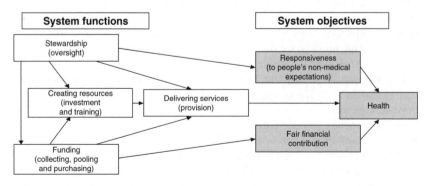

**Figure 16.1** Relations between functions and objectives of a health system

**Figure 16.2**   Health systems' objectives

and objectives in the framework can be applied in all cases due to the lack of information and evidence.

## Organizational interventions

This section reviews four major organizational interventions that are commonly introduced as part of health system reform (decentralization, ownership, integration and consumer empowerment) and their impacts on health system performance.

### Decentralization

Decentralization has been the main thrust of public sector reform and health sector reform in a number of countries. The key argument for decentralization suggests that increased local autonomy in decision making, combined with input from the population to be served, will increase responsiveness of health care to local needs and accountability for the actions of the health system to its client population in terms of both the quality of care offered and the use of health system resources. The benefits of decentralization should thus derive from two primary strategies: the space created for autonomous decision makers and the space created for the voice of the local population to be incorporated into local planning. Although a number of studies have looked at the process, evidence on the impact of decentralization is very limited (Atkinson et al., 2000).

The impact on financing has been variable, depending on the other contextual factors. The changes in financing can be explored from different perspectives, such as overall funding and allocation of resources.

In some countries, such as Ghana and the Philippines, decentralization resulted in overall increase in the availability of financial resources for health. On the other hand, some countries, such as Botswana, China and Tanzania, faced a decrease in overall funding. The decrease in overall funding sometimes accompanied a low capacity for local revenue raising, which exacerbated the situation (Bossert et al., 2002; Schwartz et al., 2002; Hutchinson, 2002; Tang and Bloom, 2000). The geographical allocation of resources to local levels has also raised concerns in terms of equity. The levels of allocation varied among regions in favour of wealthier regions in Ghana, Philippines and Uganda. In Chile, the 'Municipal Common Fund' was considered as a horizontal equity fund that redistributed local funds from wealthier to poorer municipalities based on a per capita formula in order to reorient the pattern of allocation of central funds, which had been highly skewed in favour of wealthier municipalities before decentralization (Bossert et al., 2000; Bossert and Beauvais, 2002). The decision to allocate local funds for local services is sometimes determined by political choices rather than local needs and priority services. On the other hand, this has been seen as a reduction in the range of choice of local decision makers (Jeppsson, 2001; Bossert et al., 2003; Ugalde and Homedes, 2002; Akin et al., 2001).

Inadequate financial decentralization makes it difficult to assess the impact of the interventions, as they are closely linked to financial decisions. In Botswana, districts received their funds from the government as 'block grants', with no freedom to move between and within the line items. On the other hand, financing has been fully decentralized in Uganda, but it was not supported with the necessary local government financial regulations. Central policy development and resource allocation can also be much influenced by donors (Janovsky and Travis, 1998).

Because countries have mostly been cautious in decentralizing the human resources functions, these have been the least decentralized or are decentralized later in the overall process. In some countries there was no decentralization of human resources management, with all the decisions on human resources functions remaining centralized. In countries where decentralization of human resources was implemented, the impact on human resources for health was in general less favourable. Impacts included reduced mobility of staff, low motivation and limited career opportunities, bias in recruitment and promotion of staff and reduced quality of health workers (Bossert and Beauvais, 2002; Jeppsson and Okuonzi, 2000; Tang and Bloom, 2000).

A limited number of studies explored the impact of decentralization on some priority health interventions such as immunization programs, reproductive health and child health and HIV/AIDS services. The hypothesis was thus that, in decentralized settings, health interventions would benefit from local planning and priority setting. In Zambia, a decline in immunization rates, which started before decentralization, did not reverse after increased funds had been made available through decentralization (Jeppsson, 2001). Another study found that in the low-income group, decentralized countries have higher coverage rates than centralized ones, with an average difference of 8.5 per cent for measles and DTP3 vaccines (Khaleghian, 2003).

A study of decentralization policy in the Philippines focused on the unintended consequences of devolution and the implications for reproductive health services. When looking at health outcomes at the national level five years after the implementation of devolution, the study did not find any significant changes. Infant mortality rates remained around 35 per 10,000 live births and immunization rates remained around 70 per cent. A large differential in morbidity and mortality persisted between provinces and between socioeconomic groups. The use of modern contraceptives increased only from 23 per cent to 28 per cent, and maternal mortality rates remained static around 200/100,000 live births (Lakshminarayanan, 2003). In two pilot districts for decentralization in Uganda, there was still a lack of capacity in districts to increase allocations of funds to maternal and child health services. Moreover, user fees, though entirely decided upon by districts, negatively impacted utilization of MCH services (Mwesygie, 1999).

In general, utilization rates of health services following decentralization increased slightly. In Colombia, for example, the average number of general visits increased from 0.58 in 1994 to 0.80 in 1997; while in Chile the number of visits to primary care facilities also increased, from 6.73 in 1992 to 7.16 in 1996. In other countries, such as Ghana, utilization remained unchanged (Bossert et al., 2003; Janovsky and Travis, 1998).

## Ownership

A feature of health system reforms has been the introduction of market principles into health care in the last two decades, with the expectation that market incentives would improve the efficiency and quality of care. This has led to increasing involvement of the private sector in health care. However, a distinction has to be made between financing (that is, who pays for health care) and delivery/provision (that is, who owns and administers the institutions or services that provide care). Both financing and delivery can be public or private, resulting in different kinds of public/private mix (Hanson and Berman, 1994).

There is a large body of literature addressing the issue of levels and composition of private versus public health sector, as well as the policy implications of privatization of health care services (Hanson and Berman, 1998). Far less attention has been paid to the potential influence of ownership status of health facilities on the actual performance of health systems.

The magnitude of the private ownership is unknown. Using the available published and unpublished sources of information, Hanson and Berman assembled a database on the numbers of private providers and composition of public/private mix for approximately 40 countries (Hanson and Berman, 1998). They found that, on average, the proportion of private physicians in the total number of physicians is 55 per cent, with regional averages ranging from 35 per cent up to 60 per cent. When looking at the number of beds with different ownership status, the authors found that private for-profit beds represent on average only 16 per cent of all beds, while the total number of private beds (including non-profit) represent approximately 34 per cent of all beds.

The evidence on the relation of ownership and outcomes showed minor variations. A systematic review and meta-analysis of studies, comparing mortality rates of private for-profit and private not-for-profit (Devereaux et al., 2002) involving 15 studies (more than 26,000 hospitals and 38 million patients), suggested that private for-profit ownership of hospitals, in comparison with private not-for-profit ownership, results in a higher risk of death for patients. It was also found that for-profit hospitals had a higher incidence of adverse outcomes than non-profit by 3 per cent to 4 per cent (Shen, 2002). Similarly, looking at the non-profit hospitals that changed their ownership status during the ten years of the study, it was found that the incidence of adverse outcomes increased by 7 per cent to 9 per cent after a non-profit hospital converts to for-profit ownership. Furthermore, patients in minor or non-teaching government hospitals were also more likely to have preventable adverse events (Thomas et al., 2000).

In terms of patient satisfaction, the hypothesis is, in general, that private hospitals have market incentives (are not subsidized and depend on income from their clients) and therefore are more motivated to provide good care than public hospitals. The studies show different results, however, with most studies finding in favour of not-for-profit facilities, followed by for-profit private facilities. For-profit Health Maintenance Organizations are rated less favourably than non-profit HMOs by patients who have self-reported fair or poor health (Tu and Reschovsky, 2002). In developing countries, the studies mainly show that private hospital users rated the responsiveness, communication and discipline higher than public hospital users and the difference was statistically significant in a study in Bangladesh (Andaleeb, 2000; Tangcharoensathien et al., 1999). Health care personnel in private not-for-profit hospitals were consistently thought to provide clearer explanations than personnel at private for-profit hospitals; information provided in public hospitals was rated lowest (Andaleeb, 2000; Tangcharoensathien et al., 1999; Arrow, 1963).

## Integration

Integration is one of the policy interventions that aims to improve the efficiency and quality of service provision. It is seen as a way to provide an optimum level of care. It brings together the tasks and functions within health services and mobilizes health-related activities in other sectors as well as with the activities of families and communities, and links them with health services (WHO, 1996; Adams et al., 2002).

The need for integration has arisen in different contexts for different reasons. One reason for integration arose from perceptions that services were fragmented when delivered through separate vertical programs. It has become apparent that one undesirable consequence of the vertical approach to organizing primary health care is that it sometimes fragments the overall service into specialized components. Fragmentation may reduce the efficiency of service delivery through duplication – of training programs, supervision and logistic management. Integration is seen as a process to counteract this fragmentation, reduce duplication of effort and improve efficiency.

Integration between specialist services is a concern for high-income countries with highly sophisticated levels of care, where the goal of integration is similar but the context is very different from that in poorer countries. The ever-increasing fragmentation of health care in developed countries has been explained as an effect of three major driving forces in health care development. First, decentralization has gone so far that health care could be classified as frontline-driven; that is, ward sisters and other frontline managers have extensive responsibilities and far-reaching authority to act independently. A second trend of significance is sub-specialization in health care. This is mainly due to medical development, whereby health care personnel acquire in-depth medical knowledge in an ever-decreasing area. This leads to diminished knowledge of closely related specialties among health care personnel. Finally, there is the principle of a professional organization. In health care, physicians, nurses and other personnel independently take decisions regarding the treatment of patients, and they take personal responsibility for those decisions. All three factors, individually and together, have strongly contributed to the autonomous functions of today's health care (Ahgren, 2003).

Integration has been defined in many ways in the literature. This chapter draws on three major aspects (Gillies et al., 1993, Shortell et al., 1993; van der Linden et al., 2001).

Service integration refers to the integration of service tasks within a given setting (multipurpose clinics providing primary health care as well as antenatal and infant care; pharmaceutical stores used for other purposes, that is, condoms, and so on). For example, the integration at primary level aims to provide services packaged together around a particular client group's needs – that is, sexually transmitted disease services combined with provision of contraceptives (family planning) or integrating services for mothers and their children. Integration of primary health care is a variety of managerial or operational changes to health systems to bring together inputs, organization, management and delivery of particular service functions (Briggs et al., 2001).

Clinical integration is defined as the extent to which patient care services are co-ordinated across the various functions, activities and operating units of a system. The extent to which care needs to be co-ordinated is largely a function of the nature of the patient's illness and the decisions made by the patient's physician. Continuity of care, chain of care and transmural care have been used to define various models of clinical integration in different countries.

Functional integration is defined as the extent to which key support functions and activities (such as financial management, human resources, strategic planning, information management, marketing and quality improvement) are co-ordinated across operating units so as to add the greatest overall value to the system (that is, comprehensive planning for family health, rather than separate planning for single-purpose programs; in-service staff training designed to upgrade staff skills in several areas of a service responsibility in a single course rather than many short, specialized courses; collecting and sharing health information, and so on).

Many studies assume that the feasibility of integrated care provision depends on the characteristics of the legislation, the financing system and other aspects of the institutional context, such as the existing organizations, their relationships and relative positions in the field (van Raak et al., 1999). There is a common debate about vertical and horizontal approaches in health care. Vertical programs are generally designed to address a particular disease or condition with clear objectives within a limited timeframe, making use of a specific technology. An intervention or service may be delivered in an integrated way, using the existing health system, but with a vertically organized managerial structure. It is suggested that vertical programs do not promote community self-reliance and may not take into account variations among and within countries, ignoring the possibility that a model-fits-all approach will not be feasible and the local contexts need to be taken into account during planning and implementation. On the other hand characteristics of vertical programs, such as having specific objectives, clear schedules of work, operating with well-defined techniques and under frequent supervision are considered to result in efficiency gains. In contrast, characteristics of integrated services, such as shortage of essential drugs, lack of adequate staff training and supervision and backup are considered to hamper effectiveness. Horizontal approaches, however, if adequately funded, staffed and managed, carry a strong potential for delivering technically efficient services, mainly due to economies of scope and scale (Oliveria-Cruz et al., 2003).

Though there is an extensive literature on defining integration and some sources on exploring types of integration, there is very limited information on its impact on health systems' performance and, in particular, not much evidence of its benefits. As there seems to be a suggestion from a limited number of studies that there is no advantage of integration over vertical programs in terms of patient outcomes, the important advantage of integration could be that of cost-saving (Briggs et al., 2001). Related to integrated care, some evidence is also available on improved patient and staff satisfaction, reduced costs and hospital admissions and tests, better follow-up attendance and screening uptake rates (Gröne and Garcia-Barbero, 2001).

### Information for empowerment

One important issue in the delivery of health services is the asymmetry of information between consumers and other actors of the health system.

Because consumers do not possess the knowledge or skills of health professionals, they are unable to judge the quality of service given. Dealing with this asymmetry has become a challenge in the reform of health service provision.

Providing better information can empower the users to help improve the quality and outcomes of health services delivered and help control the cost. Information is given to patients in order to equip them with sufficient and clear information and to involve them in the decision making process or to obtain their adherence to treatment by shifting patient involvement from basic informed consent to informed choice and shared decision making (Fabregas and Kreps,1999).

Different information mechanisms have been set up to deal with asymmetry of information and to involve consumers in the process of improving health services delivery. The information can be provided to the users of services at local level (health workers, family members, employers, community members, religious leaders), national level (policy makers, health financing organizations, nongovernmental organizations) or international level (NGOs, intergovernmental organizations, organizations and specialized agencies of the United Nations system).

Information provided to users generally is of three types – health education, clinical care, and health systems and services. This chapter explores the latter two. Though several successful examples of some mechanisms have been described in the literature, evidence on the impact of providing better information is scarce and insufficient for conclusions.

A randomized controlled trial concluded that giving clear information on diagnosis about cervical screening results to women had reduced the loss to follow-up of persons with cervical intraepithelial neoplasia. In the same way, an experimental intervention in Ghana has been conducted to improve the adherence to recommended chloroquine treatment regimes. However, the study has also shown that there are probably other factors beyond communication and labelling of drugs that influence adherence and should be measured, such as the patient's confidence in the prescriber (Del Mar and Wright, 1995; Agyepong et al., 2002; Tran et al., 2002).

Invitation letters and consumer decision aids (CDAs) have been used as mechanisms for empowering consumers. The invitation letter or patient reminders/recalls systems are introduced to increase the uptake of certain prevention interventions. In some studies, invitation letters have improved the use of certain interventions, such as immunization and cancer screening. (Rosser et al., 1991; Burack et al., 1996; Pearlman et al., 1997; Hawe et al., 1998; Crane et al., 2000; Dexter et al., 2001; Chan. et al., 2002; Stone et al., 2002; Forbes et al., 2003; Szilagyi et al., 2002).

The consumer decision aids have been used for people facing health treatment or screening decisions. These are interventions designed to help people make specific and deliberative choices among options by providing information on the options and outcomes relevant to a person's health status. Reviews that assessed the impact of CDAs on health services outcomes found that the CDAs influence some outcomes such as knowledge and decision making processes, but show little effect on treatment preferences, actual decision, satisfaction and other outcomes (O'Connor, Fiset et al., 1999; O'Connor, Rostom et al., 1999; Man-Son-Hing et al., 1999; Estabrooks et al., 2001; McPherson et al., 2001; Man-Son-Hing et al., 2002; Edwards et al., 2003).

It has been hypothesized that accreditation standards, clinical guidelines, and standards of competence and conduct for health professionals can be used to reduce the asymmetry of information by enhancing the availability of reliable, accessible information for service users. However, studies on this are very limited (O'Neill and Largey, 1998; Huttin, 1997; Durieux and Ravaud, 1997; Eccles et al., 2002). Standards of competence and conduct for health professionals are used in the decision making process between the patient and the provider. Such standards recognize the consumer's perspectives on quality, which include the availability of timely and appropriate care and advice; the provision of high-quality, comprehensive, whole-patient care; good communication between various levels of health service provision; respect for patient confidentiality and privacy; and ethical behaviour by health professionals towards their patients. The impact of this approach on the quality of health care and on the responsiveness of consumers is not clearly demonstrated (Carruthers and Jeacocke, 2000).

Models of patient empowerment programs have been implemented in some countries in order to increase patient choice and patient commitment. Increasing patient choice has effects at different levels, from moral persuasion (patient advice and appeals, annual patient selection of insurance carrier in HMO model, and so on) through formal political control (elected democratic control over finance and provision, request of second opinion, and so on) to countervailing power (patient choice of physician and hospital with budget links). For patient choice to be linked to true empowerment, choice must reinforce rather than undercut the accountability of health care providers to the population they serve. The use of information on providers' performance data is widely described in the literature, with the assumption that the disclosure of these data can influence the choice of consumers and increase the efforts of providers to improve the quality of their services. But this approach faces many challenges, including the provision of adequate and comprehensible performance data, the administration of such an approach, evidence that large deductibles discourage patients from seeking necessary care, and the question of equity. Even if consumers do not use performance and cost data to select high quality, efficient care, experience shows that hospital and medical groups respond to the public release of information on quality by increasing efforts to improve the quality of care. In the United States of America, a survey showed a 50 per cent increase in consumers' awareness of differences in performance among clinicians and a 25 per cent increase in consumers' willingness to change providers on the basis of performance data, as compared with an earlier survey (Saltman, 1994; Hoy et al., 1996; Anell, 1996; Marshall et al., 2000; Goddard et al., 2000; Galvin and Milstein, 2002).

Another aspect found in the literature is the information on reform of health systems. A solid communication strategy is essential to inform the public on the reforms and to manage expectations. These reforms should not be oversold and the population should not be encouraged to think that benefits will come quickly. Furthermore, appropriate information can facilitate the implementation of reforms by enabling people to take action when necessary. For example, an active social marketing campaign in Kyrgyzstan helped people to understand the changes in the system and accelerated their enrolment with the newly introduced family physicians, which was crucial in the implementation of reform (Gedik et al., 1999).

## Concluding note

The information on organizational interventions focuses primarily on process, since the evidence on outcomes is too limited to lead to conclusions. There are a number of constraints in assessing the relationship between these interventions and health systems performance.

A major caveat in interpreting changes in health systems following organizational changes is the potential coincidence of the specific intervention with other policies, which renders the evaluation of the organizational impact quite difficult, without control of the other variables.

It takes a long time to achieve fundamental health sector changes. The degree to which a health system can change a health determinant is related to the time frame of the analysis. Many health sector reforms and institutional changes may take several years to have their full effect and thus require a longer-term perspective for assessment.

Organizational reforms require comprehensive change along different dimensions of the system. Successful reform of complex systems depends on the internal consistency and coherence of the overall policy framework. Consistency and coherence relate partly to whether the different components of the proposed reforms have been adequately specified, and partly to the relationship of these components to each other as part of the reform package. Even if these issues are addressed at the design stage and aligned appropriately, implementation deficits may crop up. These may arise because policy-makers depart from their plans during the implementation or because the context is hostile. Actors may also try to delay or divert implementation because their interests are adversely affected.

Interventions or incentive regimes can be affected by pressures originating from the external environment and pressures originating from organizational structure. Managerial instruments allow systems to respond to these pressures. Organizational reforms require a strong managerial role and clearly delineated responsibilities. These interventions require a management culture characterized by a willingness to take responsibility and exercise initiative, as well as the ability to lead and motivate change. Managers and providers require information and evidence so they can dynamically innovate and adapt policies to local needs and contexts.

Managerial changes must be accompanied by institutional strengthening that will allow the reforms to be implemented. A country's prevailing institutional characteristics can contribute to the success of the organizational reforms. Institutional strengthening requires attention to areas such as appropriate regulatory framework, management capacities and training capacities.

Our initial work looking across countries suggests that organizational processes have an impact on health systems performance and different results in different contexts. Any systematic attempt to understand the performance of health systems should include a study of factors that potentially influence it. It should be noted that any fundamental change introduced to health systems demands sustained effort, commitment and a long-term perspective. Throughout the process, the interventions provide learning opportunities for further improvement, even when the outcomes on health system performance cannot be well established.

## References

Adams, O., Shengelia, B., Stiwell, B., Larizgoitia, I., Issakova, I., Kwankam, Y., Siem, T., and Jam, F. (2002) *Provision of Personal and Non-personal Health Services: Proposal for Monitoring* (Geneva: World Health Organization).

Agyepong, I. A., Ansah, E., Gyapong, M., Adjei, S., Barnish, G. and Evans, D. (2002) 'Strategies to improve adherence to recommended chloroquine treatment regimes: a quasi-experiment in the context of integrated primary health care delivery in Ghana', *Social Science & Medicine*, 55 (12), pp. 2215–26.

Ahgren, B. (2003) 'Chain of care development in Sweden: results of a national study', Paper presented at the International Conference on New Research and Developments in Integrated Care, Barcelona, Spain.

Akin, J., Hutchinson, P. and Strumpf, K. (2001) *Decentralization and Government Provision of Public Goods: The Public Health Sector in Uganda* (Chapel Hill, NC: MEASURE).

Andaleeb, S. S. (2000) 'Public and private hospitals in Bangladesh: service quality and predictors of hospital choice', *Health Policy and Planning*, 15(1), pp. 95–102.

Anell, A. (1996) 'The monopolistic integrated model and health care reform: the Swedish experience', *Health Policy*, 37(1), pp. 19–33.

Arrow, K. (1963) 'Uncertainty and the welfare economics of medical care', *American Economic Review*, 53, pp. 941–73.

Atkinson, S., Medeiros, R. L., Oliveira, P. H. et al. (2000) 'Going down to the local: incorporating social organization and political culture into assessments of decentralized health care', *Social Science & Medicine*, 51, pp. 619–36.

Bossert, T., Larranaga, O. and Ruiz M. F. (2000) 'Decentralization of health systems in Latin America', *Pan American Journal of Public Health*, 8, pp. 84–92.

Bossert, T. J. and Beauvais, J. C. (2002) 'Decentralization of health systems in Ghana, Zambia, Uganda and the Philippines: a comparative analysis of decision space', *Health Policy & Planning*, 17, pp. 14–31.

Bossert, T. J., Larranaga, O., Giedion, U. et al. (2003) 'Decentralization and equity of resource allocation: evidence from Colombia and Chile', *Bulletin of the World Health Organization*, 81, pp. 95–100.

Briggs, J., Capdegelle, P. and Garner, P. (2001) *Strategies for Integrating Primary Health Services: Effects on Performance, Costs and Patient Outcomes* (Liverpool: International Health Division, Liverpool School of Tropical Medicine).

Burack, R. C., Gimotty, P. A., George, J., Simon, M. S., Dews P. and Moncrease, A. (1996) 'The effect of patient and physician reminders on use of screening mammography in a health maintenance organization: results of a randomized controlled trial', Cancer, 78(8), pp. 1708–21.

Carruthers, A. E. and Jeacocke, D. A. (2000) 'Adjusting the balance in health-care quality', *Journal of Quality in Clinical Practice*, 20(4), pp. 158–60.

Chan, L., MacLehose, R. F. and Houck, P. M. (2002) 'Impact of physician reminders on the use of influenza vaccinations: a randomized trial', *Archives of Physical Medicine and Rehabilitation*, 83(3), pp. 371–5.

Crane, L. A., Leakey, T. A., Ehrsam, G., Rimer, B. K. and Warnecke, R. B. (2000) 'Effectiveness and cost-effectiveness of multiple outcalls to promote mammography among low-income women', *Cancer Epidemiology, Biomarkers & Prevention*, 9(9), pp. 923–31.

Del Mar, C. B. and Wright, R. G. (1995) 'Notifying women of the results of their cervical smear tests by mail: does it result in a decreased loss to follow-up of abnormal smears?', *Australian Journal of Public Health*, 19(2), pp. 211–13.

Devereaux, P. J., Choi, P. T. L., Lacchetti, C., Weaver, B., Schünemann, H. J., Haines, T., Lavis, J. N., Grant, B. J. B., Haslam, D. R. S., Bhandari, M., Sullivan, T., Cook, D. J., Walter, S. D., Meade, M., Khan, H., Bhatnagar, N. and Guyatt, G. H. (2002) 'A systematic review and meta-analysis of studies comparing mortality rates of private for-profit and private not-for-profit hospitals', *Canadian Medical Association Journal*, 166(11), pp. 1399–1406.

Dexter, P. R., Perkins, S., Overhage, J. M., Maharry, K., Kohler, R. B. and McDonald, C. J. (2001) 'A computerized reminder system to increase the use of preventive care for hospitalized patients', *New England Journal of Medicine*, 345(13), pp. 965–70.

Durieux, P. and Ravaud, P. (1997) 'From clinical guidelines to quality assurance: the experience of Assistance Publique-Hopitaux de Paris', *International Journal of Quality Health Care*, 9(3), pp. 215–19.

Eccles, M., Hawthorne, G., Whitty, P., Steen, N., Vanoli, A., Grimshaw, J. and Wood, L. (2002) 'A randomized controlled trial of a patient based Diabetes Recall and Management System: the DREAM trial: a study protocol', *BMC Health Services Research*, 2(1), p. 5.

Edwards, A., Unigwe, S., Elwyn, G. and Hood, K. (2003) 'Personalized risk communication for informed decision making about entering screening programs', *Cochrane Database of Systematic Reviews*, (1).

Estabrooks, C., Goel, V., Thiel, E., Pinfold, P., Sawka, C. and Williams, I. (2001) 'Decision aids: are they worth it? A systematic review', *Journal of Health Services Research & Policy*, 6(3), pp. 170–82.

Fabregas, S. M. and Kreps, G. L. (1999) 'Bioethics committees: a health communication approach', *Puerto Rico Health Sciences Journal*, 18(1), pp. 31–7.

Forbes, C., Jepson, R. and Marui, E. (2003) 'Interventions targeted at women to encourage the uptake of cervical screening', *Cochrane Database of Systematic Reviews*, (1).

Galvin, R. and Milstein, A. (2002) 'Large Employers' New Strategies in Health Care', *The New Journal of Medicine*, 347(12), pp. 939–42.

Gedik, G., Kutzin, K., Fawcett-Henesy, A. (1999) *Report on Implementation of Health Care Reforms in Kyrgyzstan for the period December 1998-May 1999* (Europe: WHO Europe).

Gillies, R. R., Shortell, S. M., Anderson, C. P. A. et al. (1993) 'Conceptualizing and measuring integration: Findings from the Health Systems Integration Study', *Hospital and Health Service Administration*, 38(4), pp. 467–89.

Goddard, M., Mannion, R. and Smith, P. (2000) 'Enhancing performance in health care: a theoretical perspective on agency and the role of information', *Health Economics*, 9(2), pp. 95–107.

Gröne, O. and Garcia-Barbero, M. (2001) 'Integrated care: a position paper of the WHO European Office for Integrated Health Care Services', *International Journal of Integrated Care*, 1(3), accessed 2005–07–26, http://www.ijic.org.

Hanson, K. and Berman, P. (1994) *Non-government Financing and Provision of Health Services in Africa: A Background Paper* (Washington, DC: USAID, United States Agency for International Development).

Hanson, K. and Berman, P. (1998) *Private Health Care Provision in Developing Countries: A Preliminary Analysis of Levels and Composition* (Boston, MA: Data for Decision Making Project, Harvard School of Public Health).

Hawe, P., McKenzie, N. and Scurry, R. (1998) 'Randomized controlled trial of the use of a modified postal reminder card on the uptake of measles vaccination', *Archives of Disease in Childhood*, 79(2), pp. 136–40.

Hoy, E. W., Wicks, E. K. and Forland, R. A. (1996) 'A guide to facilitating consumer choice', *Health Affairs*, 15(4), pp. 9–30.

Hutchinson, P. (2002) *Decentralization in Tanzania: The View of the District Health Management Teams*, WP-02-48 (Chapel Hill, NC: MEASURE Evaluation).

Huttin, C. (1997) 'The use of clinical guidelines to improve medical practice: main issues in the United States', *International Journal for Quality in Health Care*, 9(3), pp. 207–14.

Janovsky, K. and Travis, P. (1998) *Decentralization and Health Systems Change: Country Case Summaries* (Geneva: World Health Organization).

Jeppsson, A. (2001) 'Financial priorities under decentralization in Uganda', *Health Policy & Planning*, 16, pp. 187–92.

Jeppsson, A. and Okuonzi, S. A. (2000) 'Vertical or holistic decentralization of the health sector? Experiences from Zambia and Uganda', *International Journal of Health Planning & Management*, 15, pp. 273–89.

Khaleghian, P. (2003) *Decentralization and Public Services: The Case for Immunization* (Washington, DC: World Bank Policy Research Working Paper).

Lakshminarayanan, R. (2003) 'Decentralization and its implication for reproductive health: the Philippines experience', *Reproductive Health Matters*, 11(21), pp. 96–107.

Man-Son-Hing, M., Laupacis, A., O'Connor, A. M., Biggs, J., Drake, E., Yetisir, E. and Hart, R. G. (1999) 'A patient decision aid regarding antithrombotic therapy for stroke prevention in atrial fibrillation: a randomized controlled trial', *Journal of the American Medical Association*, 282(8), pp. 737–43.

Man-Son-Hing, M., O'Connor, A. M., Drake, E., Biggs, J., Hum, V. and Laupacis, A. (2002) 'The effect of qualitative vs. quantitative presentation of probability estimates on patient decision making: a randomized trial', *Health Expectations*, 5(3), pp. 246–55.

Marshall, M. N., Shekelle, P. G., Leatherman, S. and Brook, R. H. (2000) 'The public release of performance data: what do we expect to gain? A review of the evidence', *Journal of the American Medical Association*, 283(14), pp. 1866–74.

Marsteller, J. A., Bovbjerg, R. R., Nichols, L. M. (1998) 'Nonprofit conversion: theory, evidence, and state policy options', *Health Services Research*, 33(5 Pt 2), pp. 1495–1535.

McPherson, C. J., Higginson, I. J. and Hearn, J. (2001) 'Effective methods of giving information in cancer: a systematic literature review of randomized controlled trials', *Journal of Public Health Medicine*, 23(3), pp. 227–34.

Murray, C. J. L. and Frenk, J. (2000) 'A framework for assessing the performance of health systems', *Bulletin of the World Health Organization*, 78(6), pp. 717–31.

Mwesygie, F. (1999) *Priority Service Provision under Decentralization: A Case Study of Maternal and Child Health Care in Uganda*. Small Applied Research Paper No. 10 (Bethesda, MD: Partnerships for Health Reform Project, Abt Associates Inc.).

O'Connor, A. M., Fiset, V., DeGrasse, C., Graham, I. D., Evans, W., Stacey, D., Laupacis, A. and Tugwell, P. (1999) 'Decision aids for patients considering options affecting cancer outcomes: evidence of efficacy and policy implications', *Journal of the National Cancer Institute Monographs*, 25, pp. 67–80.

O'Connor, A. M., Rostom, A., Fiset, V., Tetroe, J., Entwistle, V., Llewellyn-Thomas, H., Holmes-Rovner, M., Barry, M. and Jones, J. (1999) 'Decision aids for patients facing health treatment or screening decisions: systematic review', *British Medical Journal*, 319(7212), pp. 731–4.

Oliveria-Cruz, V., Kurowski, C. and Mills, A. (2003) 'Delivery of priority health services: Searching for synergies within the vertical versus horizontal debate', *Journal of International Development*, 15, pp. 67–86.

O'Neill, C. and Largey, A. (1998) 'The role of quality standards – accreditation in redressing asymmetry of information in health care markets', *Health Policy*, 45(1), pp. 33–45.

Pearlman, D. N., Rakowski, W., Clark, W., Ehrich, B., Rimer, B. K., Goldstein, M. G., Woolverton, H. and Dube, C. E. (1997) 'Why do women's attitudes toward mammography change over time? Implications for physician-patient communication', *Cancer Epidemiology, Biomarkers and Prevention*, 6(6), pp. 451–7.

Rosser, W. W., McDowell, I. and Newell, C. (1991) 'Use of reminders for preventive procedures in family medicine', *Canadian Medical Association Journal*, 145(7), pp. 807–14.

Saltman, R. and Figueras, J. (eds) (1997) *European Health Care Reform, Analysis of Current Strategies*. WHO Regional Publications, European Series, No.72 (Geneva: WHO).

Saltman, R. B. (1994) 'Patient choice and patient empowerment in northern European health systems: a conceptual framework', *International Journal of Health Services*, 24(2), pp. 201–29.

Savas, S. and Gedik, G. (1999) *Health Care Reforms in Central Asia. Central Asia 2010 – Prospects for Human Development* (New York: UNDP Regional Bureau for Europe and the CIS).

Schwartz, J. B., Guilkey, D. K. and Racelis, R. (2002) *Decentralization, Allocative Efficiency and Health Services Outcomes in the Philippines* (Chapel Hill, NC: MEASURE).

Shen, Y-C. (2002) 'The effect of hospital ownership choice on patient outcomes after treatment for acute myocardail infarction', *Journal of Health Economics*, 21, pp. 901–22.

Shortell, S. M., Gillies, R. R., Anderson, D. A., Mitchell, J. B. and Morgan, K. L. (1993) 'Creating organized delivery systems: the barriers and facilitators', *Hospital and Health Service Administration*, 38(4), pp. 447–66.

Stone, E. G., Morton, S. C., Hulscher, M. E., Maglione, M. A., Roth, E. A., Grimshaw, J. M., Mittman, B. S., Rubenstein, L. V., Rubenstein, L. Z. and Shekelle, P. G. (2002) 'Interventions that increase use of adult immunization and cancer screening services: a meta-analysis', *Annals of Internal Medicine*, 136(9), pp. 641–51.

Szilagyi, P., Vann, J., Bordley, C., Chelminski, A., Kraus, R., Margolis, P. and Rodewald, L. (2002) 'Interventions aimed at improving immunization rates', *Cochrane Database of Systematic Reviews*, (4).

Tang, S. and Bloom, G. (2000) 'Decentralizing rural health services: a case study in China', *International Journal of Health Planning & Management*, 15, pp. 189–200.

Tangcharoensathien, V., Bennet, S., Khongswatt, S., Supacutikul, A. and Mills, A. (1999) 'Patient satisfaction in Bangkok: the impact of hospital ownership and patient payment status', *International Journal for Quality in Health Care*, 11(4), pp. 309–17.

Thomas, E. J., Orav, E. J. and Brennan, T. A. (2000) 'Hospital ownership and preventable adverse events', *International Journal of Health Services*, 30(4), pp. 745–61.

Tran, T. P., Schutte, W. P., Muelleman, R. L. and Wadman, V. (2002) 'Provision of clinically based information improves patients' perceived length of stay and satisfaction with EP', *American Journal of Emergency.Medicine*, 20(6), pp. 506–9.

Tu, H. T. and Reschovsky, J. D. (2002) 'Assessments of medical care by enrollees in for-profit and nonprofit health maintenance organizations', *New England Journal of Medicine*, 346(17), pp. 1288–93.

Ugalde, A. and Homedes, N. (2002) 'Decentralization of the health sector in Latin America', *Gaceta Sanitaria*, 16, pp. 18–29.

van der Linden, B., Spreeuwenberg, C. and Schrijvers, A. J. P. (2001) 'Integration of care in the Netherlands: the development of tranmural care since 1994', *Health Policy*, 55, pp. 111–20.

van Raak, A., Mur-Veeman, I. and Paulus, A. (1999) 'Understanding the feasibility of integrated care: a rival viewpoint on the influence of actions and institutional context', *International Journal of Health Planning and Management*, 14, pp. 235–48.

WHO (1996) *Integration of Health Care Delivery: Report of a WHO Study Group* (Geneva: WHO).

WHO (2000) *Health Systems: Improving Performance*. World Health Report (Geneva: World Health Organization).

WHO (2003) *Shaping the Future*. World Health Report (Geneva: World Health Organization).

# Concluding Thoughts

*Bob Hinings*

During the fourth International Conference on Organizational Behaviour in Health Care, I speculated that when considering innovation within health care jurisdictions, 'the more we change – the more we change'. Hindsight from a larger spectrum of evidence, and discussion of lessons shared as well as my own further reflections, suggest that it is more likely that there is a continuum of change experience and impact. This spectrum includes examples where significant change seems to breed even more change, but there is an equally striking and contradictory message that in some of our effort to innovate, 'the more we change, the more we stay the same'. It is this paradox that often intrigues researchers and frustrates practitioners.

The problems encountered with change and innovation initiatives in health care often arise, or are at least intensified, through the mismatch between the design of the change and what is actually required to facilitate innovation. For example, governments across the globe most often use structural interventions to induce changes within their health care systems. They change boundaries, amalgamate care sectors, designate teams and assume the change work is done. Canada is fixated on regionalization, which is a restructuring mechanism. As a result, regionalization gets blamed for everything that happens, both good and bad. The reality is that regionalization by itself has very little capacity to do more than enable a number of other complex processes that are required for changes to occur and be sustained. Until governments recognize this limitation, our political solutions will remain stalled at best.

The reality of transformational change within health care is that it occurs within high levels of uncertainty; it is loosely coupled and is riddled with unanticipated consequences (Hinings et al., 2003). One of the key issues in health care change has been, and continues to be, uncertainty. Uncertainty exists when relationships between elements are unpredictable. For example, health care is delivered through a number of autonomous professional groups, and is subject to the competing values and practices of those groups. Introducing change that emphasizes integration between these groups faces considerable uncertainty in producing the hoped-for outcomes. Loose coupling refers to circumstances in which elements of a system retain separateness in structure and identity. Denis, Lamotte, Langley and Vallette (1999, p. 111) point out that the clinical operating core in a hospital is relatively immune from managerial influence because of institutionalized power-sharing based on loose coupling between clinical and administrative activity. This produces uneven and inconsistent adoption in change. Together, uncertainty and loose coupling mean that attempted transformational change will, inevitably, produce consequences that are either unarticulated at the beginning of the process or are unanticipated by some groups and stakeholders. A primary unintended consequence is that change proceeds as a series of 'stops and starts', rather than in the linear, seamless way that is intended. Transforming change also takes a long time. We do not know whether it even makes sense for the initial period or whether it will be sustained for a much longer time. A decade or more may elapse before complex change becomes current practice or the new 'business as usual'. This is complicated by changes in the surrounding context of the specified change as that context does not remain static. The sheer scale of lasting and significant innovation makes it hard to understand ahead of time where it will really take us.

For all of the theory that exists, we seem to have a remaining deficit in our ability to support complex change in complex settings such as health care systems. Factors such as professional silos and the political contexts combine with the financial and human resource constraints to create situations where one large misunderstood change attempt triggers other change cycles and on it goes, making change the only constant. Our low level of understanding of how change unfolds in practice creates change mechanisms that ignore the difficulties of change processes and the highly political nature of attempts to change health care. Health care is a highly visible and valued social good, everybody cares and everybody has a perspective. As Tom Burns (1963) put it, 'The beginning of administrative wisdom is that there is no "one best way"'. This suggests that, for complex change in complex contexts, we have to live with differences rather than look for universal solutions, and acknowledge that everyone has a part to play.

Governments need to garner enough political will to counteract existing barriers and create new incentives for change. In health care organizations, CEOs are politically well connected, which is needed for their roles as pivotal translators for government policy makers about realistic pathways for innovation. Senior health services managers can provide stability within change processes. They provide the buffering that allows the space for innovation and experimentation. The role of middle managers is powerful and not yet well understood or articulated within the literature as the translators and managers of change. Finally, the role of the front line worker is layered and critical. They often identify, lead, implement and learn from change almost simultaneously. An Alberta-built example of this is SEARCH Canada with its learning and development programs that build capability in health regions to deal with change and promote evidence based decision making, and stimulate the production of practice based evidence as well.

I believe that part of the next step in understanding and nurturing change lies in radically altering the research-policy interface. There is an expanding interest in creating a stronger, more acceptable and more accessible strategy for exchanging knowledge iteratively between researchers and practitioners. For example, some research funding agencies are stipulating that decision making partners need to be part of the research team. This promotes change as a collective initiative, not residing solely with policy makers, or funders, or researchers, acting independently of practice, or having practitioners acting alone, separated from wider evidence and knowledge. Radical change in the way research is conducted is needed to match this radical change in the way applied research is being funded. More of our health services research needs to be in partnership with, or even led by practitioners to expand our knowledge about research in practice and to facilitate practice innovation. Some innovations that are helping to support this shift include the development of communities of practice based learning; the emergence of networks to enhance knowledge exchange; and opportunities for multi-directional, just-in-time learning. Until we develop different ways of connecting the evidence base to the practice base and vice versa, efforts to bring about meaningful change will have limited success. We will end up with change that inevitably leads to more change; or, we will end up with illusions of change where only the status quo remains real.

## References

Burns, T. (1963) 'Industry in a New Age', *New Society*, 31, pp. 17–20.

Denis, J-L., Lamothe, L., Langley, A. and Valette, A. (1999) 'The struggle to redefine boundaries in health care systems', in D. Borck, M. Powell and C. R. Hinings (eds), *Restructuring the Professional Organizations* (London: Routledge).

Hinings, C. R., Casebeer, A., Reay, T., Golden-Biddle, K., Pablo, A. and Greenwood, R. (2003) 'Regionalizing healthcare in Alberta: legislated change, uncertainty and loose coupling', *British Journal of Management*, 14, pp. S15–S30.

# A Summing Up

*Ann L. Casebeer, Annabelle L. Mark and Alexandra Harrison*

With this fourth volume in the series, there is real evidence of growth in the development of research concerning organizational behaviour in health care. The focus in this volume is 'innovation' which remains a contentious and highly debated term, as many of the book's contributions highlight. Innovation can be defined as both a product and a process; however, the mixing of these two aspects is often required if anything new is to happen. If it is to be sustained as a process in health care organizations and is to produce outcomes, innovation requires cultural change which may be confounded by organizational purpose and process – as we see in some of the examples set out in the book. In addition, the development of health care has always relied not just on innovation but rather on both creativity and innovation to sustain it; therefore, understanding the boundaries between them is important. The former (creativity) as Kuhn (1985) suggested forms something from nothing, while the latter (innovation) shapes that some-thing into products and services. A better understanding of innovation and its relationship to creativity is crucial if health care development is to continue. Clearly, creativity and innovation within complex health care contexts and cultures are not easy to research or to practice, hence our call for a 'reality check'.

## Emergent themes

A general review of what has emerged from the contributions in this book demonstrates that they have built on messages in earlier books enhancing our knowledge of both organizational behaviour research and practice. Four themes are particularly noteworthy:

1. Increased longitudinal research and practice experience.
2. The maturing of our understanding of evidence based management.
3. The notion of transitions across boundaries, especially the emergence of networks.
4. The potential of knowledge translation and exchange to help us better understand and support development in both research and practice.

Contributions found in Parts I and II of the text demonstrate real growth in our ability to undertake longitudinal research and enhance practice experience.

Many of the authors have followed long-term research and experience of health reform in the UK, New Zealand, Canada and Italy. These efforts begin to fill the gap identified in volume one – they provide evidence of research contributions that are staying the distance in the field and beginning to identify the impact of organizational change across time. For example, the work of Denis and colleagues in Quebec, as well as Bob Hinings' concluding thoughts, remind us that we are getting better at watching long enough to get inside change process. That said, Barnett and colleagues, following reforms in New Zealand, remind us that sometimes little real change emerges on the ground that can be directly attributed to large-scale health reform efforts even when we watch for a long time.

Other contributors demonstrate the capacity for existing literature to inform the framing of new change initiatives and to allow evaluative work to follow. For example, Chambers sets out a carefully constructed initiative in mental health research in the United States that has the potential to better establish and understand dissemination and use of research results in practice. And yet other authors identify some gaps between the theory and the practice reality. For example, Ginsburg and colleagues have been able to identify the existence of multiple safety subcultures within health care settings that call into question the notion that a single strong and unifying patient safety culture is feasible. This clarifies problems identified by Arah and Klazinga (2004) in their cross-national study of the safety paradigm in health care, and confirms yet again the subculture environment of health care. Indeed some might argue that safety is of itself an anathema to innovation which is synonymous with change and risk, so innovating a safety culture perhaps presents unique problems and paradoxes.

Several chapters contain in-depth examples of how change unfolds empirically – allowing additional reflection on our current approaches to organizational research and our current theory base. For example, the need for continued learning and practice in relation to understanding 'leadership' and 'leading' as opposed to fixating on 'leaders' is well described by Bolden and colleagues. And contributions from Rushmer et al. focus intently on the need for purposeful learning in support of health care practice improvement. All of these contributions at their core describe attempts to enhance our knowledge of how to innovate and how to create, or not, conditions for positive and sustained change in organizational behaviours leading to progress.

Our attempts to undertake better organizational behaviour research are being enhanced by conducting research in more robust ways, and extending our theoretical and methodological constructs. This in turn informs and improves conceptualizations of organizational and system level change, as demonstrated in the chapter by Mark and Snowden. Similarly, while various attempts to influence practice behaviours in positive ways sometime fall short of expectations, we are seeing some real and sustained examples of improvement in health care management and practice.

'Evidence based management' is a mantra within and across most health care settings – for some it has become hackneyed rhetoric, for others it remains the gold standard. The authors in Part III of the text demonstrate that, in some spaces, we do know more about what works and what does not, and we know more about the nature of accessing and using evidence. The first text in the Organizational Behaviour in Health Care series included a passing reference to 'Evidence Based Management' (EBM). In this latest volume, an entire section is devoted to this topic. The 'EBM' section illustrates an interesting dual interpretation of the concept of evidence based management. One view, evident in the chapter by Rod Sheaff et al., explores applying evidence related to organizational innovations or policies. Another interpretation examines the organizational context that facilitates or inhibits the uptake of evidence related to clinical processes. This approach is evident in the chapter by Sally Redfern et al., and a similar approach is evident in the chapter by Judy Birdsell et al., which presents a comprehensive organizational model about how health regions use research evidence in delivering services. In the chapter by David Rea, organizational and clinical aspects of health care delivery are explicitly combined in the concept of clinical governance, a set of ideas which finally unite in a meaningful way the parties involved in providing health care.

In ways that parallel our love–hate relationship with EBM, we are increasingly enamoured with the notion of 'networks'. Networks for learning, for research and for practice are developing that cut across boundaries and barriers within health care settings and across national borders, linking a variety of stakeholders interested in innovation. For example, Evans and colleagues describe and evaluate the CHAIN network that creates a community of participants in health care who are willing to share their research expertise and collaborate in order to advance health research capacities. Best and colleagues demonstrate the power of system level efforts when facing the kind of complex and multi-dimensional and layered change that is required to take tobacco control to the next level. And yet, even with these positive examples of the value of linking for learning and for making a difference, there is a sobering note from Adams and Gedik who remind us that even though 'throughout the world, governments are now assessing their health service provision . . . interventions in service provision and their impact still remain one of the least well understood of all health care reforms'. This may be why, in July 2005, the UK government set up its new Institute for Innovation and Improvement and why learning communities and networks such as SEARCH and CHAIN have been developing over the past several years. Clearly, there is more work to be done. There is continuing need to find spaces for enhanced communication capacity within and among both the academic and practice sectors concerned with making a difference to organizational behaviour in health care settings. The continuation of this book series, as part of the Organizational Behaviour in Health Care (OBHC) biennial conference, facilitates this progress.

A common theme in many of the chapters is change – not just change for change sake – but change resulting in innovation. This starts in the Foreword by Stephen Shortell who highlights a number of models of change and reminds us that, as organizational forms become more complex, our theories and practices related to change must become equally sophisticated. This challenge is taken on by Allan Best and his colleagues in the part of the book concerning managing across boundaries. The Best team applies system thinking methodologies to a transorganizational system (multiple organizations linked together) related to tobacco control. The intent is to produce systemic transformational change. The chapter stretches our notions of how to manage across boundaries and provides background on three systems thinking approaches that create a 'combined toolkit' to help address this challenge. Clearly, issues of critical concern regarding the reality of change and innovation for health and health care are raised within all of the author contributions. Each chapter highlights some research effort and/or some practice experience that has at its core the objective to make a difference – to innovate.

## Future realities

Concluding Thoughts by Bob Hinings emphasizes that successes are apparent. Sometimes we are actually changing well and better understanding the how and what of these innovations. However, we also see a continuing orientation to the illusion of change or the constant recycling of restructuring rather than evidence of deeper sustained process change. Hence the title of this book – *Innovations in Health Care: A Reality Check* – reminds us to be humble when sharing our current successes and strident in staying the distance in our future research and practice efforts. The current and explosive interest in knowledge translation and exchange may hold promise for real breakthroughs in our abilities to communicate innovation across sectors and systems, and also with the recipients and consumers of care. The revived interest in the nature of innovation and how to spread good ideas can seem somewhat confused (Greenhalgh et al., 2004) or prescriptive (Fleuren et al., 2004). It is interesting that the reality check for more populist writers such as Malcolm Gladwell in his book *The Tipping Point* published in 2000 utilizes the health metaphor of epidemics to describe three 'rules' which promote change and innovation, notably:

1. the law of the few which suggests the right kind of people rather than lots of them are key;
2. the stickiness factor which suggests ideas must be memorable if they are to move us to action; and,

3. the power of context that suggests human beings are a lot more sensitive to their environment and can be affected by the smallest details to 'tip' them.

That said, other factors are also inherent to enhancing change and innovation in the organization of health care. If we do not look harder at the entrenched power differentials and disincentives that plague many of our health organizations, our ability to innovate will remain sluggish and uneven. We also need to examine and understand better the contributions of networks, coalitions and cultures that form around and within change, and that impact on creativity and innovation. It is in part for these reasons that the fifth International Conference on Organizational Behaviour in Health Care at Aberdeen University in 2006 will address the challenges of 'Speaking Truth to Power – Who Speaks to Whom?'.

We believe that continued research, practice and knowledge exchange can make a difference. Only through continued and deliberative communication and actions that support new ways of researching and practising health care can we hope to improve the reality of health care innovation. Vigilant 'reality checks' will help ensure that progress continues to be made in the delivery of health care that, in turn, can make contributions towards the achievement of improved health.

## References

Arah, O. A. and Klazinga, N. S. (2004) 'How safe is the safety paradigm?', *Quality and Safety in Healthcare*, 13(2), pp. 226–32.

Fleuren, M., Wiefferrink, K. and Paulussen, T. (2004) 'Determinants of innovation within healthcare organizations: literature review and Delphi Study', *International Journal for Quality in Healthcare*, 16(2), pp. 107–23.

Gladwell, M. (2002) *The Tipping Point* (New York: Back Bay).

Greenhalgh, T., Robert, G., Macfarlane, F., Bate, P. and Kyriakidou, O. (2004) 'Diffusion of innovations in service organizations: systematic review and recommendations', *Milbank Quarterly*, 82(4), pp. 581–629.

Kuhn, R. L. (1985) *Frontiers in Creative and Innovative Management* (Cambridge, MA: Ballinger).

# Author Index

*Notes*: b = box; f = figure; n = note; t = table; **bold** = extended discussion or heading emphasized in main text.

# Subject Index

absorptive capacity 143, 144
academics xxxvi, xxxvii, 159, 161–5, 168f, 170, 171, 225
accident and emergency 37, 160t, 183, 208, 215, 216f
accountability xiii, 3, 125, 126, 134, 232, 234, 241
ACE inhibitors 221
action 150f, 150
need for 'memorable ideas' 254
actor-network theory (Latour) 12
actors 150f, **153**, 154f
individual attributes 150–1
acute care 103(n2), 182, 231
administration and support staff 98, 103(n2)
administrators 55, 84
age 55
Alberta iii, xvi–xvii, xxi, xxv–vi, 249
building capacity for evidence based management in health regions **142–56**
Alberta Heritage Foundation for Medical Research (AHFMR) xxi, xxix, 142, 148
alcohol abuse/rehabilitation 81, 87, 90
'allied health professionals' 98–101
'allied health professions' 161
Alma-Ata principles 231
anxiety 208, 209, 217
architecture 199
social 190, 193, 198
strategic/marketing 190, 193, 198
technical 190, 195, 198
Area Health Boards (AHBs, NZ, 1989–) 65, 66
Arkansas 47
Aspirin® 129
Assisting Clinical Effectiveness (ACE) 158, 169
assumptions 94, 95, 113, 175–6, 177, 184
Atkins diet 129
attitudes 44, 114, 114t
audit 56, 57, 125, 161

Australia xvi
autonomy **4**, 68, 97, 124, 127, 134, 234
awareness 44, 53

*ba* concept (Nonaka) 33
Banff (Alberta) xxxi, xxxvii
Bangladesh 237
barriers (to action/change) 12, 57, 74, 110t, 149
Bath 228
Battelle's Centres for Public Health Research & Evaluation xviii, 192
behaviour 93, 114, 114t, 197
cognitive therapies 215
social 129
*see also* organizational behaviour
Behaviourally Anchored Rating Scale (BARS) 107, 115
beliefs/belief systems xxxv, 114t, **151**, 175, 199
normative component 176
social 94
Berkshire 228
best practice 26, 34, 37, 85, 191
biology 35, 128, 129, 176
*Birth of Clinic* (Foucault) 32
Bonferroni correction 98
Botswana 234, 235
boundaries **xxxv–vi**, 73, 248, 253, 254
blurred 215
concept **207–9**
definitions and concepts xxxv–vi
formal (moved by structural lever) **5–6**
generational 212
geographic xxxvi
intra-psychic 207, 211–15, 217
line analogy 207
organizational 4, 10
professional xxxvi
psychodynamic approach xxxvi, 206, 207, 217
research versus practice 223
transitions across 251
violations 217